"Wait . . . what was that you said?"
I said, "Spend less time looking around and adding up the facts and being afraid and more time looking to the Lord, believing
and moving forward."
El espiritu santo

Createspace, North Charleston, South Carolina
ISBN: 978-1480236073
LCCN: 2012921038

Available through Amazon.com
samueljeppsen@cox.net

Acknowledgements

Arizona Senator Charles "Chuck" Gray
Arizona Senator Larry "Lucky" Chesley
POW and Author of "Seven Years in Hanoi"
Mayor Art Sanders of Queen Creek
Mayor Scott Smith of Mesa
Mayor John Insalaco of Apache Junction
Mayor John Lewis of Gilbert
For their Endorsement of the Fundraiser

Lindsey Jeppsen for creating
The official Arizona Charity Riders Poster and the Covers of: From Faith to Trust

Jennifer Jones of KPHO Channel 5
William Hermann of The Arizona Republic
Scott Anderson of Channel 11 "Mesa Talking"
Susan Swanson of the Apache Junction News
Becky and Tim and Willy of "KMLE Country"
Clayton Jeppsen of Infusionsoft
For Advertising and Promoting the Fundraiser

Attorney James Neal Mackinlay
For Overseeing the Funds

***Infusion**soft*
Skunk Motorsports Inc.
Joeta's Leather
Keith Salyer of American Family Insurance
Superstition Harley-Davidson
San Tan Ford
For Sponsoring the Dream

View the pictures at: www.ArizonaCharityRiders.com

It is a long, long way from *Faith* to *Trust* in the Lord. Some people spend their whole life's journey and never get there, while others seem to make it in a very short time.

There is a story of a man laden with troubles. As he walks a canyon ledge deep in thought, he tries to figure out how to solve them. As he gazes over the canyon below, he begins kicking small stones over the ledge and watches as they fall for what seems like a thousand feet, and then crash onto the canyon floor. Consumed with his troubles, he kicks another stone. This time however, he loses his balance and falls.

He tries to grab the ledge where he stood, but his hands are unable to take hold of anything that can save him. Directly below is a small branch growing out of the canyon wall. He falls on it and he manages to get a firm grip just in the nick of time. But now, he is hanging by his hands over the rocky canyon floor. He has no idea how long the small branch will support him or how long he can hang on. He looks at the canyon ledge where he once stood and sees that it is about fifteen feet above him and the face is smooth rock. He is in a remote place in the wilderness and he knows there is no chance of someone coming by or hearing his cries for help. He knows he cannot climb up and he knows if he lets go, he will fall to his death.

As he hangs there, he cries out for the Lord to come and save him. The heavens seem to be silent for what seems an eternity, as he contemplates what will happen if he lets go or loses his grip. Over and over he cries out, "Lord, help me please, please, help me!"

Then he hears a voice. It is not a loud voice. It doesn't come with thunder and lighting and it doesn't come as an earthquake. But instead, it comes as a small, familiar voice, almost as if it were from inside him. It is filled with love, peace and comfort. Amidst all his problems, his focus changes to the engulfing love he now feels inside. The voice says, "Do you believe in the Lord?" "Oh yes!" came his reply. "You know I believe, Lord!" "Do you believe that I am the Lord?" "Oh yes Lord! I can tell by the feeling within me that it is you, Lord!" "Do you believe that I can save you?" came the voice for a third time. "Oh yes." came his reply. "You know I believe you can save me!" Then the voice came again and said, "Then let go of the branch."

In each of our lives comes that moment where we find that merely having faith in the Lord is no longer enough. But moving from hanging on *or believing,* to being able to let go of the branch *or trusting,* requires a willingness to take the Lord at His word. As you seek Him, He will bring you to that point, where you are more willing to let go of the branch than you are to keep hanging on. It begins as a step by step, personalized journey with Him that is called, *From Faith to Trust.*

Dedicated to Julie, the girl I love with all my heart. She is not only the love of my life, she is my best friend. Through all my short-comings, issues and problems, she never stopped loving me or failed *to* love me. If I am a decent father and grandfather at all, it is because she taught me and put up with me, while I learned and continued to change.

Dedicated to each of my children, their spouses and our grand-children. Not only do I deeply love them but they too, have set so many examples that have helped me become a better father and they raise their children to follow the Lord. What more can a man ask?

To my brother, whom I share an uncommon experience and a deep love for. To my sisters and to Bobbie, my mother-in-law. Each follow the Lord and I love them for it. To my first FTO (Field Training Officer) Jay Close for his help and enduring friendship. To Sheila Greear, Clay and Julie Jeppsen for their help with this book. To my sister, Minna Morris, for her closeness to the Lord and for her guidance, and to an ole police buddy and his wife, Roger and Chris Sweet. Roger and I were each other's longest partners and I really grew to love him over the thousands of hours we spent together. Roger and Chris also helped make my ministry as a police chaplain, possible.

Most of all, to eleven beloved men, who took the time, trouble and patience to teach me what it means to be a Melchizedek Priesthood holder, a man of God and a feeder of the Lord's sheep. These eleven men have uncommon faith, valor, and love for others and for the Lord Jesus Christ. They are, Uncle Malcolm Seth Jeppsen, for teaching me how to unite the family. Harvey Jeppsen, my wonderful father, Bud Bernard, my father-in-law, Kevin Smith, Russell Richardson, Clynn Christensen, Hal Hanson and Joel Beckstead. And an ole police buddy by the name of, Chuck Stadler, who had the courage to call his wayward friend to repentance, now some thirty-five years ago. To Charles Bosley for teaching me, not only by word, but by example, how to have a genuine Christlike love for other people. I became his "Arizona nephew" and he became my "Uncle Charlie." To Bill Glennie, a Police Chaplain and Ordained Minister, who grew up catching Mustangs. He was taught to read and write by his wife Nadine. By both word and deed, Bill stands among the most Christlike men I have ever met.

To my mom and dad, who always loved me, were patient with me, believed in me, taught me correct principles and created in me a love for the Lord and for the Scriptures.

You will notice that no one has a title in this book. That is because this book is not about them. It is about you and the Lord, which brings me to my most important dedication of all. It is to my dearest and very best Friend ever ...His name is Jesus Christ.

Six Months Later

Hello Beth,

It's me, Sam Jeppsen, that guy from Arizona who rode his 03, One Hundredth Anniversary, rigid mount Sportster in the 2010 Hoka Hey. I just got your drawing, my certificate and your letter in the mail. I wanted to drop you a note and say thank you, to you, Jim and the entire group that made the 2010 possible. It was a dream come true for me. The event was far more than I had ever hoped it would be.

I had no illusions of ever winning and I was not willing to ride to win. The gold for me was the ride, the adventure, the scenery, the people and the memories. I stopped for every beautiful picture, took some detours and made it a point to talk to people along the way. It became an event I still find myself thinking about, now six months later. As others said it was life changing for them, it was also life changing for me.

I've ridden some fine rides, Beth. I rode the entire Baja Peninsula to Cabo and back, the Mexico mainland to Guatemala to British Honduras, around the Yucatan Peninsula, around the Gulf of Mexico and back to Phoenix. I've ridden the PCH (Pacific Coast Highway) four times now. All on two to five week motorcycle adventures, where I did as we did here, slept out along the way.

But this ride, the Hoka Hey 2010, was like no other ride I have ever taken. The rush of emotions that coursed my veins as I literally became Jim Bronson *(1970 TV series--Then Came Bronson)* has never left my mind and I don't suppose it ever will.

My son-in-law, Jim, made me a DVD of some of my pictures and put it to music and my eighteen grandkids still talk about it. I lived almost a month outside and I slept on the ground at night. Each night before I drifted off, I gazed at the stars and pondered the greatness of God and thanked Him for His continual blessings. The ride was all about me, my bike, my new friends, my freedom and being with God.

I am heavily involved in my community, my Church, the youth, my friends and family. I am also a Law Enforcement Chaplain with one of the largest police agencies in Arizona. I have had many, very choice, memorable and spiritual experiences, on a bike, in a police cruiser, at the side of those in need or on my knees, praying for help. This experience, Beth, ranked among the best.

Officer Samuel Jeppsen, #3751
Retired Police Officer and current
Law Enforcement Chaplain, #91024

The Official Phoenix Valley
Fundraiser Poster.
Created by Lindseygirl
Designed around the actual
Lakota Indian, Hoka Hey MC Trade Mark

As Hope is more than Desire, Faith is more than Hope.
As Faith is more than Hope, Trust is more than Faith.

Table of Contents

"I have been driven many times
upon my knees, by the overwhelming
conviction that I had nowhere else to go.
My own wisdom and that of all about me,
seemed insufficient for the day."
Abraham Lincoln

Chapter One

The "When-Factor"

It was just like any other workday—almost anyway. It was Friday and the alarm went off the same time as usual. I rolled out of bed, landed on my knees and started my day with prayer, as usual. I staggered into the bathroom, took my shower and put on my favorite cologne, put on my uniform, walked into the garage and raised the garage door, as usual. I then rolled out my Harley. As I was putting on my leathers, I happened to look toward the eastern sky. There, in the breaking light of the day, was one of the most incredible mornings I had ever seen. *"Oh my gosh!"* I said, as I stared in almost total disbelief at what I saw. My eyes were riveted to the fire bursting on the eastern horizon.

The whole eastern sky was coming alive with incredible color. As the sun was starting to make its appearance, streaks of light were shooting across the sky under and through the scattered clouds. The tail end of a storm, which had lasted for two days, was still moving through the valley and the sun had lit up the underside of every cloud. The Superstitions were silhouetted against the sky. The gold and yellow and orange and gray colors were everywhere. As the rays of the sun were streaking through the clouds, the brilliant lines in the sky were slowly changing as the clouds continued their journey across the sky. This is one of the most beautiful sunrises I have ever seen, I thought, as I stood and watched it evolve. The storm had left us with plenty of rain. The smell of the freshness in the air was equal to the view I beheld. My heart and mind were filled with the emotions of freedom and the prospects of just taking off for a long day's ride.

The summer had been so hot. Each day seemed to test the very limits of your ability to withstand the heat. Here we were in the fall and still the Phoenix Valley was experiencing unrelenting, record breaking heat. But now, in just a few days, the weather had gone from over one hundred degrees to a cool sixty-five degrees and in the distance was one of the most beautiful mornings I had ever seen. Watching it evolve created a burning desire in me to just get away. Around me was the smell of rain fresh earth and in front of me was a Harley. The thumping of the motor and shaking of the handlebars seemed to say, *"Let's go! Let's go!"*

I continued to watch the morning sky, as I listened to that arrhythmic thump. For the past two years I had been riding to work every day, the same time, through the same intersections and seeing the same people in the same cars. Months ago I started telling myself, "One of these days, I'm going to keep on riding. I'm not going to turn into that parking lot and I'm not going to work. I'm just going to keep on riding." Deep inside, I wondered if that day would ever really come. I always left for work a little before 6 a.m., unless I took the long way to work, which I often did. In that case I would leave by 5 a.m.

On the early days, I would usually head up Usury Pass and through the curves to Saguaro Lake. Even in the darkened early morning hours, I knew the road so well, that I could enjoy the long high speed curves, often called "sweepers" and the sharper curves often called "twisties." I usually had the road all to myself and I would be there in time to watch the sun come up and turn the lake from a dark, colorless, large spot on the ground into a giant shimmering, golden mirror. It would only last a short while as the sun peeked over the low mountains to the east.

When the sun made its appearance, I would be waiting. My bike would be turned off. There would be no one in sight and in my hand would be a thermos of hot chocolate. Surrounding me would be the calm, quiet stillness of the morning. The only sounds to be heard would be the chirping of the birds, as they too, began welcoming the new day. After about fifteen minutes of peace and reflection on just how much beauty the Lord had placed before me and how much there was to be thankful to Him for, I would mount my bike, hit the starter and head down Bush Highway. I would cut across the Salt River Indian Reservation, cut through Lehi, pass by the police shooting range and then head to work.

Well, this time, seated on my Harley and staring at that beautiful morning sky, I said to myself, "I think today is the day. I'm not going to just take the longer way to work, I think today is the day I'm going to fulfill that dream and just take off."

As I rode down the same streets, through the same intersections, seeing the same people at the same times, I just kept repeating those words in my mind. "I think today is the day." I went the same route, as usual, turning west onto Main at Lindsay as usual and continued westbound on Main. There in the distance, I could finally see my destination. It was that same eight story glass building …as usual. With each passing mile, I found myself thinking, "This is the day! I'm going to do it today!"

At Center Street and Main, I turned north to turn again into the parking lot, where I always park my bike and go to work. But this time, instead of pulling in, I pulled over and stopped. I flipped up my visor and looked into the parking lot and then looked down the road. I slowly looked back into the parking lot and then back down the road. I thought about how many times I had stopped here and just wanted to take off and keep riding.

I sat there a moment and watched some of the early-birds showing up with coffee cups in hand. Most were looking ahead or down at where they were walking, instead of looking at the beautiful sunlit morning over their heads. As I watched a few of them walk into the building, with their minds already on the workday ahead of them, I began to smile. I then flipped my visor down, rolled on the throttle, let the clutch out and took off.

I headed north, crossed the Salt River Reservation and rode through Fountain Hills, where I took the little road through the beautiful, rolling desert to Rio Verde. The narrow two lane road twists and turns and dips and often brings with it the sighting of coyotes. My eyes were peeled, hoping to see one. The traffic was very light, with a car passing every few minutes. As I rode along, I could overlook the valley to my right and had a perfect view of the majestic Four Peaks Mountain. I passed through Rio Verde to Cave Creek and passed by one of my favorite places to eat, "Big Earl's Greasy Eats." It's an old, converted, small, one island, two pump, filling station. With its ten places to sit on the inside, its dining area out front where the pumps still are, its kitchen where they stored parts and repaired cars and its bathrooms outside and out back, it's the biggest hole-in-the-wall place I've ever eaten.

Big Earl's is known for their hamburgers and people often come quite a ways just to get one. I smiled as I puttered past in second gear and remembered the chicken fried steak and eggs I ate on my last visit. Their food is good. The people are friendly. The atmosphere is calm and peaceful and the stop is worth it.

I rode to New River, then west on 74 and passed by Lake Pleasant. I could feel the morning temperatures dropping as I rode into Wickenburg. When I finally pulled over, it was chilly and seemed to be the perfect time for a Carne Asada Burrito. …It was.

Afterwards, I took out my Blackberry and sent a few emails to different friends. I told them that I was on a motorcycle, a hundred miles away, with several hundred miles ahead of me. I told them I would be heading through the mountains and I wished them a good workday. I then attached a picture of my smiling face, put my phone in my pocket and mounted up.

With the feeling of adventure and excitement coursing my veins, passing through the fresh smell of the rain soaked Desert Mesquite, Sycamore and Palo Verde trees, I headed for the town of Congress and then for Yarnell Hill. I was heading for one of the best motorcycle roads in Arizona.

As I passed Congress, I started mentally preparing myself for the long sweepers and tight curves that lay ahead. The road there is in perfect condition and just seems to beg for a good rider. The day was cool and the smell of the rain fresh earth intensified as I passed by the numerous, fragrant Manzanita bushes and Palo Verde trees. Mile after mile, the excitement inside me grew until finally there it was …Yarnell Hill.

As I leaned into my first right hand sweeper at the bottom of the hill, the ride began to take on a whole new feeling. I knew from here to where I would return home, the road was mostly curves, sweepers and switchbacks—the kind that make you motion sick if you're in a car, but the kind you live for on a bike.

All the training I had received for two years as a Professional Harley-Davidson Motorcycle Test Rider was now bubbling inside me. Though I was smart enough to leave my trick-riding on the tracks, I could not help but let myself enjoy the sweepers and curves that lay in front of me. The day was young. The sun was still at an angle and shadows and sunlight colored the dry road and the mountains in front of me. The air was crisp, cool and exhilarating and I could not breathe enough of it.

As I gracefully brought the bike down, caressing each sweeper with perfect form, I held the throttle steady as I entered each curve. Steady—steady and then at the halfway point, I began slow-rolling the throttle on. As I began to come up and out of each curve, more and more throttle was used as the motor pounded away. In my mind, I could hear the harmonica in Johnny Cash's song, *The Orange Blossom Special.* As I listened to that song, I noticed that the pounding of the motor seemed to be keeping perfect double time with the harmonica.

I leaned forward, putting my weight on the front wheel and leaned inward to decrease the bike's lean angle. I could hear the intensified sound of the heartbeat of the motor as it bounced off the pavement, now much nearer to my ears. My bike was literally in one lane and I was in the other lane as I swept curve after curve.

Form more than *speed* was my goal. Amateurs are speedy. Professionals are graceful and will sacrifice speed for grace. As a professionally trained rider, I was trying to resist the temptation to ride too fast. I wanted to enjoy the ride, but not be dangerous.

"Oops!" I said as my right foot peg touched down. The grinding of the foot peg made me realize I was going too fast on this one. I held the throttle steady to prevent a wobble and kept my weight forward and inside. When I came up and out, I braked, lost ten, shifted my weight to the left, dropped a gear and leaned into the next sweeper. Once again, holding the throttle steady through the sweeper, until the halfway point and then slow-rolling it on as I gracefully began coming up and out of the long curve.

Curve after curve I rode and then there it was, the last overlook below. Finishing that left hand sweeper, I passed the turnaround and leaned in to finish the one to my right, as well. I then slowed, turned around and went down the hill. The road is divided and the downhill is mostly single lane with steep sides and sharp curves. Some of the curves show the effects of cars hitting the shoulders and knocking dirt and gravel onto the pavement. So I slowed down and enjoyed it, but was very mindful that bikes are more easily lost on downhill curves than on uphill curves.

At the bottom of the hill, I turned around, gave it a little more throttle and came back up. I was into it now, into the curves and into the gracefulness of my riding. Sweeper after sweeper, all the way up the hill I rode in perfect form as I listened to the deep, rumbly music that was blasting in stereo from my "twice-pipes."

As I became ever more aggressive, I could almost hear the fans cheering me on as I swept each curve. I used my gears and throttle to keep a perfect wheel track and shifted my weight from side to side, leaning forward and low as I pulled the bike over again and again.

I had become one with the bike and was now *thinking* the bike around the curves, instead of riding it. I felt like a dancer, dancing with a beautiful woman on stage, while the whole world watched in awe of our talent. When suddenly, there it was again, that gut wrenching sound of grinding metal.

"Oops!" I said more nervously. There was a long drag on the left foot peg and it was followed by a deep grinding sound that I could feel in the handlebars and seat. I knew even before the bike began to react that it was a *hard hit.* I had gone past the upward, folding ability of the foot peg and had hit the frame! The bike now began a dance of its own.

Though unintentionally, I had hit the frame several times as a test rider and I was now glad for those experiences. I knew what was coming and how best to counteract it.

The bike suddenly felt like I was riding a dolphin. It was in a leaned over, high speed wobble with a hopping motion. Though there is no silver bullet solution to a problem like this, I knew if I handled this incorrectly, the outcome could be fatal.

The first time I had experienced a situation like this, I was on the High Speed, Interstate, Test Track. I had been pushing the bike too hard through a curve and it suddenly went into a high speed wobble. It's often referred to as the *Dyna Death Wobble*. I was doing a little over 80mph and I had no idea what happened. It was horrifying, but I managed to stay with it until it calmed down and came out of it. When I told other riders about it, they laughed and said, "He's new!" The most severe time I experienced it, was from a frame impact like this one. I was on the High Speed Sport Track. I had just come out of my last tight curve at over 50mph. The bike was low and I was heading into the straightaway. I had rolled the throttle on to a full acceleration, but was going too fast. The frame hit the track and the bike started wobbling and hopping. Now, on my own bike, I was experiencing a more violent reaction and I was glad for those half dozen prior experiences. I was now summoning everything my trainer, Larry Fort, had taught me. I instinctively began to follow my training.

I remained calm, did not touch the brakes and suppressed my urge to panic. I focused ahead, never looking off the road or at the edge. I had learned this tactic in an actual Arizona Highway Patrol Police Pursuit School in 1976—to never look at where you don't want to go. Instead, focus and concentrate on where you want to end up. I learned this to be a universal principle and I have used it throughout my life in various settings. It has paid off almost every time. I relearned it on the Harley-Davidson test tracks and was now praying it would work one more time.

My focus was about fifty yards ahead of me and I leaned lower and more inward—going down so I could bring the bike up and get it off the frame. I also began an aggressive roll-on, trying to use the thrust of the motor to push the bike through it. My brain began making the thousands of split second calculations needed, to create the outcome I was now desperately praying for.

I also eased up on my grip and control of the handlebars and didn't try to overpower the wobble. I steadily increased the throttle in hopes of decreasing the violence of the bike. Though my natural tendency was to brake, I stayed away from that, so I would prevent a "high" or "low" slide.

After shifting as much weight as possible inward and forward, I gave it more and more throttle—now almost holding it wide open—forcing the bike forward. I used the thrust of the motor, the now decreased lean angle, as well as the three natural gyros of the bike (the two spinning wheels and motor) to correct it. What seemed like minutes, but was actually seconds, the bike finally began coming out of it and I was once again in control.

After bringing the bike under control again, I slowed way down and now began trying to bring myself under control. Though I didn't feel the effects of panic then, I was beginning to feel it now. Just before the top of Yarnell Hill, the last overlook of the valley below, I pulled over to slow down my racing heart and the adrenaline that was now coursing through my veins. I knew from experience that the best way to slow my heart rate and my riding was to stop, get off the bike and take a break.

Though I have drug many a foot peg and muffler, even the frame and have felt my rear tire "walk" (give way) in professional settings, I seldom do it on the street. I haven't gone down since my early twenties and didn't want to now. Since I have gotten older, I try to stay *inside* my abilities and not outside them.

This time, I had failed to do that. I knew that Yarnell Hill was dubbed "Arizona's Deadliest Hill" and "A Graveyard for Motorcycles" and yet, I had allowed myself to become foolish. I had gotten caught up in the thrill of the moment and had become a danger to myself. Pulling over and backing away was the right thing to do. There is an old saying, "There are *old* motorcycle riders and there are *bold* motorcycle riders, but there are no *old bold* motorcycle riders!" The whole thing reminded me of an experience of one of my favorite apostles, the great Apostle Paul.

When Saul was converted and became the Apostle Paul, he traveled about preaching the gospel. He was not well received and often found he had to keep moving along. He left his homeland for almost ten years. Wherever he went, he found that there were those that would lay in wait for him, to catch him and persecute him and if at all possible, kill him! However, he was protected by the Lord and some of his friends. Then one day, he wanted to go to Jerusalem to attend a conference.

As Paul was preparing for his journey, a prophet from Judea, by the name of Agabus, came to him and took Paul's robe and bound his own feet and hands with it. He then told Paul, "Thus saith the Holy Ghost, So shall the Jews at Jerusalem bind the man that owneth this girdle, and shall deliver him into the hands of the Gentiles." Paul didn't listen and went to Jerusalem anyway. Within a few days the Jews found him in the Temple. Paul was pulled outside, beaten, arrested, survived an assassination plot and eluded a flogging by telling them that he was a Roman citizen. Within two weeks of his arrival, he found himself before the Roman Governor, Felix. He was then incarcerated for two years for *...just because!*

In each of us, there is an Agabus who whispers, "Don't do that." when we are thinking of doing something we shouldn't. He pleads with us instead, to stop and listen to the Holy Ghost and to rethink things. As I brought the speed of my bike down, I thought of Agabus and said, *"It's a good day to rethink things!"*

70 steps to get from Faith to Trust.

1) Make life *...an Adventure.*
2) Make wise decisions and always think things through.
3) Remain calm and keep your focus on where you want to end up.
4) Know when to stop and "rethink" things.

Chapter Two

Caught up in the Moment

As I pulled to a stop, I put my kickstand down, turned off the motor, got off and stood at the edge of the canyon wall. I looked down at the huge Phoenix Valley below. As I stood there, shaking it off and bringing my heart rate down, I realized I had made the mistake of allowing myself to get too caught up in the moment. Doing so had blurred my judgment.

My mind went back to a time when I responded to a "shots fired" call in the 1300 block of E. Broadway, in Mesa. Two men had gotten caught up in the moment and had escalated a simple argument, over cable TV, to the point that it ended in gunfire. When it was over, one man lay dead and the other under arrest for first degree murder.

My mind also went back to a time when I was about fourteen. I had been invited to a party by a friend. His parents were not going to be home and the party was in their basement. I thought it would be fun, so I went. When I arrived, there were girls and everyone was drinking. My friend had some of that fairly new stuff called marijuana. Everyone was doing things they knew they shouldn't be doing. Within a half hour, things had escalated to the point, I was now uncomfortable. I left the party and went home.

It turned out to be a wise decision and a great teaching moment for me—one I would always remember. The party got out of hand and several of the kids not only got in severe trouble, they made some decisions and did things that they regretted for many years—just because they got caught up in the moment.

Going to that party turned out to be one of my first experiences in learning that when the feeling comes to back away, *back away ... and do it immediately!*

As I stood there and looked over the canyon wall, able to see from Buckeye to Apache Junction, a third experience came to my mind. It was of a young Elders Quorum President. I have had about fifty special opportunities to sit in a Bishopric or in a Stake Presidency and High Council setting and help those who have made terrible mistakes. They come wanting to put their lives back together. They are personal and private and afterwards I pray to forget them. But this one, I prayed to always remember.

He was a tall, well built and very handsome fellow. He was loved and admired by all who knew him. His friends in the church spoke highly of him. He had served a mission, had a beautiful wife and family and a great career.

One day he noticed this wonderful woman at work. She too, was striving to do all the right things and set the right example for others. But she had marital problems and she just didn't know how to handle them. She needed the help of a wise and caring friend, someone she could count on to give her wise counsel. They worked together. In a few weeks they developed an emotional relationship with each other, fulfilling his need to help and console and fulfilling her need to be understood, consoled and vindicated. They often met for lunch or lingered in the parking lot.

Long story short, here he was, sitting in front of the Stake President and Stake High Council with tears streaming down his face. He was trying to work through a terrible mistake, one that had happened, because both had let their judgment become blurred after allowing themselves to get caught up in the moment.

With tears dripping from his chin and onto the table, he said, "I only let go of the iron rod for a minute. I thought it was right there, always within arm's reach. Then came this fog and I couldn't see clearly anymore. When the fog lifted and I could see the rod again, I realized I was more than a mile away." It was this comment, at this most critical time in his life, which made me pray to never forget my moment in time with him.

I thought of the many good people I had met throughout my police career and church experiences. Ones who had gotten caught up in the moment and made extremely regrettable decisions and afterwards suffered very painful consequences.

Though, I knew the Savior could forgive and forget, I also knew that in this life, consequences and oftentimes the scarring memories of our decisions are ours to keep and bear.

After about ten minutes of reflecting on the things that were brought to my mind, I turned away from the canyon ledge and looked at my bike. My eyes happened to fall on the black inlaid words above the golden eagle on my clutch cover, the inscription, *Live to Ride—Ride to Live.* With that in mind, a smile came across my face, as I threw my leg over my bike. I turned the key and hit the starter. As I dropped it in gear and let the clutch out, I rode away a slower and much wiser man.

As I continued up the hill, passing over the last few sweepers and riding past the turnaround, I thought of Yvon, a friend and fellow Harley-Davidson test rider, who had once raced professionally. I thought of his ride up the beautiful Apache Trail that led to Canyon Lake. From the Apache Lake turn off, there are about seven miles of gentle sweepers. In the next eleven miles, from the first "Slow to 25 mph" sign to Tortilla Flat, there are one hundred and thirty-seven switchbacks and curves. While taking one of the curves, he got caught up in the moment, lost control and sent his new Harley Softtail Night Train over the edge and into the canyon below. Fortunately, he walked away but almost went over the edge with his bike. "It can happen to anyone." I said. "It's a good day to ride ...and yes ...it's a good day to live."

With that, I made a promise to myself that I would never again allow myself to get so caught up in foolish moments, that I ignored the warning signs to back away. I also promised myself I would never again push my bike to the point, that I hit my frame or even the pegs. "It is indeed, a good day to live." I said as I rolled on the throttle and began shifting gears.

I continued on through the curves and sweepers until I popped over the hill and into the town of Yarnell. There, I slowed to 35 mph to look over the little sleepy town. It was just before 10:00 a.m. The streets were lined with little shops and people were beginning to move about. On the road through the center of town were two cars, a kid on a bicycle and a dog. To my right was the *Ranch House*, a mom and pop restaurant, famous for its breakfast. On any given weekend, I could find a dozen bikes out front with as many riders inside. Not far from there was the roadside, *Cornerstone Bakery*, a fun stop for great pastries.

As I entered the center of town, I turned left onto Shrine Road and rode up to see the Stations of the Cross at the Shrine of St. Joseph. It is a beautiful and peaceful place, nestled into the rocks, trees and mountainside. I always stop there. As I walked the pathway, I reflected on the many things the Savior had done for me personally, throughout my life. I thought of how blessed I was at every turn and how things always seemed to work out for my best.

After about thirty minutes of reflection, I returned to highway 89 and turned left. As I left the sleepy, little town behind, I rolled the throttle on and made my way toward Prescott.

The road from Yarnell to Prescott is one sweeper after another, until the last fifteen miles or so, before you enter the town. There, the sweepers become curves and twisties with occasional switchbacks. I knew from experience that on this stretch of road, paying attention was very important. It would be easy to misjudge and find myself entering a switchback too hot. Remembering my promise to never touch down again, I slowed my pace and enjoyed the journey through the picturesque mountains and canyons. As I got closer to Prescott, I gazed in envy at the little homes on the mountainsides. My ride was leading me through the mountains, the valleys and grassy hills, the meadows, the Pine trees, the dips and the twisties. As I came through the last curve and out of the trees, there it was—Prescott. Prescott is the "Cowboy Capitol of the World" and the home of the world's oldest rodeo.

As I entered Arizona's very own, mile high city, I rode through the hills and dales, until I entered Whisky Row, a historic area from the mid 1800's. It received its name because of all the bars that once lined the west side of the street. I chuckled as I rode through, because Whisky Row had burned down in 1900. Legend has it, that when the patrons found out Whiskey Row was on fire, they took their drinks from the bar, ran across the street to the Capitol grounds and watched it burn—while finishing their drinks.

As I turned north on Gurley Street, I passed the Capitol building. Arizona became a territory in 1863, during the Civil War and Prescott became the Capitol in 1864. As I rode past the beautifully crafted, stone County Courthouse, I looked at the steps leading up to the entrance. I chuckled again, at the Prescott Town Ordinance, which still reads, "No one is allowed to ride their horse up the stairs of the County Courthouse." After passing by, I climbed the steep street and headed northeast to Jerome.

The road out of Prescott is through a long valley and the climb, up over Mingus Mountain and into Jerome, is a slow road with tight curves and switchbacks and steep mountainsides. As I rode, I stopped from time to time to take in all the beauty of the mountains, trees and canyons. The road, though slow and tedious for cars, was perfect for motorcycles. And with this being a Friday, I had the road almost all to myself.

I followed the steep descent down the mountain and into the town of Jerome. As I rode along, I marveled at the incredible ability and ingenuity of the hands of yesteryear, which literally made it possible for homes and buildings to be built on the steep mountainsides.

Most of the homes had no front yards and a fall from the small, narrow front porch could cost you your life. I marveled again, as I thought about the tenacity of those early residents, building those homes and doing whatever it took to earn a living. I remembered the paycheck I had once seen in a Jerome museum. The recipient of the paycheck had received eleven dollars for a week's work in the mines, during Jerome's heyday. As I pulled over to the side of the road, to look at some of the homes, I wondered how safe they were and was amazed that people still lived in them.

The town of Jerome is America's most vertical city and America's largest ghost town. It's an old copper mining town that sits on the side of Cleopatra Hill. The old mine is directly under the town. In 1930, a whole city block, including the jail, slid down the mountainside, because of an underground blast. The buildings were all but totally destroyed. Oddly, the Town Jail slid an entire block—intact! Being a retired cop, I had to laugh, because Jerome was dubbed, "The Wickedest Town in the West" by the *New York Sun* in 1903. I laughed because I guessed that the good Lord knew that they still needed their jail. But like other western towns, that received that kind of brand, it turned into a ghost town. Like Prescott and Denver, Jerome is a mile high city.

I rode through the narrow, almost one lane streets, making my way down the singular steep road out of town. I then rolled on the throttle and headed for the red land of Sedona. Once there, I stopped for gas and water and looked at the reddish-orange colored dirt. I then sat on the curb, drinking my water and watched the seemingly countless stream of out of state cars pass by.

Sedona is a very beautiful and unusual place. The valley is surrounded by greenish-brown high desert landscape. Yet, in the midst of all the brown and green is this valley of green trees with red dirt and rocks. Even the mountains look like stacks of red boulders, just like the *Vermillion Cliffs* in northern Arizona.

Sedona's first postmaster, T.C. Schnebly, gave the settlement his wife's name, in 1902. Sedona is also the home of one of my favorite John Wayne movies, *Angel and the Badman.* Another one of my favorites, filmed in Sedona, was the movie, *Broken Arrow,* with Jeff Chandler and Jimmy Stewart.

I like movies where it actually means something to be a good guy and the hero of the movie, stirs the hero within you. Movies where the heroes are men of honor, unlike movies where the hero is just a few cuts above the bad guy. In the John Wayne movie, *The Cowboys,* he was a principled man with high ideals and he was a great example to those boys, as opposed to the movie, *True Grit.* There, John Wayne was the hero, but he was also *El Borracho,* "The Drunk." I like true hero movies like *The Cowboys, The Streets of Laredo, The Man Who Shot Liberty Valance, The Magnificent Seven, Chisum, Ben Hur* and believe it or not, *Spiderman.* Movies where the good guys are *good* guys!

One of the hero movies, that really stirred me, was about a soldier named Todd, played by Kurt Russell. It was an extremely sad story of a man who was stolen as an infant and was denied any love. He was horribly brought up and trained to be an uncaring, extremely disciplined, experimental soldier. What impacted me was that through it all, despite all the evil and wickedness he had been through—*who he was deep inside*—emerged. And in the end, there stood a man of great honor and integrity that others could count on!

The fictional character, Todd, reminded me of Richard, an ex-gang member from Southern Cal. I had met him when I was the Neighborhood Services Coordinator for Buckeye, Arizona.

Richard had been stabbed seven times, shot eleven and had all the scars to prove it. He had also been to *camp* twice, once for attempted murder. Today, Richard is supporting his wife and family. He is a respected member of the community and is spending his life trying to reach out to troubled youth. He travels to boys clubs throughout the Phoenix Valley and spends his own time and money to make a difference in their lives.

Richard is a great man, whom I deeply respect. Though he had a very hard time starting over, a very hard time getting people to give him a chance, he just kept pressing forward, one struggling step at a time. Like Todd in the movie, Richard too, was denied so much in life. He was surrounded by so much evil, yet in the end, *who he was deep inside,* emerged! And Richard today, is a man of great honor that others can count on!

Richard and the fictional character Todd, had a deep need to do good that didn't manifest itself until later on in life. It was the tragedy they went through that brought out their genuine love for their fellowman. It has always amazed me, what genuine love can do in a conflict and the power it has to soften hard hearts.

In my police career, I had answered about a thousand family fights or boyfriend/girlfriend or neighbor fights a year, as either primary or backup officer. I figure I responded to over twenty thousand all total. I was always amazed and impressed with the very few that had the love and courage to be the first to cross the battle line and extend true love and forgiveness and be a peacemaker. It is a rare trait that requires love and understanding.

After finishing my water, I threw my leg over my bike and headed up Oak Creek Canyon. It happens to be one of my favorite rides. Drivers don't get the full feel, because they can't see the depth and width of the canyon that riders can see. The trees line the road much of the time and only spots of sunshine make it through. As always, but especially here in this canyon, I was awed by the panoramic view that kept unfolding before my eyes.

I followed the winding road up the canyon, smelling the freshness of the rain washed mountains and trees. Passing through patches of sun and shade, I was engrossed in the beauty of this natural wonder and the sound my pipes made as they bounced off the canyon walls. The sound was music in stereo to my ears. And by the looks on the faces of the drivers that I eased past, I could tell it was music to their ears, too …*well…*

At Mile Post 380, the trees start arching over the road. At MP 386, I began my climb out of the canyon. The road is literally cut into the canyon walls. To my left was cut rock and mountain side and to my right was the drop off into the canyon floor. The road twists back and forth like a snake. It reminded me of the road I traveled, from Durango to Silverton, while on my three thousand mile ride through Colorado.

As I came out of the canyon, south of Flagstaff, I rolled the throttle on and roared onto the famous Route 66. Before 1917, ninety-eight percent of America's roads were dirt. Most were merely graded over wagon trails. At the end of WWI, a road to connect the east to the west was commissioned. It was called Route 66. The work began in 1926 and was completed in 1938. Route 66 ran from Chicago to Los Angeles and was nicknamed, *The Mother Road* and *The Main Street of America*. Arizona has the longest stretch of original road that is still in use today.

I smiled as I rode and thought of one of my favorite, TV series, *Route 66*. An old series about two guys with a love for adventure and the open road. Up ahead, was a man and woman in a red convertible. I crunched the throttle and as I rolled past, I pretended they were Todd Stiles and Buzz Murdock in their 59 Corvette. As I passed by, I gave them a nod and a salute.

I left Route 66 and rode by the land, Julie and I had once owned, near Snow Bowl. There, I found a beautiful home, someone had built on the two acre lot that was to be our final home site. It is a beautiful, brown, log cabin style home with an A-frame entry and huge windows that face the San Francisco Peaks. The home had a perfect unobstructed view of the almost thirteen thousand foot mountain. As I stopped on Abert Way, I looked at the beautiful home and dreamed of what it would have been like if we lived there. It was a place where the air was fresh and clean! "Someday!" I said as I enviously looked on. "...Someday!!"

I then rode back into Flagstaff, had lunch and headed down the road past Lake Mary and Mormon Lake. I was glad to see that Lake Mary was still about fifty percent full. Until I was forty years old, Flagstaff had about a half dozen lakes that were good for fishing and small boats. Mormon Lake was the largest of them all. The locals that live around the lake will tell you that something strange happened during the 1989 earthquake in San Francisco. It was as if someone pulled the plug in a tub. Each lake got lower and lower until within a few years, some dried up. Now, some of the lakes are just large, deep, grassy holes in the ground.

I continued south on 87 crossing the Mogollon Rim, down into Strawberry, Pine and Payson and then back into the valley, arriving home a little after suppertime. The day was filled with great memories, passion and exuberance. Each little town I passed through began a brand new adventure for me.

With each mile, I lived the *Great Escape.* I smiled as I rode and saw myself as Steve McQueen as he jumped his 1961, TR6-650 Triumph over the German, POW prison fence at Stalag Luft 3. The movie was based on a true story of captured airmen during WWII. Their unquenchable thirst for freedom would be something I would always remember.

As I pulled into my neighborhood, I beamed, knowing I had done what I had dreamed of, for the past two years. I had ridden a little over four hundred and fifty miles and had the time of my life and never once felt bad. I pulled into the driveway a little later than usual, went inside and hollered, "Honey, I'm home." I then sat down for dinner as usual, with no guilty conscience at all, for what I had done. I was smiling from ear to ear and was almost unable to contain my joy. Of course …it was my day off…but so what!! …It's what I always wanted to do!!!

When I showed up for work on Monday, everything was fine. My job was still intact. My good name, my standing in the Department and the trust they had placed in me was still there. Everything that was important to me was the same as when I left. Nothing was negatively impacted by the choice I had made. Not necessarily so with the decisions I had often seen others make.

As a young boy, I dreamed of being a cop or a soldier someday. I dreamed of being one of those brave souls that wore a uniform and stood the line between good and evil and protected good *from* evil. I knew, even then, there were those that didn't feel as I felt toward officers and soldiers. Later on, during the Vietnam era, I knew cops and soldiers were quite often despised. But to me, they were heroes …and would always *be* heroes.

However, in my career as a police officer, I had seen many police careers go down the river. Maybe as many as one hundred cops *go-away* by getting the *Either—Or.* Every one of them, for choices the officer made, while facing a decision. It always began, "Should I do this …or should I do that?" It was such an easy question, yet it often brought unimaginable consequences.

I had seen six officers get arrested and had even arrested one myself. I had seen three of the six go to prison. One of the three was a great man and a great street cop, by the name of Al. He was a real man's man. He printed like a typewriter and he was fearless. Al was the best backup officer anyone could want. He even designed the current, Mesa PD, uniform shoulder patch.

It is out of love and respect for a friend and a great street cop that I don't mention Al's last name. But it was the foolish choice he made, while caught up in the moment, which caused him to spend twenty-five years of his life in prison.

From getting the *either—or*, to going to prison for twenty-five years, most of what the officers did, resulted in getting caught up in foolish moments. Surprisingly, many of those things would have been just fine, if their timing had been different.

In a way, being a cop, being one of the protectors in life, was like this ride I had just taken. It was one of the things that I had wanted to do, long before I ever did it. But had I taken this ride on a regular work day, it could have cost me my job. I would have been AWOL and at very least would have been reassigned. But doing it this way, I was not in trouble at all. It was as if I never did it. Nor did my family suffer because of a selfish, careless and unwise decision on my part.

Some of life's most important lessons have their roots in the simplest of principles. Things like; listening to the Agabus inside us, exercising good common sense, making wise and well thought out decisions, not getting foolishly caught up in the moment and, the proper timing of our decisions! Collectively I call these five things, *"The When Factor."* They are also some of the first few building blocks, the Lord needs to see *within* you, so that He can begin to build trust *in you.*

Trust is very fragile. It is quite hard to build and easy to destroy. Trust is also a two way street. In building a relationship of trust with the Lord, *He* must be able to trust *you.* Your ability to keep private information private, the true desires of your heart, the choices you make when facing a decision and the timing of your decisions, begin to determine the amount of trust *He* can place in *you.* The first step in your journey from Faith to Trust begins by being worthy of the Lord's trust. As you grow in your relationship toward Him, you find …even the little decisions you make *matter.*

5) Recognize foolish moments and don't get caught up in them.
6) When the feeling comes to back away, do it immediately.
7) Never let your decision making process become your enemy.
8) Be trustable. Create, live and be the *good-guy!*
9) Apply *"The When Factor"* to your decisions.

The Centurions...

When all God's children began to come forth,
there had to be those who would stand and take an oath.
An oath of great risk to protect and serve all the others
who would come to earth, once sisters and brothers.
The Protectors would be called Centurions, their duty full of fear,
their training beginning now for their dangerous earthly career.
They'd be going to a violent world, these centurions receiving birth.
They'd have to be willing to take another's life, in uniform on earth.
Some would carry a rifle and fight for freedom in foreign lands.
Others would stay at home and fight criminals and armed bands.
These centurions would walk into the bloodiest and dirtiest of scenes
to solve people's problems and somehow keep their own lives clean.
They would have to listen to and be with those who mournfully cry,
willing to reach out to them, even wiping a tear from their eye.
They'd have to be the kind who could seem mean and stern.
And yet also have compassion for others as well as concern.
And then as they would come to the end of their embattled tours,
they'd find few who understood their emotional sores.

Where once they had been kind, forgiving and gentle,
they now seemed to be angry, cynical and judgmental.
They've seen and lived things that others can turn away from and hide,
but they had to deal with, their best friend, the weapon at their side.
Even those who know and love them have accused them of being cold,
not able to understand, no matter the times they've been told,
that some of the world's dirt and soil has rubbed off onto their soul,
making them rough and sometimes hurting others who try to console.
But there is one thing that all centurions have to come to understand.
They have to return to who they were before they agreed to this plan.
That no matter what they have seen or what they have gone through,
there is Someone who understands, loves you and has died for you.
He will wipe away your inner pain and mend your hardened soul,
and give you what you had before, that soft inner glow.
You'll have to do what you did in your pre-existent life,
focus on the good, follow the Lord and walk toward his Light.
Of this I bear testimony of the truthfulness of what I say,
hoping you will listen to a centurion who's learned to pray.
Ofcr. Samuel Jeppsen #3751

"Blessed are the peacemakers: for they shall be called the children of God."
Matt 5-9

The Debriefing…

"How are you? It's good to see you, even though it's late.
I saw what happened, so I thought I'd meet you at the gate.
I can see you have several questions you want to ask of Me.
Like: What happened? Why you? And what about your family?
There is a lot you won't be able to understand right away.
So you'll have to trust Me and take solace in what I say.

It's no surprise you are here. You've been called home for a reason.
The loved ones you left behind will be with you again in a season.
It was all part of the plan, you know, that you chose to be one to fight.
You were called from the beginning to protect others with your might.
You see, I warned everyone of evil and that evil was cunning.
I warned the others to turn away, to hurry and leave running.

But if everyone turned away, and from evil they ran,
then evil would rule, because they'd know they can.
So, I had to ask some of you to run not. But instead, stay and fight.
This, that evil be stayed, even turn and take flight!
I asked you few to do your duty, be fair and don't make the mistake,
of becoming cynical or callous, though it is one many did make.

I told you few would understand the call to duty I put in you,
and most would question your values and your love of family too.
I told you some of you would fall and to take no worry of that.
That I'd take care of you and your families where ere they're at.
I'm aware that your death there tears at the hearts of your family.
But trust Me, they'll receive love and peace from Me personally.

Your children will be watched over. I'll take care of them too.
And in time, they'll understand what it was I asked of you.
That you be one of those to take up the sword and protect the rest.
That you were chosen because you were among My bravest and best.
Yes, though I asked the others to run from evil with all their might.
I thank you …for being one who was willing to stay the line and fight."

Officer Samuel Jeppsen, #3751

"Then the word of the LORD came unto me, saying,
Before I formed thee in the belly I knew thee…"
Jeremiah 1:4, 5

"Remember, we work for God." Lt. Commander Vernon J. Gerberth, NYPD
Dedicated to all those who gave their lives for the cause of Justice or Freedom,
with special dedication to Cory Justin Jenkins, KIA: 08/25/2009, Afghanistan.

Chapter Three

The Power of a Dream

In the movie *The Neverending Story,* all of the people are leaving their homes and fleeing in a wild panic. They're leaving everything behind and running for their lives to escape the total devastation that is fast coming upon them. There is panic everywhere except in the heart and mind of a young warrior by the name of Atreyu. Atreyu is about fourteen years old, but he is fearless and has chosen to defend his homeland, even though he is the only warrior that will even try. He gets clues about his foe but no clear answers. All he is told is that the enemy is *The Nothing* and that it is wiping out everything and leaving nothing behind.

To learn how to defeat his foe, he travels through the *Sea of Despair, the Swamp of Sadness* and many other obstacles. Finally, he reaches the Empress, who sends him on, in hopes he can stop *The Nothing* from destroying everything. As Atreyu travels, he is confronted by Gmork, a huge wolf sent by *The Nothing* to destroy him! But if Atreyu is to die, he tells Gmork that he first wants to know what *The Nothing* is!! Gmork tells him, "It is the lack of hopes and dreams in the hearts and minds of the people. When these things are gone *...there is nothing left.*"

Of all the tragedies, I have seen in my police career and in my prison ministries, the saddest of them all, are the people who have lost their hopes and dreams. They either had them stolen or they gave up on them and discarded them as trash. They begin to doubt that the Lord could be interested in them. Soon, they feel they amount to nothing …so nothing matters!

As a young boy, I had lots of dreams for myself. One in particular, was inspired by the Culligan Water Softener Company and their slogan *"Hey Culligan Man!"* The commercial showed a big strong man wheeling large, heavy, metal bottles inside the homes of the customers. I dreamed of being the Culligan Man and of being so strong, I could carry the heavy bottles in my arms.

My dad had a large metal, galvanized pipe that was about chest high to me. It had an elbow and another short pipe on the lower end, connected to another elbow. It was big and heavy. I would pick it up and carry it up and down the driveway, seeing myself as being the strong Culligan delivery man.

Several years later, when I was in my early twenties, I was in Dad's basement, in his odd parts and pieces section. It was the place he kept things he may use one day. While looking around, I came across that piece of pipe. I recognized it immediately, but stood and stared at it in almost total disbelief!

The pipe that was so huge, so very heavy for me to carry, was in reality, quarter-wall, two and a half inch pipe, about twenty-four inches tall and weighed only about five or six pounds. All my life I had lived with the mental image that I was unusually strong for my size. That image came from a dream I had of who I wanted to be. It was fed by my carrying that pipe up and down the drive-way as a kid and seeing myself as a strong man. Seeing the pipe now, made me realize just how powerful having strong dreams are and how important having a good self image is.

As I grew, I went through a stage, where I felt that most of the dreams of greatness that young kids have, are childish and foolish and need to be set aside for the reality of adult life!

As life continues to pass, like Atreyu, I have come to realize just how important dreams of greatness are and that keeping them alive is critical to our will to press on and to our ability to be happy. After all, the number one tool for prisoner control in POW camps is the smashing of hopes and dreams.

I believe that many of our dreams are given to us by the Lord. Joseph of Egypt saw his family bowing to him. Jacob had a dream of prosperity. Lehi dreamed of the Promised Land. Each received those dreams during times in their lives, when they did not actually need them. Yet, having those dreams then, gave them something to hang onto during the times that followed, when their lives would be so turbulent and full of setbacks.

The effect a dream can have on us is incredibly powerful. Even a resurrected dream of yesteryear can supply the hope and energy to overcome a seemingly impossible situation or turn a dismal future into an exciting adventure for you.

Early in the marriage of my oldest daughter, Katina and her husband, Jay, they found that trying to make ends meet was very difficult. They came to a point where their uphill battle *looked harder* than the reward for pressing on *looked enticing.* They were living in a small little duplex in a rough part of town and their bills were piling up faster than income was coming in.

One night, both had a dream of living in a beautiful home. In the morning, they shared their dream, only to find that each had had the same dream and had seen the same home. It had a big and majestic, old-fashioned wood and tile entry. It had high ceilings, chandeliers and a staircase to the left with oak railing. It had a huge open room beyond the top of the staircase. Standing at the top was a little boy, looking down at Jay, as he entered the home. At the far end of the main floor, on the family room side, Katina was at a large countertop, preparing dinner.

That dream created hope within them and a passion for finding that home. For years, they searched several different new and used homes, looking for that home, but never found it. As time moved forward, Jay graduated from law school and became a successful attorney. They moved from one new home to another. Years later, living in a big, beautiful, new home, they got to the point where they no longer needed that dream.

One day, many years later, Julie and I bought a new home. It was big and beautiful and in a wonderful neighborhood. We had such great and wonderful feelings about it before we bought it. Every feeling inside us bore the signature of the Holy Ghost. The feeling telling us that it was right, was almost overwhelming.

However, shortly after we bought the home, troubles began. While it was being built, we were confronted with one disappointment after another. It got to the point that Julie and I were both sorry we had bought it and wished we had never seen it. Not understanding what was happening or why, I went over and over those feelings we had before buying the home. I knew we had followed the Spirit and had made the right decision, but I was totally confused and not understanding the problems we were now facing. I knelt in prayer time and again seeking understanding.

Jay and Katina, busy with their life, their family of four and Jay's career, had not had time to come and see our home being built. When it was finished, they finally came to visit. When Jay stepped inside, he suddenly stopped and stared. The look on his face was as if he had just seen a ghost. He then called Katina who was busy with her little family, to the front door, where he stood. He then said, "Look!" They stood there with looks of amazement on their faces for several moments. Afterwards, they joined the family and never explained what had just happened.

One day, while voicing our regrets for buying the home, Jay and Katina told us about the dream they had when they lived in that little duplex in the bad part of town. They said when they stood at the door of our home, they realized that it was *our* home, they had seen so many years ago in their dream. They described what they had seen then and how it matched everything, now. Even Luke, their three year old son, was standing at the top of the stairs looking at Jay when he came in. They said that it was the dream of that home that gave them the energy to keep pressing forward through the hard times. Jay then said, "Sam, I tell you this because we no longer need that dream, but I feel you and Julie do."

Their dream totally changed our feelings about our home and our outlook on the frustrations we faced. Their dream not only became our answer to prayer, it became a confirmation that we *had* made the right choice, after all. It became our very own dream. It testified to the four of us, just how great and loving, all-knowing and wise the Lord is. He was able to give a dream to *them*, when they needed it, which became a confirmation to *us*, later on.

Just as I believe that we are often given dreams to hang onto, often long before we need them, I also believe that our hopes and dreams can come through a third party. Someone else's hope or dream, or a story in the Scriptures, can become our own and it can supply the energy to move a mountain. More importantly, it can become a tool for the Lord to work miracles in our lives.

I have noticed that many of my own dreams have come to pass even as I dreamt them. Some dreams are unfolding now. As more and more dreams unfold, it confirms my belief that they were placed in my mind *then*, for direction in my life *now!* And I think that the *writing-off* of our dreams, is the tossing aside of future gifts from the Lord. Future gifts that first come in visual form, long before they come in physical form!

I have tried living with and without specific hopes and dreams. I have found that living without them, makes me as a pool of stagnant water, still and motionless, getting smaller each day and having less and less value. Without hopes or dreams, people are like a ship without a rudder. It is as American Idol judge, Steven Tyler said during the 2012 American Idol season. "If you don't have a dream, there is no way to make one come true!"

I have learned to not laugh at lofty dreams or to treat them lightly. I have learned to keep them alive and to keep them sacred and dear and to know that someday, the *how* to achieve them will open up when the time is right. As I have been doing this, I have found pathways for these dreams to become possible. First seeing them visually, then finding a pathway, brings a feeling inside me as if I were keeping an appointment with destiny.

As a kid, I had four hopes or dreams that I envisioned for myself. 1) To know God. 2) To help others and be the guy others could count on to protect them. 3) To marry a beautiful girl. 4) To live a life of adventure. Now, at over sixty, I can say that everything good in my life has stemmed from those four childhood hopes and dreams.

Growing up, many of my heroes were the fictional characters, portrayed by John Wayne. And like the days of the old west, where there was a big difference between good guys and bad guys and the good guys actually had high standards, it made me want to be a good guy. It made me want to wear a white hat, do the right thing, be the hero, stand tall, ride hard, shoot straight and all the other hero stuff.

Standing in the way of these desires coming to pass was just one little problem. I have a learning challenge and have struggled with it my whole life. I could read things two or three times and not understand them as well as others who had read them only once. It made school very difficult. If I grew up in this day and age, I would have been labeled.

I was fortunate that I grew up in the time that I did. I had stern teachers that told me that I needed to stop being lazy and to work harder. They said that I needed to pay more attention and keep up with the rest of the class and stop goofing off. I remember getting those talks regularly. I was put in several remedial reading and math classes. I failed the fourth grade and averaged C+ grades throughout school.

Having teachers that told me I needed to stop being lazy and pay more attention, instead of giving me a label, was a huge blessing. To me, it was just a habit that I needed to break, not a deficiency in my ability. All through life, I have tried to do just that. Do I fall short? I do! So what do I do about it? I continue to try harder, to pay more attention and stop goofing off.

Though I still struggle with this challenge, through it has come my greatest gift from the Lord. So great, that I developed a huge dependency on Him and a strong relationship with Him. This dependency and relationship has been as a sweet fruit I was able to enjoy anytime I wanted. I have learned that I never have to be afraid again. I know that He lives and that He will always help me. I can trust Him and be calm in my troubles because He will come.

To add to my problems, I left home when I was seventeen and moved to Arizona to start a new life. The decision was not made out of rebellion. Financially speaking, things were very tough at home and it seemed the right time to get started in life. To further complicate things, I didn't have any college. High school was as far as I got.

Eight years later the Lord blessed me with the opportunity to become a police officer. In law enforcement, much of my need to protect others was fulfilled. That need even kept me from trying for rank. Rank would have taken me off the street, out of the homes, away from the family fights, away from the bullies and the mean and ugly people who make life miserable for others. I had a deep need to continually block their path and keep them away from those who were good. It also helped satisfy my strong need for adventure, as each night at work, was a new adventure for me.

I also managed to marry a beautiful girl. She is as beautiful as a person, as she is to behold. Falling in love and marrying her was one of the best decisions, I have made in my life. We've had our ups and downs, our good times and our bad, but we've gotten to the point where we don't even argue anymore.

Roberta Randall Stapley is a marriage counselor, public speaker, CEO of Family Dynamics Inc. and more. She said that anytime there is trouble in a family, she starts by looking at the marriage and works to strengthen it first. She said men are natural givers and women are natural nurturers and when a marriage begins to fall apart, it is because the man has stopped giving and the woman has stopped nurturing.

In the thousands of family fights, I have been to as a police officer, I have found Roberta Stapley's words to be true. Even though you can't change someone that doesn't want to change, if two people are willing to change themselves, their marriage and home can become a heaven on earth.

Motorcycles also helped me fulfill my desire for adventure. It occurs because of the feeling of freedom that comes when you ride. It is hard to explain if your preferred method of travel is in an environmental envelope (car.) In a car, you basically have three television sets that you're trying to watch at the same time. You have the front windshield and the two side windows. The wind you feel is the AC and what you smell is the inside of the car.

Riding is totally different. Your vision is not blocked at all and the world appears as a panoramic theater. You feel like a low flying angel, flying through the living and ever changing art gallery of the Lord. You feel and smell, life itself. You feel like a participant in nature. You feel ...awakened!

Through my great love for motorcycles, I have learned that the feeling of being awakened is a natural euphoric feeling. It is a powerful motivator that stirs something deep inside. I have learned that when this awakening is coupled with a dream, the dream becomes the launch pad for desire. Desire is the starter button for action, which is the first step of succeeding at whatever you try to do. Without a dream, everything is troublesome and labored. But with a dream, everything is an opportunity to get closer to that dream. In pursuit of a dream, life itself changes and because your attitude changes, you have a newfound energy and enthusiasm. It all becomes the perfect open door for the Lord and the perfect fertile ground for Him to work miracles in your life.

With three of my four childhood dreams fulfilled, my last was to know more about my God, to follow Him and to have a personal relationship with Him. In all honesty, this was also my most important dream. It is the dream that I have thought of most often and it is the dream that is the foundation of all others.

Wanting to know more about Him, was always hampered by my feelings that I had fallen short of His interest in me. I was one who had made several mistakes in life and who had lots of shortcomings. This had become a roadblock in my mind. Yet, in my quest to learn more about Him, I have not only learned how much He loves us, but how little our shortcomings matter to Him.

Maybe you didn't make all the right choices and decisions! Maybe you feel you have made too many wrong choices or that your mistakes are too big or that you are unimportant! Maybe you still take yourself out to the gallows and hang yourself on a regular basis! Maybe you've given up on your dreams for these or other reasons. Well ...maybe you shouldn't!

Your Heavenly Father and His Son Jesus Christ, love you so very much and more than you can ever understand. Your Dear Heavenly Father has a plan called, *The Plan of Happiness* and it targets you. His Son, Jesus Christ, Creator of heaven and earth and Savior of all mankind, stands at the head of that plan. And because of His atoning sacrifice, He has a way, already worked out for you. The Plan of Happiness is not a plan of dashed hopes. Instead, it is a plan of fulfilled dreams. Our loving Lord did not die in vain and He did not give you those dreams way back *then*, just to rub them in your face *now* or to show you what you *could* have had. He gave them to you then, to hang onto, for the times later on, He knew you would so desperately need them.

It is this foreknowledge He had of you and the love and blessings He still gives you that is the proof that you can trust Him. As you place your hand in His, on your journey from Faith to Trust with Him, you will find a whole new life, filled with adventure. It will be one that is filled with dreams and excitement all the time.

So, maybe you still have an appointment to keep with Him. Maybe your dream is still waiting for you, a wonderful dream with none of the pieces missing. Maybe He patiently waits for you to keep your appointment with Him.

It would be just like Him, wouldn't it? It would be just like Him to love you so much that even after a major mistake in your life, He would still give you that old dream back. It would be just like Him to catch you as you tried to write yourself off, to remind you that you are His, to let you know that if you will follow Him, in time, you could be right where you would have been anyway.

Wouldn't it be just like Him ...to love you that much?!

10) Don't curse yourself, compare yourself or write yourself off.
11) Recognize shortcomings as huge blessings in disguise.
12) Create a new you. Start seeing what isn't ...until what isn't ... is!!
13) Cherish your dreams, use them as roadmaps, appointments with destiny.

Chapter Four

Creating a Partnership

> "Intelligence, Patriotism, Christianity, and a firm reliance on Him, who has never yet forsaken this favored land, are still competent to adjust, in the best way, all our present difficulty."
>
> *Abraham Lincoln*

In creating a partnership with someone, you must first begin a friendship which requires that you get to know them. In order to get to know them, you have to study them. Developing a partnership with Christ involves the same step by step process. I study from the Scriptures every day, just for that reason.

I am also very religious and there is much that can be said about religion. I am Christian and though I have not seen Christ, I know some very basic truths about Him. One is that I know for a surety that He lives. I don't hope this or just believe this, I *know* this! Like a blind man knows by his senses, that the sun has risen and a new day has begun, so too, do I know that the Savior lives.

Even so, every religion believes in a God and one can argue beliefs, scriptures and facts all day. But at the end of the day, all you will have is what you began with—an argument. There are seventeen major religious groups in the world, with Christianity being one of them. That not being enough, there are over thirty-two thousand different denominations inside Christianity. With all this, there certainly seems to be a lot to argue about.

To simplify things, here are six easy steps to follow. Step Number One: *Decide for yourself what you should believe.*

My Scriptures were given to me by my mother in 1978. In my Bible she wrote, "Always stay very close to the Lord, My Son, and He will always be your Shepherd and your constant guide and will bring you forth triumphant." My old Scriptures and her words to me are the most valuable possession I have from her. Tucked away in the pages, next to a favorite verse, I keep her picture.

My Bible is the *King James Version* which is important to me. Modern versions are easier to read but modern words can change the meaning of very significant teachings.

On January 13th, 2012, as a Law Enforcement Chaplain and a retired police officer, I went to the funeral of Maricopa County Sheriff's Deputy, William Coleman in Phoenix, Arizona. He was an exceptional father and contributor to the community. He was also the first *Line of Duty* (LOD) death in Arizona for 2012. He was killed by an assailant who also killed two people in Sedona, Arizona, with a possible link to a forth slaying.

The pastor who performed the service did a remarkably wonderful job. In his sermon he said we should not worry about Bill. He quoted the Savior in John 14:2 from the 2005, *Today's New International Version* (TNIV) the updated version of the 1984, *New International Version* (NIV). It reads, "In my Father's house are many rooms; if that were not so, would I have told you that I am going there to prepare a place for you?"

In my old, 1978—1611, *King James Version* (KJV) the verse reads, "In my Father's house are many mansions: if it were not so, I would have told you. I go to prepare a place for you." The differences between the two versions are interesting. In the first example, the Savior makes a statement followed by a question. In the second example, the Savior makes a statement followed by two more statements. There are also differences in the punctuation which is designed to emphasize the writer's meaning. Changing the punctuation can change that meaning. But the most important difference to me is the change of the word *mansion* to the word *room*. The mental image that comes to my mind with the word *mansion*, is totally different from the mental image that comes with the word *room*.

I suppose the word *mansion* was changed to *room* in the newer version because the scholars who rewrote the scripture couldn't see how you could have *mansions* inside a *house*. So using their logic, the translators changed *mansions* to *rooms*. The mental image that comes to mind, "In my Father's house are many rooms …" is one where I have a room waiting for me in my Father in Heaven's house, like a bedroom. But in the case of there being millions of children, comes the image of an enormous dormitory. My mental picture is a dorm having endlessly long hallways and my room being someplace, down one of them.

When I think of my own house, I not only think of the structure itself, I also think of the beautifully landscaped property the structure is on. *All of it* is my house. We once owned thirty-five acres in Colorado where we planned on living one day. *All of it* would have been our home.

When I think of the words of Christ, as quoted in the KJV, "In my Father's house are many mansions ..." I think of Heavenly Father's house as being an entire world and my mansion being on some beautiful hillside, overlooking a beautiful green valley with trees and a small river running through it. There, winding through the valley and trees is a little road, leading up to my mansion.

I don't have a big problem with these kinds of changes. The gist of the two verses is similar and *both* versions will draw the reader closer to Christ. But these kinds of changes are partially the reason I choose to study and quote from the KJV.

I love the KJV Bible my mother gave me and I always will. It is my Bible of choice. Wikianswers.com said of the KJV, "This is the most widely used version; however, it has a large number of errors given that none of the writers had a decent understanding of Hebrew." Even though Wikianswers made that comment, I know that the Spirit of the Lord is throughout this holy book.

There are eight versions of the Bible that are considered to be, "the Primary Versions." They are: *The Septuagint*, written in Greek in 250AD, *The Vulgate*, written in Latin in 400AD, *Luther's German Bible*, published in 1534, *The King James Version* (KJV) published in 1611, *The Young's Literal Translation* (YLT) published in 1862, *The Revised Standard Version* (RSV) published in 1952, and *The New International Version* (NIV) written in the late 1960's and early 1970's and updated in 1984 and again in 2005. From these eight versions of the Bible have come approximately fifty other English translations.

According to Amazon, their top ten sellers are, *The New Revised Standard Version* (NSRV,) *The New Living Translation* (NLT,) *The Message*, *The Amplified Bible*, *The Orthodox Study Bible*, *The New American Bible* (NAB,) *The New International Version* (NIV,) *The King James Version* (KJV,) *The New American Standard Bible* (NASB,) and *The Revised Standard Version* (RSV.) There are also two more popular versions, *The New American Standard* (NAS) and *The English Standard Version* (ESV.) To me, it is a surprising amount to choose from.

There are others besides these Protestant Bibles. And according to The History Channel's program, "Banned From The Bible," there are several books that never made it into the Bible, including ones about Christ. So the differences began in 325 AD, at the Council of Nicaea, where the Bible was formalized.

Wikianswers.com said, "Each [Bible] chooses different translations the authors felt were most important or most accurate, based on the documents they had at the time." Therefore, Step Number Two is: *Decide what Bible you want to study from.*

Another reason I prefer the KJV, is because it is the Bible of our Fathers. It was translated by the order of King James and it took 47 to 55 scholars, over five years to complete the work. They finished it in 1611 and it was *that* Bible that inspired the men and women in 1620 to board the Mayflower and set sail for America. Before disembarking, they created and signed the Mayflower Compact. All forty-one adult males signed it and the remaining fifty to sixty passengers ratified it. Interestingly, like the different versions of the Bible, there are three different versions of the Mayflower Compact. The original that was signed on November 11th, 1620, has been lost. In all three of the later versions, (1622, 1646 and 1669,) the word "God" is found four times.

The passengers were not only adventurous to some and foolhardy to others, they were religious people with great faith in Christ. They were Christians, just as our founding fathers were. It was Patrick Henry that said, "It cannot be emphasized too strongly, nor too often that this great nation was founded, not by religionists, but by Christians, not on religions, but on the Gospel of Jesus Christ ..." Thomas Jefferson said, "I have little doubt that the whole country will soon be rallied to the unity of our Creator, and, I hope, to the pure doctrines of Jesus also." He said that it was the God of the Bible, who founded America, in his 1805 inaugural address. He also said, "I shall need, too, the favor of that Being in whose hands we are, who led our forefathers, as Israel of old, from their native land and planted them in this country."

Abraham Lincoln, though not a founding father, was like our Founding Fathers. This incredible man that I admire, made a statement that I resort to often. He said, "I have been driven many times upon my knees by the overwhelming conviction that I had nowhere else to go. My own wisdom, and that of all about me, seemed insufficient for the day."

It was the *King James Version* of the Bible and the Pilgrim's love for Jesus Christ and their hope for freedom that ignited the dream that began all of this. You see, I not only love my Bible, I love my Country and I love the righteous that followed the Spirit of Freedom so long ago. It was the KJV and their hope in Christ that made these dreams a reality for me and my family.

My favorite apostle in the Bible is the Apostle Paul. There are many things about him and his life that really inspire me. In Paul's letter to Timothy, he told this truth that is often overlooked by people today. He said of the Scriptures, "All scripture is given by inspiration of God, and is profitable for doctrine, for reproof, for correction, for instruction in righteousness; that the man of God may be perfect, thoroughly furnished unto all good works."

One of the things, in particular, that I really like about Paul is that he reminds me of the many people I have met who were once *Sauls* and who became *Pauls*. Paul said of himself, "For I am the least of the apostles, that am not meet to be called an apostle, because I persecuted the church of God. But by the grace of God I am what I am: and his grace which was bestowed upon me was not in vain; but I laboured more abundantly than they all: yet not I, but the grace of God which was with me."

As I ponder Paul's summation of himself and as I travel life's highways, I often run across these *Sauls to Pauls*. In almost all cases, they were basically good people who were on the wrong track. In each case, the Lord was able to reach out and touch them and turn them. Afterwards, each one in their own way became a mighty servant of the Lord.

Another reason I like Paul so much, is that he had such a deep understanding of Christ and spiritual things. When he spoke of Christ to the Corinthians, he said, "And that he died for all, that they which live should not henceforth live unto themselves, but unto him which died for them and rose again." A scripture later he said, "if any man be in Christ, he is a new creature: old things are passed away." And just two scriptures later he said of those who follow Christ, "Now then we are ambassadors for Christ."

Paul is also one of the reasons I know we have a Father in Heaven and that Jesus is His Son. He taught of God the Father and of His Son Jesus Christ throughout his entire ministry but perhaps no more plainly than he did to the Hebrews in the first ten verses of Hebrews, chapter five.

It is in this chapter, Paul spoke of Christ, of High Priests and of the Melchisedec Priesthood (KJV.) When Paul taught the Ephesians, he said, "Cease not to give thanks…That the God of our Lord Jesus Christ, the Father of glory, may give unto you the spirit of wisdom and revelation in the knowledge of him…which he wrought in Christ, when he raised him from the dead and set him at his own right hand in the heavenly places."

Peter and John taught the same doctrine, as well. When they healed the lame man on their way to the temple, they were arrested and taken before the high priest, Caiaphas. It was during their second arrest that Peter gave his strongest and most rebuking testament to Caiaphas, of Christ. He said, "The God of our fathers raised up Jesus, whom ye slew and hanged on a tree. Him hath God exalted with his right hand to be a Prince and a Savior, for to give repentance to Israel, and forgiveness of sins. And we are his witnesses of these things; and so is also the Holy Ghost, who God hath given to them that obey him." In fact, if you read the Bible yourself, you will find that all the apostles taught the same doctrine concerning Christ and His Father. So, Step Number Three is: *Study the Scriptures for yourself, instead of letting me or someone else tell you what they say.* One of the reasons King James ordered the Latin Bible to be translated into English, was so the common man could read the Bible, himself and learn for himself, what it said, without having someone else's interpretation added in.

If you KJV word-search or Google search any of the quotes I have used in this book, they will bring up the verse and those around it and you can read for yourself and develop your own understanding and form your own beliefs.

Though *faith in* and the *understanding of* who Christ is, has to be based on *all* the scriptures and not on isolated verses, it was Christ Himself who said, "No man can come unto me, except he doeth the will of my Father who hath sent me" and "My meat is to do the will of him that sent me, and to finish his work."

In His great intercessory prayer, He said, "Father, the hour is come; glorify thy Son that thy Son also may glorify thee…And this is life eternal, that they might know thee the only true God and Jesus Christ, whom thou hast sent. I have glorified thee on earth: I have finished the work which thou gavest me to do." As He hung on the cross, His last words were, "Father, into thy hands I commend my spirit."

After His resurrection, He appeared to Mary at the sepulcher. When she realized it was Him, she ran to Him. As she did, Christ said, "Touch me not for I am not yet ascended to my Father; but go to my brethren and say unto them, I ascend unto my Father, and your Father; and to my God, and your God."

You will notice that I have stayed away from any personal interpretation of the Scriptures. My belief in *who* Christ is, is rooted in what the Scriptures say. It has grown from there through prayer, fasting and personal experiences. I am a simple man and I believe simply and I don't let myself surmise answers to the deep and philosophical questions I may have. Unfortunately, like the evolution theorists, who are constantly surmising one thing after another, I know many good religious men and women who are doing the same thing. A wiser man than I once said, "Cling to the trunk of the tree. There is safety there, and don't get out on the branches." So I do. I avoid Think-Tank friends and Think-Tank philosophy. If it's not Scriptural, I set it aside.

In studying the Scriptures, what I do know for a surety is that Christ said to pray to our Father in Heaven. When Christ was transfigured before Peter, James and John and they saw Christ speaking with Moses and Elias, Peter suggested that they build tabernacles for Christ, Moses and Elias. The suggestion was to honor all three, Christ, Moses and Elias. As Peter was speaking, a cloud came over them all. It was then that a voice from the cloud said, "Behold this is my Beloved Son: hear Him." In other words, Christ is totally in charge and we are to follow Him—period.

The Scriptures also tell us it was the Lord that was in the furnace with Shadrach, Meshach and Abednego and it was the Lord that appeared to Gideon and told him to prepare for battle against the Midianites. It was the Lord that gave Samson his strength. It was the Lord that appeared to Abraham and later to his son, Isaac. It was also the Lord that went before Moses and freed the Israelites. It was the Lord that led the Israelites, "by day in a pillar of a cloud and by night in a pillar of fire."

When the Israelites saw the Egyptians in their chariots, coming to slay them, they murmured against Moses. They said it would have been better for them to live in Egypt as slaves than to die in the desert. Moses told them, "Fear ye not, stand still, and see the salvation of the Lord, which he will shew to you to day: for the Egyptians whom ye have seen to day, ye shall see them again no more for ever. The Lord shall fight for you, and ye shall hold your peace." It was also the Lord that parted the Red Sea. It was the Lord that rained bread from heaven upon the Israelites and it was the Lord that called unto Moses from the mountain.

It was the Lord that appeared to Solomon, to Samuel, to Mary, to the eleven apostles, to Paul, to the brother of Jared, to Alma and Amulek and many others. It is also in the Lord's name that all blessings are given and miracles are performed.

Perhaps one of the most powerfully descriptive Scriptures of Christ is given by King Benjamin as he addressed his people. He said, "Behold the time cometh and is not far distant, that with power the Lord Omnipotent who reigneth, who was, and is from all eternity to eternity, shall come down from heaven among the children of men, and shall dwell in a tabernacle of clay ..." He also said, "And he shall be called Jesus Christ, the Son of God, the Father of heaven and earth, the Creator of all things from the beginning; and his mother shall be called Mary" and "that salvation might come...even through faith on His name."

I don't pretend to know all the answers, but I do read the Scriptures and I believe what they say. Perhaps one of the most important Scriptures we can remember is, "For God so loved the world that He gave His only Begotten Son that whosoever believeth in Him should not perish but have everlasting life." And when Christ said these words during His Sermon on the Mount, "Ask, and it shall be given you; seek, and ye shall find; knock, and it shall be opened unto you: For everyone that asketh receiveth; and he that seeketh findeth; and to him that knocketh it shall be opened," He gave the basic solutions to all of life's questions and problems. ...*All* of them!

When Christ followed that with, "Or what man is there of you, whom if his son ask bread, will he give him a stone? Or if he ask a fish, will give him a serpent? If ye, being evil, know how to give good gifts unto your children, how much more shall your Father which is in heaven give good things to them that ask him," He gave the promise of our prayers being heard and answered. So, Step Number Four is: *Prayerfully decide who Christ is.*

Remember that in your journey to build a partnership *with* Christ, you must spend time getting to *know* Christ. I can think of no better way to begin, than by reading the Bible. The Bible is our Basic Instructions Before Leaving Earth book.

Most people spend very little time in the Bible and very, very few have ever read it page to page, cover to cover. It can easily become one of your most favorite books, as it is mine. The words of Christ bring electricity to my heart and soul. In my very best attempt to explain it, I am reminded of the words of Jeremiah when he said, "…his word was in mine heart as a burning fire shut up in my bones…" That is how you will feel inside when you feast on the words of Christ.

The thing in this chapter I want you to remember most of all, is the great benefit that can become yours if you will take the time to know the Savior and then to follow Him. The trek from Faith to Trust is an incredible journey of happiness. As you travel the path toward trust, you will find that the trail is heavily traveled by angels. It is a trail that relieves fear and heartache. It is a trail that when troubles, uncertainty and pain come-a-knocking, there will also be the quiet calmness of attending angels that have been sent by the Lord. You will feel them to your right and to your left.

One of my favorite Bible stories is the story about Elisha and the Syrian army. The king of Syria was angry with the prophet Elisha because he had been forewarning the Israelite army of the strategies of the Syrians. So the king searched until he found where Elisha was living. Then, by night, the king surrounded the city with his armies. He had his army stand motionless and let the break of day announce their presence. He used the silence and his overpowering presence as a psychological weapon to strike fear into their hearts. The Scriptures record that the Syrian king, "…sent he thither horses, and chariots, and a great host…" The very next verse says, "And when the servant of the man of God was risen early, and gone forth, behold, an host encompassed the city both with horses and chariots. And the servant said unto him, Alas, my master! How shall we do?"

The Scriptures do not say whether or not Elisha even went to look for himself. Instead he calmly said, "Fear not: for they that be with us are more than be with them." Elisha then said, "Lord, I pray thee, open his eyes that he may see. And the Lord opened the eyes of the young man; and he saw: and, beheld, the mountain was full of horses and chariots of fire round about Elisha." Notice that the Scriptures never say that the Lord opened Elisha's eyes. Elisha didn't need his eyes opened. He didn't need to see. Elisha already knew the Lord and he knew that he could count on Him.

Elisha learned through a lifetime of experiences that he could trust the Lord. This was not his first experience or his first crises. This particular story of Elisha is one of my most favorite stories because of the magnitude of trust Elisha must have had in the Lord. It is one of my favorite stories because I don't believe Elisha ever did see, what the servant saw and—that he didn't need to see. It is one of those precious stories that is dear to my heart because here was a man, who because of the trust he had in the Lord, could be calm in a raging storm.

King David said, "Yea, though I walk through the valley of the shadow of death, I will fear no evil: for thou art with me; thy rod and thy staff they comfort me." David, like Elisha, knew from personal experience that he could trust the Lord.

Knowing who Christ is, is the foundation of understanding what He can do for you and it is the most important thing you will ever learn. Your trek from Faith to Trust requires a friendship and then a partnership with the Savior. Your partnership with Him can only come with effort on your part.

Our Savior lives. Christ is The Way. He is the Only Begotten Son of God. He is the Lord Omnipotent. He is the Savior of all mankind. He is the Creator, the Father of heaven and earth. In order to get to know Him, you must *want* to know Him. So, Step Number Five is: *You have to want!*

You must spend time studying the Scriptures and you must spend time praying. When Christ taught the disciples of our Heavenly Father, afterwards, some of them came to Him and asked, "Lord, teach us to pray…" He told them, "After this manner therefore pray ye: Our Father which art in Heaven, Hollowed be thy name…" Prayer begins that simply. It was James that said, "If any of you lack wisdom, let him ask of God, that giveth to all men liberally, and upbraideth not; and it shall be given him." So, Step Number Six is: *You have to ask!!*

14) Read the Scriptures, learn who the Savior is, learn for yourself what He taught.

Chapter Five

The "Lester Gift"

I am a people watcher by nature and a retired police officer by trade. Police work is nothing more than the people-problem-business. It is dealing with the end result of their bad choices. With over twenty-five years of trying to help people from behind a shield, I learned a lot about understanding them. In my learning to understand them, I would also watch the decisions they made concerning Christ. It was in my watching of their decisions *concerning* Christ, which has given me hundreds of hours of reflection, on the need to partner *with* Christ.

Some people feel they don't need to partner with Him and that they do just fine without Him. Many more are so successful and prosperous, that they live lives I can only dream about. I have always admired people who are so gifted, that life is easy for them. "Why wasn't I like that?" I have asked myself. "Why not me?" For years I have wished to be like that. But fortunately for me, however, life is a struggle.

Struggling to keep up with others has turned out to be one of my greatest gifts from the Lord. At my very best, I'm only a ninety percenter. I have just about ninety percent of what it takes to put a normal life together. I have always had to pray and call out for help for the rest. I have realized that this seemingly great downfall in my ability is in reality a marvelous blessing from the Lord. It is one of His special blessings to me that I think of often.

I am *still* very self conscious of the fact I have some learning challenges, but because of what they do for me, I have nicknamed them my *Lester Gift.*

In junior high, I had a small group of friends and Lester was one of them. One of our pastimes was to tepee a friend's home. Lester was a bit short and round and could not scale the property fences. He always got stuck on the wall and would cry out for help. Somebody always had to help him over. He never cleared a single wall on his own. So we agreed among ourselves that we would help Lester first, before we jumped over.

One day, we were teepeeing a friend's home and the police came. Our lookout yelled, *"Police!"* We took off running through the backyard and through the Oleander hedge—or so we thought! When we hit the Oleander hedge, we found that it had a six foot chain-link fence running through it.

We were so scared! Without a thought we were over that fence and running down the street. We were a whole block away, before we remembered we had forgotten to help Lester.

The other guys kept running, but one other fellow and I went back for Lester. Sure enough, there he was, still standing in the backyard. Now however, there were two big cops standing in front of him, shining their flashlights in his face. Lester looked terrified. He was standing with his hands clasped together, swaying back and forth from foot to foot, like an elephant. The look on his face was one of total fear. The owners then came outside and we had to clean up the mess. That turned out to be the last home we ever teepeed. I would never forget that experience because *Lester's* story became *my* story.

All through my life, in trying to achieve anything important, jobs, high test scores, success in business ventures, etc., I have found that I was Lester. No matter how hard I tried to scale the wall myself, I always got stuck near the top. I could never clear a single wall alone. After doing my very best, I found I could only make ninety percent of the minimum requirement needed to succeed. I have always had to depend on the Lord's help. Many people talk of how much they need a relationship with the Lord, for their spiritual understanding, guidance, relief and forgiveness, etc. But for me, it was more than that. I needed the Lord for everything and in every single area of my life.

Absolutely *needing* Him for everything has brought me hundreds of cherished moments *with* Him. It has also brought me the knowledge that He lives, as well as a deeper and more personal relationship with Him.

I have always loved the story of David and Goliath. When the Prophet Samuel, under the direction of the Lord, was looking for a new King of Israel, the Lord sent him to a Bethlemite, by the name of Jesse. Once there, he invited Jesse's sons to come before him. When he saw Eliab, he said to himself, "Surely the Lord's anointed is before him." But the Lord told Samuel, "Look not on his countenance or on the height of his stature; because I have refused him." Apparently Eliab was a big, strong and mighty man and he must have had all the command presence of a great warrior as well as the countenance of a leader.

The next thing the Lord told Samuel is something I have thought about hundreds of times throughout my life. He said, "For the Lord seeth not as man seeth; for man looketh on the outward appearance, but the Lord looketh on the heart."

Samuel goes through all seven sons and is confused because the Lord rejects them all. He then asks Jesse if there are any more sons. Jesse says, "There remaineth yet the youngest, and behold, he keepeth the sheep." Samuel sent for him and when he saw him, the Lord told Samuel, "Arise, anoint him: for this is he." David becomes the chosen of the Lord, to be the next King of Israel. The lesson to learn here is that the Lord does not choose His leaders by their greatness or by their stature or talent. Instead, He chooses them by their heart. ...Something *anyone* can have.

As the story goes on, the Philistines come against Israel. Goliath, a man from Gath, who stands six cubits and a span tall, stands at the border of Israel and begs Israel for a challenger. The Scriptures say, "All Israel ran," which included David, as he was there. It was not until later on that evening, after hearing the king's reward, for the man who killed Goliath, three different times, that David made the decision to fight Goliath.

There are two important things to learn here. One, David had a dream—and so must you! Regardless of how great a reward may be, if you don't have a dream, a strong *want* inside you, even the enormity of the reward will make no difference to you. Some of David's dreams were obviously, to own a horse and never have to walk again, to own land, marry the princess and to be someone important, as those were the rewards. Two, because David already had a faithful heart and had built a great deal of trust in the Lord, he was not afraid to depend on the Lord in this life and death crisis moment—which is exactly how you and I should live *our* lives.

When David made the decision to fight the mighty Goliath, he asked King Saul for the chance, but Saul tells him, "Thou are not able to go against this Philistine to fight with him: for thou are but a youth and he is a man of war from his youth." David replies, "The Lord that delivered me out of the paw of the lion, and out of the paw of the bear, he will deliver me out of the hand of this Philistine."

Through these two prior experiences and the many smaller experiences he must have already gone through, David had built a strong and powerful relationship and then partnership with the Lord. When David fearlessly walked across that battlefield and stood in front of the mighty Goliath, he knew that the Lord would be with him. For David to boldly say to Goliath, "I come to thee in the name of the Lord …" took far more than faith. It took a tremendous amount of trust in a God he had never seen.

David knew that the Lord lives and he knew that the Lord would come to his aid. His step by step partnership building process with the Lord began by trusting here-a-little and there-a-little, until one day he could fight a bear, then a lion and then his biggest problem ever …Goliath!

My desperate need *for* the Lord's help in my life has become my greatest gift *from* the Lord. It has become my very own Jacob's ladder, where Jacob dreamed of a ladder to Heaven and saw the Lord standing at the head of it.

Perhaps the very first time I realized what a blessing my shortcoming is, occurred just before I was hired by the City of Mesa, as a police officer. I was never afraid of work, but I was always afraid of taking lengthy written tests. On the day of the police exam, I went into a room with over six hundred and forty other applicants, for thirty slots. The written portions of the test were scheduled to take the whole day. There were several tests totaling almost six hundred questions. Only someone, who has the kind of shortcoming I have, can understand the fear this can bring.

Realizing that I needed help, I prayed and poured out my heart and pleaded for it. I prayed until I got that feeling that He would be with me. In fact the feeling was so strong with me that when I showed up that day and found six hundred and forty other applicants, I remember actually feeling bad for the six hundred and ten that would not make it. I knew for a certainty I was going to be one of the chosen ones …and I was.

Realizing this great need *for* Him, to help slay my own goliaths, is my greatest gift *from* Him, has caused me to create a partnership *with* Him. The fruits from that partnership are so great, I have come to feel sorry for those who are so sharp, competing in life is a breeze. Of the two gifts, I have the greater.

If you have this gift or this need, this great shortfall on your part, *learn to cherish it*. It is the gateway to miracles *if* you create a partnership with the Lord! Nobody can create that partnership for you. It is something you have to do for yourself. Just as no one can test or interview for a job *for* you, creating your partnership with the Lord, has to be done *by* you.

Many times when life has been the most challenging, because of Him, it has also been the most rewarding and the very sweetest. I have learned that in my trials and tribulations, to look for the gold nuggets, among the rocks, as they will always be there.

Search your own life. Look closely and see if that isn't true for you as well. Look back at the challenges you faced, the trials, the devastating heartaches and at your darkest moments. Were you really ever alone in them? Wasn't there a feeling inside you that told you the Lord was nearby and that you could depend on Him? Couldn't you feel Him reaching out to you and placing gold nuggets of Hope and Light in front of you and beckoning you toward Him?

In the story where Christ healed the blind man with clay and spittle, His disciples asked, "Master, who did sin, this man or his parents, that he was born blind?" The Savior's answer was as usual, very profound. He said, "Neither hath this man sinned, nor his parents: but that the works of God should be made manifest in him." That is often the way it is with us too. The weaknesses we have and the challenges we experience, are there so that the works of God can be made manifest in us.

15) Never lose heart, believe everything in life is for a good reason, even shortcomings …and chomp at the bit—to believe as David believed.

"Behold, I have refined thee, but not with silver;
I have chosen thee in the furnace of affliction"
Jesus Christ

Chapter Six

The Wish List

I have learned that if things are going well, with not much adversity in my life, to compensate by trying to obtain something on my *Wish List.* It is a fabulous way to develop or increase my faith and understanding in the Lord. Trying for a wish, increases my need for Him and it increases the intensity of my prayers. It also ultimately builds and deepens my relationship and partnership with Him. Lastly, it not only helps me obtain more out of life, it does what having a crisis in my life will do for me. It tests and taxes me and improves me as I struggle along. I can often learn the same lesson trying for a wish …that I can learn in a crisis.

It is not that important to the Lord that you have a wish come true, but it is important to Him that you seek Him. And it is much more important to Him that you seek Him because you *want* to, instead of seeking Him because of a crisis and now *have* to.

In early 2010, I was invited to become a law enforcement chaplain. The invitation came from a senior chaplain by the name of Bill Glennie. He has been a law enforcement chaplain for forty years. He has served with the Arizona Dept. of Public Safety (AZ. Highway Patrol), as well as the US Marshal's Office and has served at Ground Zero and at the Katrina disaster.

He told me once, "I was nothing before I turned my life over to Christ. I was just a cowboy, catching wild mustangs and selling them for twenty-five dollars a head, if I green-broke them first. But when I turned my life over to Christ, door after door began opening for me. It was literally one blessing after another."

I have found this to be true in my own life. I can almost point to the dates on the calendar, where I had made an increased commitment to surrender *my* will to *His* will and to do things His way, instead of my way. It was during those times of increased commitment to Him, that the "Doors of Increased Opportunities" began opening around me, and for me. The periods of increased commitment on my part, would come as I faced crisis moments or as I was trying for something on my Wish List.

I use the term partnership in addition to relationship because the term relationship encompasses a broad spectrum of meanings from passive to being deeply committed. The term *partnership* is an *action* word and has a narrower meaning that signifies a two-sided commitment to work together. After all, it is one thing to *love* the Lord, it is a whole other thing to *need* Him.

When you desperately need the Lord, it brings an intensity of emotion within you. It brings an unusual closeness to Him that is hard to explain, but easy to discern. This draw toward Him, also creates a greater distance between you and the world.

Paul said, when he spoke to the Romans, "For of him, and through him, and to him, *are* all things." In short, Christ is the way and the only way! Following Christ, creating a partnership with Him and doing things His way, is not only a major principle of success—it is the very key that opens the door to happiness.

When you make the commitment to follow the Lord and to partner with Him, you will not only have increased help in your crisis moments, you will find that in every area of your life, you will actually live beyond your ability to achieve. You will also find a spiritual nudge to go after the things on your wish list. If you seek Him in all things, He will adorn your life with gifts.

Dieter F. Uchtdorf tells the story of a man who had the lifelong dream of boarding a cruise ship and sailing the entire Mediterranean Sea. He dreamed of being one of the very few that ever experienced living on a ship in the Mediterranean and seeing every port and country. He dreamed of walking the streets of Rome, Athens, Istanbul, Barcelona and more. He saved every spare penny until he had enough to finally fulfill his dream.

He packed an extra suitcase of food, so he could save money on the cruise. The man ate from his suitcase and watched in envy at the passengers who ate in the fine dining rooms and went to the wonderful shows.

On the last day of the cruise, he was asked which of the farewell parties he would be attending. It was only then that he realized that all the fine dining and shows and activities had been included in the price of the ticket. He realized that all along he had been living far beneath his privileges.

Without the Lord's help, regardless of our natural talents, we *all* live far beneath our privileges. We could all have so much more than we do, including things on our Wish List ...*if*... we just built the partnership. When John, the brother of James, asked the question, "Who is he that overcometh the world, but he that believeth that Jesus is the Son of God?" he gave the secret behind the partnership! Because who *can* overcome the world except he that believes that Jesus is the Son of God!

When Limhi recounted the slaying of Abinadi, he said, "And because he said unto them that Christ was God, the Father of all things, and said that he should take upon him the image of man…and that God should come down among the children of men…and go forth upon the face of the earth, and now because he said this, they put him to death…" But Abinadi's words, coupled with the words of Alma the younger, "Yea, every knee shall bow, and every tongue confess before him. Yea, even at the last day, when all men shall stand to be judged of him, then shall they confess that he is God…" are the light over the pathway that leads to a bright and happy future …and forever.

The point is, whether you are needing help with a crisis, a Wish List item, or you are seeking eternal life, Christ is the answer and He has always *been* the answer. He stands at your door and knocks. But your journey from Faith to Trust requires that you let Him in. Regardless of your need, His hand is outstretched but you have to take hold. Creating a partnership with Christ means; first, having a desire, second, studying Him to learn who He is, and then third, taking His hand and doing things His way. When you do, the result is a lifelong journey through …*The Land of Miracles!*

16) Use your Wish List to create a series of learning environments.
17) Seek the power that comes with *really needing* the Savior and want something so bad, that your need becomes a constant yearning for Him.
18) Create the partnership with Him. Open the door and do things His way.

Those Little Signs…

I found myself wondering as I thought over my day,
"How do I really know the Lord knows what I pray?"
In Bible times, it was easy. His followers always knew.
He performed many miracles showing what they should do!

"Yes, but only very few people ever saw miracles of that kind,
raising the dead, parting the Red Sea or healing the blind!
Everyone else had to travel by faith, moving one step at a time,
following the path I laid out, something I do for those who are Mine.

If you'll think back, you'll remember the signs I left along your way,
so you wouldn't get lost, become discouraged or go astray.
I know you saw every one of them, for I placed them with great care.
And I placed them so only you would know that I'd been there!

And though you haven't seen a sign like the parting of the Red Sea,
do you really need a sign like that to know I know of your plea?
With each sign you passed by, I placed a feeling in your breast,
that I was aware of you, loved you, and once again you'd been blest."

"Yes!" I said. "I remember seeing those signs many times before.
How foolish not to remember and need to be reminded once more."
As I looked over my life, it was obvious that He knows what I pray,
for there stood all those little signs ...scattered along my way.

Ofcr. Samuel Jeppsen, #3751

"...I am with you alway, even unto the end of the world. Amen."
Jesus Christ

Chapter Seven

The Language of the Spirit

Learning to follow the feelings or impressions of the heart is such a precious talent and an absolute must in your journey toward trust. Much is said about this and many don't believe in it. Some think it is little more than just your own internalized thought process and that it is no more than weighing things out in your own mind and making the better choice.

Though some of that is true, I have learned the language of the Spirit is an actual language we can understand, acquire, live by and depend on, just as any foreign language. And like a foreign language, it is only understood by those who learn that language.

WWII has always had an unusual appeal to me. I believe it is because it was such a conflict between good and evil. Though not a WWII quote, one of my favorite military quotes is one credited to Gen. Colin Powell. Whether it is accurate or not, it is the exact sentiment of how I feel about our military and our great Country. The quote is, "Over the years, the United States has sent many of its fine young men and women into great peril to fight for freedom beyond our borders. The only amount of land we have asked for in return is enough to bury those …that did not return."

One of my favorite WWII stories and one that has helped shape my life for good, is about Desmond T. Doss, a Seventh Day Adventist. I still remember reading the comic book adventures of his WWII story, when I was a kid. Desmond was an Army Medic and a Conscientious Objector. He was also the recipient of the Congressional Medal of Honor.

When WWII broke out, Desmond wanted to do something to help his country. Being a Conscientious Objector, he was offered a deferment, but he declined. Throughout basic training he was heavily ridiculed by virtually everyone in his unit. After the ridicule, he was offered more chances to leave the Army but again refused. He was despised, insulted, cursed and even told by some of his fellow soldiers, that they wanted to shoot him, themselves.

He passed boot camp and was sent to the battle front. He would not carry a gun, but volunteered for dangerous missions. On one of them, he and two other soldiers climbed a hill, while their platoon stayed down below. The three men then pulled heavy, naval, rope ship ladders up the hill for the troops below to climb.

During vicious battles, where no one was allowed to leave their foxholes at night, Desmond would crawl out onto the battle-field and would treat and retrieve the wounded. He would even treat wounded enemy soldiers who were on the field. This was learned by his leaders upon finding enemy soldiers in the daytime with U.S. bandages on them. If someone needed help, he would help them, regardless. He was that Christ-like.

On Hacksaw Ridge in Okinawa, approximately one hundred and fifty soldiers ascended up onto the ridge. Once there, the shelling got so bad, that the Americans had to retreat down the hill. Of the one hundred and fifty that climbed up, only about fifty were able to climb down. The rest lay wounded on the battlefield.

Desmond was the only soldier that remained behind that was not wounded. He worked all night, crawling along on his stomach, listening for the groans of soldiers. When he heard one, he would crawl to them, drag them to the edge of the cliff, tie a rope around them and then lower them off the ridge to the troops below. He was told several times to come down off the ridge, but he always turned and went back out onto the battlefield for one more soldier. He averaged one soldier every ten minutes and managed to save the lives of seventy-seven wounded soldiers.

When Desmond was asked where he got the courage to do all the things he did, he said, "I just trusted God and trusted that feeling in me that said God would protect me." Desmond was more willing to *trust* in the Lord than he was willing to be *afraid.* This incredible man was the first Conscientious Objector to ever receive the Medal of Honor. To date, there have only been three. The other two were Army Medics and were killed in Vietnam.

Of all the great stories of valor and honor during WWII, Desmond's story is my most favorite. His story is the story of an incredibly faithful man, who not only had great honor and valor, but who had an uncommon faith and trust in God.

I have come to believe that there is really no such thing as luck and that everything happens for a purpose. Though I know that the Lord does not cause anything bad to happen, I know that because of our gift of free agency, good things can happen to bad people and bad things can happen to good people! Agency is so essential to the plan of happiness that it has to be that way. We are here to experience life, agency and consequences. Oftentimes, the consequences of agency can take years to understand and bad things often become great groundwork for future blessings.

Another thing I have noticed is that some miracles are extremely obvious, like Desmond's. While most, however, are very subtle and sometimes so subtle that they can be easily over-looked or excused away. I am positive it is done that way on purpose, so we can choose or not, to recognize the miracle.

I have also noticed that usually only the receiver of the miracle knows for certain it was a miracle. I believe it is done this way because the miracle was not intended for anyone else. Others can easily explain away the miracle, because they didn't feel the feelings and experience all the events leading up to the miracle.

The second of four police officer involved shootings, I was involved in, took place early in my police career. I had chased a suspect on a motorcycle northbound on LeSueur from Main St. He was a long haired, biker looking fellow and turned out to be a violent offender. He ran into his house and I went after him. My sergeant was with me. As I took one step inside, a very powerful feeling came to me to s*tep back! Step back! Step back!*

Without seeing or knowing what was on the other side of the door, I quickly took one step back, just as the center of the door where I had been standing, exploded into dust. The lamp to my left exploded and then I heard the sound of the shotgun blast. It all took place in milliseconds, but it happened in that order. It was an obvious miracle, but had I not listened to that prompting and stepped back, that shotgun blast would have hit me in the side just above the beltline. I was not wearing a ballistic vest, but it would have made no difference. The blast would have struck between the two panels. I would have been dead before I hit the floor.

Several years later, I was sitting in my little blue Chevette at the intersection of Brown and Recker, waiting for the light to turn green. I received a strong feeling to look to my left. As I did, I saw a loaded dump truck heading west on Brown, approaching Recker. Before there was any sign of anything amiss, I got the distinct feeling that the truck had lost its brakes, that the driver was going to turn right (northbound) onto Recker and that he was not going to make it. He was going to crash and I was to move.

I saw no signs of trouble with the truck, but I decided to follow that feeling. Long story short, it happened just as I was told. The heavily loaded dump truck had lost its brakes. It turned, without slowing down and rolled over. His bed landed right where I had been. Had I not listened, I would have been crushed.

Years later, while hunting deer in the Kaibab National Forest, I got lost. It was during an evening hunt and just before sundown. I realized I was walking in circles when I passed the same set of downed logs twice. I tried to get a bearing on where I was by landmarks, but every direction looked the same. The clouds had come in and were literally sitting on top of the trees. They were so dense, that I could not tell where the sun was. The sun had turned the ceiling of clouds to a brilliant gold color. It had become cold and I was partially wet. I was unprepared for what I faced and knew I would not survive the night.

So I did the only thing I knew how to do. I knelt and prayed and asked for guidance, believing I would receive it. I did not need north, south or east or west, as I had no idea where those directions were in relation to where I was. I needed one degree in a 360 degree circle. After my prayer, I stood and waited for the inspiration to come. I contemplated the possibilities of what could happen as I waited for the answer. I knew that if I didn't receive an answer or followed the wrong feeling, I could end up more lost and deeper into the forest, fighting to survive the night. But to be honest, I was calm, as there was a feeling of peace within me.

Finally the feeling came and I looked in the direction I was to go. I lined up three trees and walked to the first. I then chose another third tree that lined up with my remaining two trees and walked to the next tree. I repeated that process over and over, never taking my eyes off the trees I picked out. I finally came to a dirt road, looked to my right and saw my brother-in-law, Olin. I laughed as he began yelling at me for being late.

These three experiences have one common denominator. In each experience, I listened to that still small voice inside me *and lived!* I could have just as easily shrugged the feeling off. With over 110,000 accidental deaths each year, I would have been just one more. But instead *...I listened and lived!*

Miracles come, but often they come *after* listening! Learning the language of the Spirit is not only a prerequisite for communication through prayer, at times, *it is lifesaving!* The ability to listen and follow enhances everything that is important!

In 1971, Julie and I had the opportunity to move to Alaska and work for Pete and Sandy Bigelow in the concrete construction business. As a reward for my hard work, Pete bought a 300 Winchester and a fly-in caribou hunting trip for me. It would be my first time in a float plane. I don't remember the exact location, but I remember it was off the Glenn Highway, also called the Tok Cutoff, not far from Gunsight Mountain.

Pete was much bigger than me, so the pilot could not fly us both in together with all our gear. So I was flown in first with the gear. Pete and the food were to come on the second trip. Shortly after being dropped off, a big gust of wind caught the plane and flipped it up and swept it to my left. The pilot came out of it, but that gust of wind was followed by another and another, making it impossible for Pete to be flown in or for me to be flown out. I was stuck there in the middle of a huge windstorm that lasted three days. My home was an eight by eight wooden shack, of sorts. It was wood for three feet up and canvas for the next three feet. There was no door, just a flap over the opening. Inside were two, two foot wide wooden bunks. So there I was with no food, except for a package of Fig Newtons, most of our camping gear, a box of ammo and my brand new 300 Winchester.

Every day, they flew over to check on me and every day it was cold and windy. Luckily, the cold seemed to remove my hunger, but it also made for a terrible time outside the hut. Because of the wind, I could not light a fire to stay warm. The nights were even colder than the days, so I sat in that little wind-break for most of every day with nothing to do, but try and keep warm without food or water.

Knowing there were bears in the area, I prayed that I would be protected. At night, I slept in my sleeping bag with the zipper down and my 300 Winchester in my bag and aimed at the opening.

On the second morning I awoke to find a marmot about two feet tall, eating my Fig Newtons. So very carefully and slowly, I raised my arms, took careful aim and shot him ...with my camera. I then yelled, *"Hey!!! Go get your own Fig Newtons!!!*

Later that morning, after the fly over, I left camp and decided to find a trophy caribou. I hiked to the top of the ridge behind the camp and glassed the open, tundra covered valley.

I saw a herd on the far side of the valley. I decided to make my way around the backside of the hills surrounding the valley. In time, I came up over the ridge and on top of them. I was now down wind and they were totally unaware I was there.

I had a perfect view of the herd and a perfect choice of a trophy. I picked a nice one, laid the bead at the front shoulder and with a press of the trigger, the beautiful animal was mine. I then walked the one hundred and fifty yards to where he lay and realized I had no knife. But, I did have my camera. So, I took my picture with the caribou and crossed the valley to see if Pete had landed yet. But he was not there and there was no knife in any of the gear. All of a sudden, the wind started blowing like crazy.

On day three, the winds died down. The plane was finally able to land, but instead of dropping Pete off, they picked me up and flew me out. I told the pilot about my caribou. He said, "We know! We saw it. It's bear food!" He then told me that from the air, they had seen a bear in the area around the camp. When I shot the caribou in the valley, the bear made his way over to it. He then said, "That caribou probably saved your life. If you had brought the animal back to camp, you would have been bear food too."

I never forgot that experience or those words. I was also amazed at how not having a knife was such a blessing. Since then I have often wondered, what if the bear had gone unnoticed? Or what if they never told me about the bear? It all would have been just another unnoticed miracle like the millions of others that occur throughout our lives!

In these and many other events in my life, I have learned this most precious truth. When you seek the Spirit, you begin to notice help that was not there before *and* it begins coming more frequently. You will also notice unusual phenomena taking place in your life. Oftentimes the difference between disaster and miracle is only a thin line apart. It is often divided by a single decision or incident that is too coincidental to be coincidental.

You will also notice that there is an understandable language that is beginning to develop inside you. A language that you realize you can trust and rely on. It is an intriguing language that makes you *want* to learn more about it and to test it more often. The language is the language of the Spirit and *impressions* and *feelings* are the *tongue* and *ears*. They are the lines of communication. The Lord *could* tell you verbally, but He uses *His* way of communicating, instead of ours. Learning the language of the Spirit requires faith, patience and practice.

The language of the Spirit is always accompanied by a feeling of peace. It is a confident, deep feeling of peace that is laced with love, even if it is corrective. If you ponder the thoughts that come into your mind, you will feel the peace and love, *if* it is from the Holy Ghost. If you have a hard time recognizing it, perhaps life is too noisy for you to hear spiritual messages. In that case, push all the distractions away from you ...everything! Push back everything that is confronting you in life. Then sit back and feel the feelings at the end of the thoughts you are thinking. If the feelings, at the end of the thoughts or impressions you have, contain peace and give you confidence, then those thoughts or impressions have the signature of the Holy Ghost.

The Adversary is the Great Deceiver. He too, has a discernible signature. His impressions will give you ninety percent truth and ten percent lie, just to mislead you. He too, can place thoughts and feelings in your mind and heart, but his impressions are always void of the feeling of peace. He is the great imitator of truth and Godly attributes.

He imitates self esteem with arrogance, self confidence with ego, joy with pleasure, Godly sorrow with self degradation, indignation with anger and enmity with hatred. He imitates love with lust and the desire for prosperity with greed. He also imitates honor with fame and admiration with envy and more. But the one feeling he absolutely cannot imitate, is the feeling of peace. Peace is the one feeling that is reserved strictly for the Holy Ghost. The Holy Ghost is the testifier of truth and light. Most importantly, He is the Testifier of the Savior Himself and of His ways.

The promise that we can trust the feelings of peace is throughout the Scriptures. When you receive a feeling or a prompting to do something, you can always tell if it is from the Adversary or from the Holy Ghost by a foolproof test.

To perform this test, push away all the stimuli and input around you. This includes separating your emotions from your feelings. They are not the same. Your emotions can often cloud your feelings and can quite often, mislead you. So take yourself out of the equation and be willing to be wrong. If with your *wants* removed, it feels right *or* wrong, it most likely is.

Next, examine the feeling that is left. Your thoughts and decisions will have one of three feelings associated with them. Either the baseline feeling of the thought, impression or decision will be one of peace and confidence or it will have a stupor of thought or it will have a feeling of anxiety or despair. The stupor of thought means it's not your best choice. The feeling of anxiety or despair means it has the signature of the Adversary. The feelings of peace and confidence means that it has the signature of the Holy Ghost. The test is that simple and it will always work.

The Holy Ghost speaks to us Spirit to spirit and brings with Him the feeling of peace, confidence, love and the direction of the Lord. His peace is as a signature at the bottom of a letter that someone sends you and it is easy to recognize. The signature of peace from the Holy Ghost is the signature of the Lord in your life.

When the Lord called Elijah and told him to anoint Elisha to be the new prophet, Elijah recorded, "And, behold, the Lord passed by, and a great and strong wind rent the mountains, and brake in pieces the rocks before the Lord; but the Lord was not in the wind: and after the wind an earthquake; but the Lord was not in the earthquake: And after the earthquake a fire; but the Lord was not in the fire: and after the fire a still small voice."

When the Savior walked on the Red Sea and met the apostles in the boat, at first they were frightened. His words to them were, "Peace be with you for it is I."

At the last supper, after the Savior taught the principle of serving others by washing the feet of the disciples, and after Judas Iscariot had been identified as the traitor, the Savior said this to the remaining eleven, "Let not your heart be troubled…" One of the last things the Savior left the disciples with was, "Peace I leave with you, my peace I give unto you…let not your heart be troubled, neither let it be afraid." He constantly used the word *peace* in referring to Him or the Comforter which He said was the Holy Ghost. The *feeling of peace* is the signature in the message you are looking for.

Through testing this language, you learn that God lives, that He is actually there and that He loves you. You also learn that the Holy Ghost communicates Spirit to spirit. You realize that if you could just become an expert at listening and following, you could live without ever having to make another mistake again.

The Savior is there! He is always there and He is always reaching out to you. He communicates to you in *His* language, not yours. He does that because you must have *your* free agency to choose whether or not to listen to Him and follow Him. This life is about your choices, not His dominion. This is why you have so much freedom of choice placed before you. This is why you are allowed to choose good or evil and why the rewards for both, are often so slow to follow your actions. Like at the beginning of a rain, the first drop from heaven falls a long time before touching your face and when it is over, the last drop falls a long time before touching your face, so too are blessings and consequences.

Following the Savior is the key to happiness. Choosing to follow Him begins with a desire to learn the Language of the Spirit. He communicates to you, through the Spirit. Learning the language of the Spirit means learning to discern feelings and impressions from the Holy Ghost. The Language of the Spirit comes with a discernible signature. It takes time and patience to learn it, but it is a real language and it not only can save your life, it can fill it with joy, peace and happiness.

Boyd K. Packer said, "If all you ever know is what you can see with your eyes and hear with your ears, you will never really know very much." It's a true statement. Understanding the language of the Spirit is paramount in your journey from Faith to Trust and it is just like understanding any other language. Others can point the way, even tell you how to do it. But no one can learn the language for you and no one can practice it in your behalf. *You* must do that! Learning this language, is the key that will unlock the door to a new and incredible future *...patiently awaiting you.*

19) Uncommon valor begins with uncommon faith.
20) Learn and practice the language of the Spirit.
21) Remember that impressions are the pathway of communication.
22) Believe, then test and track your own results.
23) The signature of peace, is the signature of the Lord in your life.

Walk Forward…

He said, "Walk forward on faith!"
I said, "How can that be done?"
He said, "Easier than you think,
you've been doing it since you were one."
"A silly statement." I replied!
"You want me to walk on what I can't see?"
"Yes, that's right." He said!
"You've done it your whole life—believe me!
For instance, you didn't know you could walk,
until the first time you tried."
"Yes, but that was a slow process,
and I fell down a lot and cried!"
"But you kept getting up, time after time,
until finally you got it right!
If you chose instead to quit trying,
that wouldn't have been very bright!
Just as gaining strength to walk
came day after day and bit by bit,
gaining faith is the same way.
It will come as you begin to use it!

Every success first began as faith.
That's true from the beginning of time!
From the simplest task,
to the highest mountain you ever wanted to climb.
But there's only so much you can do,
when you accomplish things alone.
So learn to use the power of the Lord,
instead of just your own!
To help gain the faith that He will help you,
one that will always last,
just think of all the things He's done for you,
that now lay in your past!
So if you can't walk forward on faith,
then use your own remembrance
to gather your blessing in front of you
and walk forward on the evidence!"
Feeling the truth in His words, I asked,
"Stranger, who are you and what do you do?"
"My Name you already know." He said.
"I'm that still small voice inside you."

Excerpts, Walk Forward, Ofcr. Samuel Jeppsen, #3751

Chapter Eight

Bikes and the Savior

I am a *Rider*, not a *Biker*—and *yes,* there is a difference! To say I love to ride motorcycles is an understatement. I have been riding bikes since I was fourteen. My first bike was an old Allstate 150 in 1965. It was painted canary yellow with a three-speed on the grip. It was also the beginning of my love for bikes.

My first big bike was a chopped 1954, Matchless 500 single. I bought it in 1966 when I was fifteen. Neat to own today, but then it was just an old, oil leaking, hard starting, English bike. But it was the Matchless that ignited my love for the open road.

There were three riders in my life that lit matches that ignited my fire for motorcycle adventures. The first match was lit by a guy we called Mr. Beezer. We called him Mr. Beezer because he rode a 1965, 650 BSA, twin. He lived on the street just north of me. His BSA was one of the most beautiful bikes, I had ever seen. It was candy apple red with a chrome gas tank and fenders. It had twin trumpet pipes that made an incredibly beautiful sound. I remember stopping and listening, every time he fired it up. You could almost say I had a love affair with Mr. Beezer's *Beezer.*

The second match on the smoldering embers was the 1969 television series, *Then Came Bronson,* with Michael Parks. Jim Bronson, rode a red 1968, 900 Harley Sportster—a bike I dreamed of owning. The show was little more than a half hour Harley commercial, but I loved it. The beginning of the show always began with Bronson pulling up to a red light. He had one duffle bag tied to the handlebars and another to the rear seat.

As Bronson waited for the light to change, in the lane next to him was a guy in his mid to late forties with a suit, tie and hat. He was seated in a station wagon. The look on his face told a thousand words. I can still recite their conversation.

> The guy in the wagon has his window down and is looking Bronson over and then says, "Taking a trip?"
> Bronson doesn't hear him and replies, "What's that?"
> The guy repeats, "Taking a trip?"
> Bronson replies, "Yeah."
> The guy in the station wagon says, "Where to?"
> Bronson says, "Oh, I don't know. Wherever I end up, I guess."
> After a short pause the guy says, "Man ...I wish I was you."
> Bronson smiles and replies, "Really?"
> Longingly the guy softly says, "Yeah!"
> Bronson smiles graciously and says, "Well, hang in there."
> The guy nods, the light turns green and Bronson rides off.

Various shots of Bronson riding the open road are shown as the credits are mentioned at both the beginning and end of each program. Though I never saw the credits and remember very little about the stories themselves, I very distinctly remember the strong feelings I felt at both ends of each show, as I watched him ride. As I watched him, I was seeing me. My love affair with bikes and for adventure was now deeply embedded.

The third match that made my passion for motorcycles completely unquenchable was lit by a lone rider I found alongside the road south of Anchorage, Alaska, in 1971.

I was standing next to a small river along the old, narrow, two lane, winding Seward highway, near Portage Glacier. My wife and I, along with some friends, were watching the salmon run. The salmon would come upstream in large schools. As we were watching the two to three foot long, orange and red colored salmon swimming past, I heard the sound of a small motorcycle engine. I looked up and saw an older man wearing a white helmet and green insulated overalls. His little bike was heavily bagged up and he looked like he had been on the road quite a while. The bike with its huge bag tied on behind, looking more like a camel than a motorcycle, was a small, green, Cushman Eagle.

The Cushman Eagle was a 318cc, 8 horsepower, two speed scooter. It would do about forty mph. I had seen only about a half dozen of them. The US Military used them during WWII.

Like me, this traveler had stopped to watch the salmon run. Thinking that he was a local from the Kenai Peninsula and heading for Anchorage, I smiled and said, “Where are you from?”

He smiled back and said, “I’m on my way back to the Lower Forty-eight.” He told me he had ridden all the way up here to Alaska. His Cushman had seventy-eight thousand miles on it. I asked him how old he was and if I remember correctly, he was fifty-nine. I was so impressed! His great love for adventure showed all over his face as he told me of his travels and of his journey to Alaska on his Cushman.

As I listened to him talk, I felt a burning inside me. I promised myself that one day, I too, was going to go on a great adventure such as his. One day, it would be me that some young fellow would be talking to about his cross-country ride on his motorcycle *…one day…*

Those three experiences created in me an image, a visualization in my own mind, that one day I would be Mr. Beezer! I would be the guy in the neighborhood with the beautiful bike! I would have the bike with the incredible sound, the one that made all the kids stop and stare! I would be Jim Bronson! I would be the guy at the traffic light! With my bags tied to my bike, I would be the guy people looked at in envy, as I headed down the road into another adventure! And one day, I would be an old, lone rider, thousands of miles from home, stopped alongside the road and watching nature at its best. I would be the guy, free to follow a dream, the wind, the winding roads and his desire for adventure! I would be free ...at least free for awhile! There would be no time clocks, no projects and no deadlines—just free!

Now several years later, having traveled about two hundred and fifty thousand miles on motorcycles, or the equivalent of ten times around the world, I realized I had become all three of the images. I had become Mr. Beezer, Jim Bronson and the old lone rider alongside the road, thousands of miles from home.

I’ve often thought about that as I have looked over my life. I have noticed that the times I was *driven by a dream*, I was happy, motivated, productive and of service to others. The times I *wasn’t,* I was unmotivated, tired or lethargic and usually unhappy.

So powerful is this truth, that I monitor my life constantly, monitoring and measuring my happiness. When I am down or depressed and life has become too much for me, I change my focus back to my dream. It is this tool that always changes my attitude, returns the smile to my face and makes the load on my shoulders, light again. It even has a greater, faster and longer lasting effect on me, than taking some "R&R."

I also noticed that the image I had of myself, who I saw myself as being, is the person I became! It was an interesting realization about just how powerful dreams, desires and actually visualizing them, is.

I have learned that what I dream of, what I dream of being, has more power and influence on my mind and life than all the positive affirmations I can come up with. I have realized that we are as clay in the sculptor's hand and to a large degree, we are the sculptor. I have learned that everything we dream of, everything we hope to be or believe is possible, changes that sculpture! Be it positive or negative, good or evil, grand or small, marvelous or hideous, that sculpture is ours to create, and becomes *what* we create. As we create our own sculpture, the powerful chisel in our hand, is what we see in our mind, followed by the choices we make and then the actions we take.

Perhaps the greatest thing I have learned from having these dreams, is that it gives the Savior the greatest avenue to work in, while working with me. I believe that is true with all of us. Unless you *want* something, it is almost impossible for the Lord to have impact in your life. The truth is, regardless of all the wonderful gifts He has to offer, regardless of how wonderful heaven will be, if you just don't care ...it all makes no difference!

It's like a wealthy man giving his son a beautiful $450.000, V-12, 8-speed, Rolls-Royce Phantom, that his son cares nothing about. You have to want the Lord's gift before His gift can have any value to you. You have to want His help before He can help you. *Wanting* for yourself and having a dream, gives the Lord the perfect avenue to work His miracles in your life!

24) Create a beautiful sculpture by creating *a want.* Creating a want, creates an avenue for the Lord to enter your life.

Chapter Nine

The Secret Room

I often tell people that I spent two years in prison. I did! I spent two years in the capacity of a prison minister, serving with the Gila River Prison Ministries Program and with the Arizona Department of Corrections. I was assigned to lead the ministries program for two yards inside the Eyman Complex, in Florence.

One day, I had an experience, I will never forget. After services, an inmate approached me. He asked for a Priesthood blessing. That is not terribly unusual in itself, but I did not know this man at all, nor had I ever seen him.

After he asked me, I said a prayer to ask for guidance. I then laid my hands on his head and spoke the words that came to my mind. After I closed the blessing, he said nothing. He slowly rose to his feet and kept his back to me for a few moments. At first, I thought that was odd. He then took off his glasses and began cleaning them, with his back still to me. After what seemed like ten seconds of silence, he slowly turned around and I noticed that tears had been running down his face. He was very emotional. As he stood there, trying to control his emotions, without looking at me, he said with a trembling voice, "I have dreamed many of the things you said ...but to actually hear them in a blessing…." He then stopped, tried to again regain control of his emotions, placed his glasses back on his face, then turned and walked away.

I had never seen him before and I never saw him again. But that experience left me with the knowledge of just how much the Lord knows us and loves us. Through dreams He can reach us and guide us and through His deep love, He can be there for us.

After retiring from law enforcement, I had some really unexpected challenges occur in my life. I entered a time period where I began having failure after failure and criticism after criticism. I didn't understand what was happening or why. I thought I could change things by going to college, but I had failures and criticism there too, even beyond my control.

Emotionally, life was very difficult for me and my self-confidence began suffering severely. Without going into it, it was the second worst time period of my life. Things were unraveling, instead of coming together and constant criticism became my companion. I sought the guidance of the Lord, who I knew understood all things, even me, my feelings and my hurts.

In December of 03, I walked into Superstition Harley-Davidson, as I had done numerous times before. On the row of used bikes, I saw a Sportster, a 100th year, 03-Anniversary Special, 1200 Custom that had been customized. I had seen hundreds of Sportsters before and dozens of Anniversary Specials. All beautiful, but all of which had very little impact on me. But this one was totally different.

I had dreamed of owning a Sportster since Junior High, but only a certain one. In my mind was a vivid picture of a particular Sportster. It had been there for over forty years. In all the thousands of Sportsters I had seen, I had not seen the one I had in my mind, nor was I looking for it. But now, I was looking right at it! The very bike I had seen forty years ago was now right in front of me! It was literally déjà-vu!

Coincidentally—or not, we happened to have the money to buy it. So after a few extra gizmos and doo-dads, Julie wrote them a check and I rode it home free and clear.

The bike, itself, is just a compilation of nuts and bolts and parts. Though beautiful, it is just junk on its way to the junk yard. It just hasn't gotten there yet. But I cannot explain what seeing it and having the opportunity to own it, represented to me. When I saw the bike, I had a huge rush of emotions. I was looking at the very picture on the wall of my secret room.

In my mind is a little room where I keep all my dreams. They are in picture form and pinned to the walls. No one has been in that room and seldom do I tell anyone about my special and private dreams. They are just there, patiently waiting for me and ever so constantly, beckoning me toward them.

When I saw this bike, I realized that the Lord knew about my special room. I also knew, that He knew about the picture of the bike I dreamed of one day owning and had pinned on the wall. As I stared at it, full of emotions and in almost total disbelief, I knew that the Lord had come into my little room, had taken my picture, turned it into a reality and placed it before me.

Seeing it then, standing right in front of me, especially during a time period when I was struggling and pouring my heart out in prayer, was a manifestation to me that the Lord knew me. He not only knew me, He knew everything about me and He knew that when I saw it, I would immediately recognize His hand. And most important was the fact that I knew that I mattered to Him!

Do I believe it is important to the Lord that I have the bike of my dreams? *...No!*

Do I believe it is important to Him that I know that He knows when I am struggling? Do I believe that it is important to Him that I know that He knows every single thing about me? Do I believe that it is important to Him that I know that He even knows about my dreams and wishes, even one that I have been secretly carrying around in my mind for over forty years? *…Yes!!!*

Seeing that bike and owning that bike has been a constant reminder to me that the Lord not only knows me, He knows all about me! And He knew that when I saw the bike …I would know that it was Him, testifying of Himself, to me.

Please understand that the bike was not the gift! The gift was realizing that He knew me that well. It was a tender mercy experience for me that I remember each and every time I ride the bike or even look at it. In fact I never pass by it without stopping, looking and remembering, "He knows me and everything about me!" If He knows that about me, He knows everything about you too, which means you can follow Him in total faith and trust!

The bike loses monetary value each and every day and will one day end up in the junk pile. However, the memory of it, the feelings I felt when I saw it and the meaning behind it, will remain with me forever. It was also the predecessor to even greater gifts. I had served on the Stake High Council before we moved but here, a few months later, I was called to serve as the Ward Mission Leader. From there, to the Bishopric of a young single adult ward. Later, I was called to serve on this Stake High Council and until mid 2010, I served in the Bishopric of our home ward.

In early 2010, I was asked to serve as a Law Enforcement Chaplain. I happen to be the only one of my faith in this agency for the entire state. I sought none of these things. I was asked if I would accept them. They were things I was given and they were given me by the Lord. I call them, *His gift to the Twenty.*

Many sports teams have as many as thirty or so players on the team. But each team has only about ten players that are the best. In the games, it is usually the same ten that get to play over and over. It is based on personal talent and skill. Though it is great to make the team, it hurts when you don't get to play. A coach who plays his best players will end up with the best scores at the end of the season. However, he will also end up with twenty players that never got to play.

The Lord is not that way. Yes, He is very interested in the overall performance of the team, but He is also very interested in the individual! In any calling I have had, I have never been the best choice! There was always a better person standing by.

Interestingly, the Lord in His tremendous love for each and every one of us, will often sacrifice score, for the individual. If you watch, you will notice that He often calls from His twenty instead of His ten. He often passes up a better person, to give a lesser person a chance to serve. Who, but someone who loves you, more than they love the high scores or the bottom line, will do that? Who? …There is only One!

To sacrifice score or bottom line, so a person might be lifted up, requires someone who loves you very dearly in spite of all your faults and shortcomings. Yet, He does it quite often and all who faithfully walk after Him will see it and experience it.

In the movie *Lion King*, King Mufasa is killed and Simba, his son, flees from guilt and lives in shame for years outside the kingdom. In his search for happiness, he seems to hide and turn his back on the things he knows are right. One day, his father's spirit comes to him and tells him, "Simba, you are more than you have become!" In everyone I have ever met, regardless of their station in life, I have not found anyone who has not felt that same feeling inside. That feeling, that call, is from the Lord. It is the Lord, reminding you that you are an actual child of God and that as such, you are actually endowed with Godly gifts and privileges. You are indeed, more than you have become. And seeing yourself as who you really are, is a critical step toward Christ.

Seeing yourself as whatever you are trying to be, and most importantly, an actual child of God, changes your attitude, your behavior, your expectations of yourself and your performance. It is the very first step to *becoming*. Seeing yourself *as,* is the root or the seed of greatness. It is the soil that grows permanent change, spawns vision, and then brings the endowment of blessings from on High. Simba, never became the Lion King, until he first saw himself as one. In my own life, whenever I am failing, it is usually because of my fears about my inadequacies. It is at those times, I have to rebuild myself, before I can rebuild my life or move up. In love and tenderness, the Lord is always there with me, helping me to believe in myself, reminding me that I am a child of God and that I am more than I have become.

Christ knows all about you too, even your secret room and all the pictures you have pinned to the wall. He knows all of your dreams and passions. If you will heed His call, He will help you make them come true and He will lovingly remind you that you are more than you have become and that with His help, you can be more than you ever dreamed possible.

The Savior lives and if you will seek Him, He will manifest Himself to you in your journey from Faith to Trust toward Him. He reaches out to you in your interests and in your dreams and begins making the connection. *What your dream is*, makes little difference to Him. If you have a passion, He has an avenue! In that avenue, if you look, you will find Him reaching out and calling you toward Him and through a series of events, turning a weak and defiant Simba, into a powerful and majestic Lion King.

When Paul was in Athens, he stood on Mars Hill and spoke to the people about changing the things they believed in. He said, "That they should seek the Lord, if haply they might feel after him, and find him, though he be not far from every one of us." He is not far at all. In fact, He is closer than you think. You see, He too has a dream. What's His dream? …To help you!

25) Choose your dreams wisely …and then visualize them. Visualizing your dreams brings more power than all the positive affirmations you can use.
26) Remind yourself often that you are more than you have become.
27) Forget the past and start seeing yourself *as*__________ (fill in the blank)
28) Let the Lord help and remember, see what isn't, until what isn't …*is!!*

"Behold, I am the law, and the light. Look unto me,
and endure to the end, and ye shall live; for unto him
that endureth to the end will I give eternal life"

Jesus Christ

The Mark of His Hand…

Ever wonder which road to take?
Which path for you is right?
There is a way you can know,
a way you can follow His Light.
It's a very simple way,
though you may not first understand.
But here is a way you can never miss,
...the loving mark of His hand.

You already know to listen,
and to follow the feelings in your heart,
to remove your wants from the equation,
and take the disinterested part.
You know if wants aren't removed,
you'll prejudice the feelings that come.
And then you will follow your own path,
instead of the path of the Son.

Well, there are three more things to know,
that will confirm the right direction.
Three more things once learned,
will increase your faith and expectation.
It requires your faith though,
you see, the Lord must know you believe in Him.
But with faith, trust and knowing He will not fail,
this is where you begin.

First, the path of the Lord will be easy.
But not the easiest way of all.
He wants you to work, struggle and grow,
and not just see where the chips fall.
But His path,
after all others have been weighed and presented,
will be the best overall,
most successful and easiest implemented.

Second, the feeling will come with a unique calmness,
a quieting of the soul.
As if you were standing in the eye of the storm,
and watching the storm clouds roll.
And as you stand in the midst of it all,
you are protected by the walls of the eye.
Inside, you feel the love of the Lord,
and above, you see the calm blue sky.

Third, is that you will see His path,
will have the best long range effect on your life.
It will solve the problem, create spiritual growth,
and ultimately reduce strife.
You'll see where the other paths <u>could</u> work,
and <u>might</u> come with more ease.
But His path will be the best in the long run,
and will increase your capabilities.

Remember, <u>all three</u> of these marks have to be there,
not just the one you like best.
And once you've found the mark of the Lord,
you'll feel peace, excitement and rest.
I know that these things I tell you are true,
for as I live and breathe and stand,
I have the witness of the Lord in my life,
...and I bare the mark of His hand.

Officer Samuel Jeppsen, #3751

"Be strong and of good courage, fear not, nor be afraid...For the Lord thy God, he it is that does go with thee; he will not fail thee, nor forsake thee." Deut 31:6

Chapter Ten

"Potato-Potato" and Spiritual Experiences

Harley-Davidson has long been known for its *Potato-Potato* sound. The sound was unique to Harley for a long time. So unique to the motorcycle industry and so sought after by V-twin cruiser riders, other manufactures have gone to great lengths to copy the Harley sound. It stems from using a single pin crank-shaft instead of what most manufacturers did, creating a crankshaft similar to bicycle peddles. Harley basically connected both pistons to the same peddle, making it where both go up and down at the same time. It created a very odd sounding motor at an idle.

It was an idea Harley came up with while looking for the most economical way to produce a V-twin engine. The fluke decision created an arrhythmic sounding and shaking motorcycle. However, it also gave it a heartbeat and it was an instant hit.

Until the EVO engine came out in 1984, comparatively speaking, Harleys were noted for being an oil leaking, high maintenance and undependable motorcycle. You often heard the slogans, "You ride—you wrench" and "If a Harley isn't leaking oil, it's because there isn't any oil in it." In fact, their nicknames were "Hardly-Ridable" and "Hogley-Ferguson." From Hogley Ferguson came their nickname of today, "Hog."

However, despite their undependability, prior to 1984, it was also the most famous and sought after motorcycle in the world. Harley was the bike seen in the movies and the motor heard in the sound tracks. It was the only motor in the world that said "Potato-Potato—Potato-Potato" as it idled. This unique sound and its romantic image still reigns in the world of motorcycles today.

The true story of the Harley fame is a perfect example of what can happen when one goes searching for one thing, only to discover an even greater thing. This exact concept occurs in life all the time. In fact, it happened with me. I went searching for great motorcycle adventures. What I found was life changing experiences with my dear Friend, the Lord.

In my youth, my spiritual experiences and my interactions with the Lord, had not been very defining. Even though I loved Him and wanted to know more about Him. But up to that point, I did not have much experience with Him or with prayer. There was nothing that I had really wanted bad enough in life, which had caused me to stretch enough to seek His help.

Wishing I was like those who had made wiser choices earlier on, I also felt that I had made too many mistakes and not enough right choices for the Lord to be too interested in me. It is the exact same way so many others feel after examining their life and tallying up their own mistakes.

What I found is that, though mistakes bring a ton of misery to ourselves and to others, we cannot make enough mistakes where the Lord stops being interested in us. Nor will our mistakes and bad choices stop Him from reaching out to us. Neither will they stop Him from trying to help us overcome and begin anew.

I learned this while serving in the Arizona State Prison in Florence. These were men who had been cast away by society and cast into *The Land of the Forgotten,* where more times than not, even their families forgot about them. Yet, here was the Lord. His presence here was as strong as in any place I had ever been. I realized then, that we cannot do anything that will make the Lord stop loving us or throw in the towel on us. I have relearned that truth while serving for the past ten years in Church government and in the many police and clergy related situations in which I have been involved.

In serving others in these capacities, either in Church government or as a Prison Minister or as a Police Chaplain, I face many challenges that are guilt related. Sometimes the guilt is so strong, it becomes self-crucifying. One of the greatest challenges of them all is getting people to believe that the Lord could actually love them, no matter what they have done. You must begin with the hope and faith that the Lord honestly knows you and deeply loves you …or a trek from Faith to Trust, is impossible.

One of the last things Paul taught the Hebrews, was to have faith. He said, "Now faith is the substance of things hoped for, the evidence of things not seen…Through faith we understand that the worlds were framed by the word of God…By faith, Enoch was translated that he should not see death...By faith Abraham, when he was called to go out into a place which he should after receive for an inheritance, obeyed…Through faith also Sara herself received strength to conceive seed and was delivered of a child when she was past age. By faith Isaac blessed Jacob…By faith Jacob, when he was dying, blessed both the sons of Joseph. By faith Moses, when he was come to years, refused to be called the son of Pharaoh's daughter. By faith he forsook Egypt, not fearing the wrath of the king…By faith they passed through the Red Sea as by dry land…By faith the walls of Jericho fell down…And what shall I more say? For the time would fail me to tell of Gideon, and of Barak, and of Samson, and of Jephthae; of David also, and Samuel, and of the prophets: who through faith subdued kingdoms, wrought righteousness, obtained promises, stopped the mouths of lions, quenched the violence of fire, escaped the edge of the sword, out of weakness were made strong, waxed valiant in fight, turned to fight the armies of the aliens…" and more.

There is simply no leap to trust, without first having faith. And though many people feel the two are one in the same, they are not. However, gaining trust, begins with having faith. The faith to believe that Christ lives and loves you no matter what, *is the key to the Gospel of Jesus Christ!* When people turn on the Lord, when something devastating happens in their life, it is because they don't understand what the Lord is doing or allowing. They think instead that He should just solve all their problems. If we were zoo animals and He was a zoo keeper, they would be right. But He is not a zoo keeper and we are not zoo animals. We are the children of God and He is teaching us …to be just that.

There is a story about a Silversmith. Though no one knows the author, I believe I know something about her. I believe the story was written after a tender mercy moment in her life. I believe she wanted to share the love the Lord had bestowed upon her, but also wanted to keep the experience sacred and private.

The story is about some women discussing the verse, Malachi 3:3. "And He shall sit as a refiner and purifier of silver." After their discussion, she decides to go talk to a silversmith.

She locates an old man who has been a silversmith for many years and is well known for his talent as a true craftsman. She asks him about the process of refining silver. After the silversmith explained the process to her, she asks, "Do you watch while the work of refining is going on?" "Oh yes!" he exclaimed. "I must sit and watch the furnace constantly. For, if the time necessary for refining is exceeded in the slightest degree, the silver will be injured!" The lady ponders his answer, as well as the scripture in Malachi. She then asks, "How do you know when the refining is done?" He replies, "That's easy! When I can see my own image in the silver, the refining process is finished."

Unfortunately for me, I was a lot like the unrefined silver in the story. Partially due to poor choices I had made and partially because I hadn't had many reaching out moments. So my refining and growth had to come through a different avenue. Like Harley-Davidson who looked for a cheaper way to build a V-twin and discovered an American heartthrob, I went looking for adventure on a motorcycle and discovered the Lord my Savior, my God. I found Him reaching out to me constantly and drawing me closer to Him, mile after mile and adventure after adventure. In fact, I even made another discovery. It was as a sign alongside the road that read, *The Road to Forgiveness.* When I saw that sign, my heart and my hope, leaped. When one starts reaching *out* to the Lord, one starts learning many things *about* the Lord!

Allen, one of nine police officers in our family, had been a homicide detective for fifteen years. He could have shared many different homicide stories with me, but this is the one he chose.

Allen said, "It began as a double shooting in a City park. A young man by the name of Ralph and his girlfriend, Jenea, had been shot by a gunman who had fled the scene by the time the police arrived. Ralph had been shot twice and was in very critical condition. We were unsure he would live. Jenea had been shot in the head and would never see her twenty-first birthday.

Before Ralph lapsed into unconsciousness, he was able to give the officers the name of the shooter. The two had been friends in high school. David had a history of being violent and was now a cold blooded killer. We expected a shootout when we finally found and arrested him. On the fourth day we received a tip as to where he was hiding out. We surrounded the home, called in the SWAT team and after awhile he gave up.

David waived his rights and began to sob and cry. During his confession, he took responsibility for taking the life of Jenea. He begged for forgiveness and expressed his sorrow for what he had done in such a sincere manner that I could actually feel the anguish of his spirit inside him. I have interviewed hundreds of violent offenders in my career and I pride myself in being a 'tough guy.' But David's anguish was so great, that I found myself being moved with compassion for him.

Everyone is sorry when they are caught, but this guy was actually repentant. I remember thinking as I sat there, that I had never seen in my entire career, someone with such a broken heart and contrite spirit, just as the Scriptures talk about.

Suddenly this tough guy began to crack and tears began to well up in my eyes. My partner looked at me as if I were nuts. But I felt somehow spiritually connected with David and I couldn't control it. Then suddenly, a thought entered my mind that was not my own. As I sat there spiritually connected to a man I knew was a murderer, the whisper that came to my mind was, *'Yes Allen! Even for him He was crucified."* And so it is for you, and so it is for me. His great sacrifice and His life's work, was and is, to make things better for you and me. Better both temporally and eternally.

It was through my love for motorcycles and motorcycle adventures that I happened to discover a relationship with Christ. That discovery led to the much needed discovery of forgiveness, so I could stop feeling guilty for the poor choices I had made. Step by step, I began to understand the magnitude of just what Christ has done and what He can do. I also discovered just how much He loves us.

Something else I discovered was that, if all you have to offer Christ is a deep love for Him, a pile of mistakes, a broken heart and a contrite spirit, which means you are now willing to follow the Lord *and stop trying to lead,* He will forgive and forget. He will then make your blemishes ...as if they never were.

29) Recognize highly unusual phenomena in your life, the repeating patterns in the phenomena, and begin experimenting on the feelings and patterns.
30) Practice reaching out and yielding *your* will to His.
31) Don't believe that past mistakes are a crystal ball to future behavior.
32) Remember that the sacrifice of the Savior *was for you personally.*

He Stayed…

This happened during a forest fire or perhaps shortly thereafter,
in a place called Yellowstone and it was quite a disaster.
Somehow a fire got out of control and burned with rage and wrath,
consuming wildlife and trees, burning everything in its path!
The fire caused great alarm and panic in both man and beast.
Everything fled from its coming, from the greatest to the least.
As the rangers began walking the burn area, assessing the damage,
in forest kings and animals, there was devastation and carnage.

Then one ranger, looking for smoldering embers to extinguish,
had a startling experience that he could not relinquish.
He came upon a burnt and statuesque bird at the base of a tree,
standing, as if saying to the fire, "You can come but I won't flee."
The ranger was puzzled as to why this bird seemed willing to stay.
Curious as to why it hadn't done like the others and flown away!
Surely it had to have known what was about to take place?
Couldn't it feel the heat of the flame upon its face?

Yet, it stayed behind and braved the fire. What a curious thing to do!
To knowingly accept death and the pain it must have gone through.
Sickened, the ranger took a stick and knocked over the little bird.
From under the wings ran little chicks, one—two, and then a third.
It was then he realized what the little bird had bravely done.
She had sacrificed her own life …to save her little ones.
As he thought about what he just saw, a quickening came to mind,
of a much greater sacrifice for the saving of mankind.

Like the bird, Christ knew what was coming and He willing stayed.
He could have left; no one would blame Him, for when He prayed;
He said, "O my Father, if it be possible let this cup pass from me."
He said this prayer not once, not twice but a total of three.
And no one had the right to ask Him to do for us what He did.
He could have gone and left us behind or run or even hid.
But He stayed … and He suffered …so you and I could be saved.
He stayed so our road to eternity …could be opened and paved.

Ofcr. Samuel Jeppsen, #3751

Inspired by a true story as reported by The National Geographic.
"He shall cover thee with his feathers, and under his wings shalt thou trust…"
Psalm, 91:4

Chapter Eleven

Sur de la Frontera en Mexico

When I was in Alaska in 1972 and 73, I bought my first road worthy and dependable motorcycle. It was a red and white 1972, Yamaha, 650-twin. It was a BSA style bike with Japanese dependability. When I left Alaska in 73, I shipped it home.

While in Anchorage, I became friends with a guy by the name of Steve Arduser. Steve was a bulldozer operator, owned a 750 K-model Honda and wanted to ride, "Sur de la frontera en Mexico." If at all possible, he also wanted to ride all the way to the Panama Canal. When he told me I said, "What a great idea!"

We joined dreams and our plans were very simple. We would meet at my home in Chandler, Arizona, head south on a five or six week journey, continue south until we ran out of time or money and then turn around and head back home. Some plan!!

Steve and I both left Alaska in late October. It was during the beginning of the OPEC oil embargo. The oil embargo came about as a result of the U.S. support of Israel in what was called, the Yom Kippur War. We met in early November and headed south with a plan to be home before Christmas.

When I really started riding a lot, I started praying a lot! In fact, being very aware of the dangers of riding, I started each ride with a prayer. My faith in Christ has always been very simple. If Christ said something, I believed it. I never changed it or said He meant something else. Instead I believed whatever He said and just as He said it. This simplistic part of me would later become a huge part of my life and would open a huge doorway of blessings for me throughout my life.

Consequently, before Steve and I met up again to fulfill our plan, I did a lot of praying. I asked that I would receive a feeling that we would be protected. I was not so naive as to not understand at least some of the great dangers and situations we could encounter. I was also very aware of the havoc they could play in our lives if those possibilities became realities.

In addition to believing in prayer, I also had a strong belief that God would protect us. Having the feeling of His protection with me was extremely important. This motorcycle ride became my very first real …reaching out moment.

As time came closer to our leaving, that feeling slowly came that we would be okay and that the Lord would watch over us. Once I received that feeling, I never looked back or worried again. My faith in Christ was that simple. I didn't need a voice from Heaven or some other sign. All I needed was that feeling.

Learning to believe and learning to feel, was a gift I received from my mother. A love for the Scriptures and the treasures that were stored in them was a gift I received from my father. These two precious gifts have been the greatest gifts I could have ever received from my parents.

Receiving this feeling, this very unmistakable feeling of peace, comfort and assurance that I felt, would leave a mark in my memory that I would never forget. It would be the first step in a staircase of testimony and faith building experiences with the Lord. With each sequential experience, I was spiritually added upon and made stronger than the time before.

When Steve and I met at my home, we rode south from Chandler, Arizona and crossed into Mexico at Nogales. Entering Nogales was a shock to the system. Compared to the U.S. it was very poor and rundown. The visual difference of the two standards of living was something I never got used to and never stopped taking in. I could not understand how just crossing an imaginary line in the dirt made all this difference and yet, it did.

Another huge difference was the *Mordida.* In my pocket, I carried about forty dollars in singles. I was told that a few here and there would help me in certain legal situations. …It did!

The need for Mordida (not to be confused with the word *Propina* meaning to tip, as in a restaurant setting) stopped shortly after the border. And fortunately for us, most of the officials didn't need to be *tipped* at all.

After the border stops and towns, we headed for Hermosillo and then down to the ocean side city of Guaymas, where we spent our first night. Getting away from the border towns totally changed everything. It was on day one, of this five to six week journey, that my love for the Mexican people began to develop.

I was somewhat leery, being a gringo from the U.S., on my first trip into Mexico. This was my first trip past a border town. Prior trips into border towns gave me the perception that Mexico was as her border towns. The border towns I had been in were dirty, rundown and overcrowded. They had too many banditos and too many people trying to take advantage of me.

What I came to realize is that Mexico changes once you get past the border and *completely* changes again about a hundred miles in. The people there were just like me. They were just trying to make it day to day. They had a dream they were hanging onto and were continually pressing toward. They believed in something greater than themselves and they loved their families and struggled to provide for them.

What I found most remarkable of all, was the look in their faces! There was an unusual softness and kindness in their eyes. And though I could see they were an impoverished people, through it all, they had the ability to be happy. "What an amazing trait!" I said. "To be able to be happy with so very little!"

I could also tell that they demonstrated the attributes and principles of love, faith and charity to others. Most interesting to me was that they so easily and openly seemed to have a great faith in and love for, my dear Friend, whom they call, "Jesucristo."

The people were humble and kind to me. I learned that I could be safe among them. Another great realization I had, was that the border towns often drew the worst of people from both sides of the border. It was not just a phenomenon unique to the Mexican side of the border.

Having never gone on a mission, it was during this trip that I began to dream of one day being able to serve as a missionary, S*ur de la frontera* (south of the border.)

As different as Mexico was from the border, to the point we were a hundred miles in, Mexico changed that much again from Mazatlan, south. Mazatlan is over seven hundred miles south of the border and is very beautiful. There is a lot of development and catering to the tourist industry, between the border and Mazatlan.

As beautiful as these vacation cities are, to go to them and say you have seen Mexico, is like saying you have seen California because you have been to Los Angeles. In fact, from Mazatlan south, the country and her people change as much as California changes from San Francisco north. It was here and south of here that my greatest memories were created and my greatest love for the Mexican people occurred.

Each nationality has a particular common thread that is fairly consistent throughout. The people of Mexico are the same. Though *los lobos* (the wolves or criminals) lurk everywhere, the Mexican people have a peaceful way and very sincere humility about them. The people I continually came across had so little and yet, they were able to be so happy. Their smiles were genuine and from their hearts. I didn't know what to expect in my travels through their country, but I had not thought to expect this. The deeper I went into Mexico and Guatemala, the more I found this common thread.

It was here, I first learned that happiness has little or nothing to do with the facts. It is a decision of the will. I found this to be a true statement in village after village and in face after face. The journey was becoming a series of discoveries.

While Steve and I rode along, we looked for places to sleep. No preplanning, just look, get a feel and either pull over or move on. Most of the time we slept in a field near the road or someplace where we could park our bikes in a "V" configuration and sleep inside the V.

Often we would cover our bikes with brush or we would find some bushes to sleep behind. Usually it required some off-road riding, to get to where we felt safe enough to bed down. Sleeping out each night under the stars, usually just outside of some little town along the way, allowed me plenty of opportunity, to just watch and observe life in *small town* Mexico.

Sometimes before bedding down, we would go into town. We visited the shops, ate at the little roadside restaurants and just moved among the people. We would watch the children and the old women and old men who often were more visible, as the younger generations seemed busier with life. These little communities along the way were so drastically different from what I was used to in the States. So impoverished, yet, the people always seemed to have an uplifting smile to give.

Nobody put on any airs with us. We never found ourselves fighting someone's holier-than-thou attitude and I was never snubbed or put down. Instead, I always received a warm smile. I began to count on it. It was that way wherever I went.

I didn't understand Spanish and Steve knew only ten to fifteen words. So, to say the least, we had some real challenges. However, we learned as we went and you can go a long way with patience, a smile and hand signals. Somehow we managed to buy food, gas, find directions and keep moving along. We felt and looked like *los dos vagabundos* (the two vagrants.) *...What a life!*

There were many times in our travels, just before dark, we would sit on a hill, overlooking a town or village and watch from a distance. Many times, after finding something to eat, we would watch the community until finally drifting off to sleep. I remember they watched us as much as we watched them. Where we were traveling, *blanco (white) americanos* were seldom seen. And Steve and I, just returning from Alaska, looked pretty ...well...

The city of Guadalajara is about the size of Phoenix, Arizona. It is the only city I know of, that was moved three times. The first locations turned out to be too inhospitable. The name, Guadalajara, actually means *The Valley of Stones.* Guadalajara is where the Mariachi music or *wedding* music comes from. At Guadalajara, our speedometers said we had traveled a thousand miles since the border. Wow! I remember thinking. If this was as far as we managed to get, it would still be a fantastic journey!

Guadalajara is a very beautiful city where the temperatures average between sixty-five and ninety degrees year round. However, large cities with millions of people and skyscrapers were not what we came to see, so we tried to steer clear of them. We often rode the fringe of the cities or took some longer, less traveled roads through smaller towns to see the simpler communities instead.

If I was surprised by any city in Mexico, it was Cuidad de Mexico, or Mexico City. It is the third largest city in the world by population and the largest city in the *western* world. It has an elevation of 7400 feet, five hundred feet higher than Flagstaff, Arizona. I was awed by the skyscrapers in the city. I could see a distant snowcapped mountain that turned out to be the second highest in Mexico at over 17,000 feet. Mexico's highest mountain, at over 18,000 feet, is Mt. Pico De Orizaba, which is also the tallest mountain in North America.

If I was negatively impacted by Mexico City, it was that traveling her ultra crowded streets, made traveling in L.A. seem safe and simple. And their smog made L.A smog, seem like a clear day. I had been to L.A. several times and had always noticed their smog. But Mexico City's was so severe, I could almost taste it. Their smog burnt my eyes and lungs constantly.

The thing that made traveling Mexico City streets worth it, was when we stopped to see the ruins of Teotihuacan. I was awed to see the third largest pyramid in the world, the Pyramid of the Sun. At its base is a street that is about a mile long and perfectly straight. It runs from the Pyramid of the Moon at the north, to the Temple of Quetzalcoatl to the south. The name of the street fascinated me. It was called *Calzada de los Muertos*, or *Avenue of the Dead.*

It was here in the once thriving community of Teotihuacan, at about 400 BC that the worship of Quetzalcoatl was first documented. The name, Quetzalcoatl, means *feathered serpent.* There are several different ideas as to what is meant by the words feathered serpent, but about the only thing that everyone can seem to agree on, is that Quetzalcoatl was Deity. With several theories as to whom he was, there is even a Christian theory. Many Christians feel it has reference to Christ, Himself.

In the New Testament, after Christ raised Jairus's daughter from the dead, healed the blind man and performed many other miracles, He told His apostles to go and preach to the people and specifically to the lost sheep of the house of Israel. He tells them to heal the sick, cleanse the lepers, raise the dead, cast out devils and to freely give as they have freely received. Then He tells them, "Behold, I send you forth as sheep in the midst of wolves: be ye therefore wise as serpents, and harmless as doves."

As I walked the ruins and climbed the steps and sat on the stone walls, I began pondering the feelings inside me. In my mind's eye, I could see and feel the people as they walked about this ancient city. In the wind I could almost hear their voices. Inside me sprang a bubbling interest in the people that had been here and what had taken place.

There are a lot of theories of what happened here, but the fact is, no one really knows. The structures were built by the Teotihuacan people in about 50 to 100 AD. They were discovered by the Aztecs several centuries after they were abandoned.

The Native American and the Mexican people have always impressed me with their faith and their simple way of explaining things. Not far from where I live is the City of Tucson. The name, Tucson, is Spanish for the Papago Indian word *Chook-soon.* It simply means, *the black rocks where the water goes in.* Though being simple has it shortfalls, so does being complex. Two of the most brilliant men I personally knew, had the shortfall of being so brilliant, so complex, so caught up in the theories of science, they could not believe in God. Like the evolution theorists, the concept was just too simple for them. Interestingly, it *is* simple, but neither one could see it. The proof that He lives, was all around them and in everything they looked at, but like the theorists, they continually looked beyond the mark. The Native American and the Mexican people are not that way. They have the ability to believe in God by a feeling inside them that tells them He is there.

As I sat there looking over the remains of this ancient civilization, I thought of my two extremely brilliant friends and thought about their lives after they turned from God. I could not help but think of God as well. As I did, I thought of the many civilizations that had passed away after they too, turned from Him. Their morals fell into decay, their lives fell into decay and their laws and their leaders became corrupt. Then, like the Roman Empire, their once great city and way of life was now just a pile of empty buildings and streets for tourists to walk around and for scientists to theorize about.

Mexico changed again after Mexico City. After we left Teotihuacan, the towns had either very poorly paved roads with huge chuckholes and missing pavement or stone and dirt streets. The density of population and the number of small towns also changed. Mexico is almost three times larger than Texas and with over one hundred and ten million people, it is eleventh in world population. Most of her population is between Mazatlan and Oaxaca (O-walk-a.) The drastic difference from the congestion of the big cities, to the beautiful green density of the countryside is amazing. Most people think of Mexico as being primarily desert. That's only true in the top half. From Mazatlan south, it is green and later on, it becomes tropical. In many places it looked like photos of the jungles of Africa. That is probably why there seemed to be a thousand small towns and villages there and it was the small towns and villages that we came for.

Through it all, my fascination and love for the Mexican people grew, as day after day, we traveled through these little towns and villages. Other than the occasional reminders that I was in the 20th Century, like an occasional car or patches of pavement, it was like traveling in a time machine. It was like going back to the days of the Old West. Through the desert parts, I remember thinking as I rode along—this is just like being in a Western! It's almost as if I were a Texas Ranger in the 1949 movie, *The Streets of Laredo* or perhaps like being with John Wayne in *Rio Grande* as he rode his trusty steed across the frontier.

The feeling often changed when I was in the heavy jungle sections. There, I kept my eyes peeled for Johnny Weissmuller and a stampeding herd of elephants. Just my luck! Here I am in Mexico, I'll hear some goofy scream and I'll get run over by a herd of wild, rampaging elephants and then eaten by one of those buzzards that keep circling overhead, when we stop!

Mingled among the small homes and often dirt streets were beautiful, little, archaic looking, stone and mudded churches. Many of them were smaller than the home I currently live in and sometimes they were the largest building in the village. We often pulled over and spent a few moments just looking and feeling the spirit that accompanied them. I would usually turn and look over the surrounding area and see the impact the church had on the lives of the people. The influence of Christ in their lives was evidenced by almost everything I saw. I found being around the people and the old church buildings to be a joy. Most of the churches were adobe construction and many had missing pieces in their exterior walls.

In my mind, I have a vivid memory of one church, in particular. It was in a little and very poor village, with dirt and cobblestone streets. It was along the way, southeast of Oaxaca. I could see the entire village, one end to the other, from where I sat on my bike. We stopped in front and guessed the building to be between three to four hundred years old. Pieces of the building had either fallen off or had been washed away by the rain. On top, was a small, chipped, stone cross. Yet here it stood, in the center of the village as a constant reminder of to whom the people should look. It reminded me of the brazen, serpent, figure on the staff of Moses. The serpent to the Israelites, represented the Lord and His matchless power and His ability to protect them.

When the poisonous snakes came among the Israelites, all they had to do was to look upon the brazen serpent and they would be healed from the snake bites they had received.

I have often thought of how easy, looking at Moses' staff would have been and yet how many, intentionally, did not look. Instead they chose to suffer from the snake bite and chose to die rather than look. I suppose they thought, "Looking, is just too simple—so how could it work?!" That story of Moses and his staff has reminded me of the many people today that won't look to the Lord, either. I suppose they too think, "Looking is just too simple—so how could it work?!" Rather than do so, they choose to suffer and sometimes even die from the poison in their souls.

In much the same way, these little churches I kept passing, seemed to say the same thing. They pointed the way toward hope and healing, because like Moses' brazen serpent, they pointed the way toward Christ. As I sat there on my bike and looked over the small village, this little old church offered that same hope. The lives these people lived were primitive by U.S. standards, but in the faces and in the hearts of the people, I saw hope, peace and charity toward others. This hope, peace and charity intrigued me. It was evidenced by the smiles, they so easily gave away and their ability to be happy in such poor circumstances. Of all the many wonderful things I ever saw south of the border, this phenomenon was always the most fascinating.

After a few moments of reflection in front of that little church, southeast of Oaxaca, I took a picture of it and of my bike on the cobblestone road. Steve and I then saddled up and hit the starters. I then turned, took one last look, tipped my head and gave the old girl a friendly salute. With the sun now low in the west, we dropped our bikes into gear and moved along.

33) Step out of your comfort zone. Create a "Reaching out Moment."
34) Develop tolerance and a genuine love for others.
35) Believe in the Lord and don't overanalyze His teachings.
36) Be observant to the quiet things in life and learn from them.

That Someone…

It's really funny how life works out,
so full of worry and silly little doubts.
Worrying over every problem that comes your way,
wishing they'd disappear and you could start a new day.
Yes, we all know that trials help make us strong,
but life would be much easier if they never came along.
Oft times you find yourself starring off into the sky,
trying to figure out what to do and asking yourself why?
Why did your life get derailed and how do you get it on track?
And how did you take one step forward and get two steps back?

It's then that something always seems to come through.
A coincidental something, just as if someone were with you.
In trials where I had no choice but to persist to the bitter end,
it was then I realized I had been helped by an unseen friend.
That unseen someone would meet me and help me to carry on,
lifting my spirits and hopes, encouraging me to be strong.
It was during these times, that I realized I had not been alone.
I felt Someone who loved me, reaching down from His Throne.
That's why it's so important in needs, wants or desires to achieve,
that in Him, who grants life and miracles ...you always believe.

Excerpts, That Someone, Ofcr. Samuel Jeppsen, #3751

"For verily I say unto you that I am Alpha and Omega,
the beginning and the end, the light and the life of the world.
A light that shineth in darkness and the darkness comprehendeth it not."
Jesus Christ

Chapter Twelve

Guatemala and British Honduras

As beautiful and intriguing as Mexico is, Guatemala is even more so. It is the size of Tennessee. Everything is green and the trees are so thick, that walking through the forests is like trying to pass through a jungle. True to the meaning of its Mayan name, Guatemala is *The Land of the Trees.*

Her towns and villages are similar to the small Mexican towns and villages, with a very definite Guatemalan flavor. The country is a little more native Indian and a *lot* more primitive.

The Mayan-Guatemalan people are very short in stature. Being around six feet tall, I was often a foot or more, taller than the people I was walking among. They were shorter than the Mexican people and often a little rounder. Also, as bad as the average road condition was in Mexico, the average road condition in Guatemala was several times worse. Many times huge sections of roads or entire lanes were missing. But the missing pavement, the giant potholes and the little, wooden, one lane bridges only added to the great adventure. Even so, it was the people and their kind ways that fascinated me the most.

As we were bouncing along near the border, we pulled into a little village and saw an old man in his mid to late sixties. He was leaning against a wall, watching us pass by. He was standing next to a bale of hay, by a rundown building. He wore a pair of slacks with the cuffs turned up, a jacket, a Humphrey Bogart hat and had a Sherlock Holmes pipe in his mouth.

His facial expression was striking. As I passed by, I noticed that he even looked like he was trying to solve a mystery. I yelled at Steve and we turned around and went back to take the old man's photo. Steve stood next to him for the picture as the old man began to grin. We jabbered and motioned to him, but he never said a word. Instead, he just smiled and looked at us. The look on his face was of a wise old man, watching two frolicking children at his feet. From his heart came a huge, warm smile as he let us take his picture. Through it all, he was so very kind to us. I still have that cherished picture today. The picture in my collection of photos—and the one I keep in my mind.

Crossing into Guatemala brought another new experience for us. There was a lot of political unrest at the time. In fact, they were in the middle of civil war. Because of this, there were lots of Military Troop Carriers on the road and they were filled with soldiers who were carrying full-auto assault rifles.

There was also a very obvious animosity toward the *Norteamericanos* (North or US Americans) because of some of our political backing in their governmental affairs. And here we were, two, grungy looking gringos on motorcycles, in our early twenties, from America. We had long hair, needed a shave and looked like stereotypical rebellious youth of the 70's. We waved and smiled at the troops as we passed, but they never waved or smiled back. In fact, their look was one of contempt. It was a very uneasy feeling as Steve and I passed the often slow moving troop carriers.

There were four groups that were fighting for control of the country. The four groups were the Guerrilla Army of the Poor, the Revolutionary Organization of Armed People, the Rebel Armed Forces and the Guatemalan Labor Party. Over two hundred thousand people were killed during that civil war and Steve and I were riding our motorcycles through the middle of it. So we made sure we were on our best behavior and tried to be careful by keeping an extra low profile. During all the political unrest in Guatemala, staying on our best behavior and keeping a low profile was critical and much more important than it had been in Mexico.

Old, green, Vietnam era, US Military field jackets were popular jackets at the time. They could be purchased at any US Military Surplus Store in America for around ten dollars. I wore one throughout Mexico, but I took it off and tucked it away the entire time I was in Guatemala.

The high concentration of troops in Guatemala was my only time for concern throughout the ride. However, I still had that feeling that we would be fine, so I didn't worry.

At the end of a long day's ride, we stopped for dinner at a beautiful roadside garden style restaurant. It was the nicest and most inviting restaurant we had eaten at. We had chicken sandwiches. They were delicious. We then spent the next three days in a hotel room in Guatemala City, deathly ill. Even then, I didn't worry and knew we would be fine. Somehow, I knew our bikes outside would be fine, also. After three days of lying on our beds, so sick we could not move, we finally emerged from our room. When we went outside, we found our hotel was surrounded by soldiers. They were standing about every ten feet apart. This high concentration of soldiers was also on neighboring city streets.

We had no idea what had happened or why the troops were there lining the streets. All we knew, was that the troops were here, everything was quiet and no one was smiling. In our room we had heard yelling and fireworks. We just thought it was some sort of street party. But to be honest, we were just too sick to care. We were miserable. All we did was lie on our beds and stagger to and from the bathroom, unable to eat or drink. I had never felt so sick, dizzy and incapacitated in my life. After finally feeling better and walking outside and then seeing the soldiers, we realized it was probably gunfire and a riot …and not fireworks and a party.

Standing there on the sidewalk in front of the Hotel and next to the soldiers, we also noticed that the streets were quiet and almost void of citizens. The troops didn't look friendly, but they didn't stop us either. Our bikes, stored behind the hotel fence, were totally fine, as well. Everything was just as the feeling I had received at home had promised—that we would be just fine!

I honestly believe the extreme illness we experienced, was a blessing in disguise from the Lord. It kept us out and away from the disturbance. It kept us safely locked inside our hotel room, away from the soldiers and away from the troublemakers.

We never did find out what all the trouble was about. But when we opened the gate, fired up our bikes, mounted them and rode away, every eye of every soldier, carrying an assault rifle, was on us. We smiled. They didn't! We waved. They didn't! But they let us pass and we slowly rode away, very careful not to break any traffic laws as we left them and all the trouble behind us.

When we took off from Guatemala City, we headed for British Honduras. As we rode, we came across an old man carrying a large bundle of straw up the steep mountain highway. He was a Guatemalan, about four and a half feet tall. The bundle of straw he was carrying was about three feet by four feet and about two feet thick. It probably weighed as much as he did. The straw was supported by a strap he had around his head, causing him to bend way forward to try and keep his balance as he carried the straw up the hill.

When I saw him, I was reminded of the huge army ants I had seen carrying big leaves across the dirt highway, soon after entering Guatemala. When I came upon them, I thought it was a thick, black, rope or a snake lying across the road. As I got closer, I could see it was moving. As I got closer still, I could see it was a thick line of insects. I stopped to look at it and saw that it was large, black, army ants about the length of my thumbnail. They were carrying leaves and little pieces of debris that were several times larger than they were. The ants were marching in two perfect east/west traffic patterns. I noticed that it looked like a freeway from the air during heavy, rush-hour traffic. As I stood and watched, I was amazed that the ants were not crossing into the oncoming lane of traffic. I was intrigued by their order.

To me, the ants were a reminder that everything in life, this world and in the universe has incredible order. It all added up, that there had to be a God in heaven that organized everything. There is just too much Swiss watch precision in life for me to believe otherwise. After a few minutes I photographed the ants and moved on. But now, here was this old Guatemalan man doing the same thing as the ants. The bundle of straw was larger than he was yet, up the hill with his heavy load, he went.

As I passed by, I noticed he had one of the greatest smiles of anyone I had ever seen! What right does he have to smile? I thought. By our standards, he should be miserable. His life is so hard and unfair. At the time of his life, when he should be able to retire, there he was, with this incredible load upon his back and head. The load was so heavy, he had to walk bent forward, yet on his face was this remarkable smile. What an incredible man! What an incredible spirit! I again yelled for Steve to stop. I smiled at the old man, as we got off our bikes. Saying nothing, he smiled back. I then bent down and took my shot.

As I tried to communicate with him, all he did was smile. He never said a word, even in his own language. He probably realized it was futile, long before we did. But my desire to know more about him was peaked. The reason I kept trying to communicate with him, was that I was so fascinated by his ability to smile, regardless of his miserable circumstances.

In his eyes, as I looked into his soul, I could see that he was truly a happy man! A man who was willing to press on and willing to try to improve his life and the life of others around him! What a great inspiration he was to me. I then waved goodbye to my little friend, threw my leg over my bike and continued on.

The road to British Honduras, renamed Belize, the year we rode through, was absolutely incredible! Absolutely incredibly bad that is! I could not believe the road we were on, had so little pavement and was often no wider than a good Jeep trail. This little country is four thousand square miles smaller than the *county* I live in, but the country was worth every bump and chuckhole I hit to get there. It was the beginning of an exciting mystery, where we would enter one ancient city after another.

The pictures I took during this time, bring with them not only the remembrance of the sights, but the remembrance of the panoramic views, the dampness that always seemed to be in the air and the smell of the land and the jungle. This experience also breathed a spiritual connection to the past with my own spirit. As I rode, I thought of one Scripture story after another. I thought of the Lord who is not only the Savior of all those who believe in the Bible, but who is also the Savior of every nationality and people in the world! I also thought of all the great and marvelous things He has done for those who follow and love Him.

For us, visiting the city of Belize, was probably not the delight it is for those who fly in on vacation and wind up at the most beautiful hotels and on the pristine beaches and eating at fine restaurants with gracious, well dressed waiters, who serve drinkable water …and edible chicken! Throughout the entire trip, whenever possible, Steve and I stayed totally away from those places. We stayed away from the tourists as well. We went to the places where the *mercados* (markets) were open-air and the stores had no fronts, only tables heavily laden with goods to sell. We went where the vendors met you on the street, selling their goods to you, face to face.

We focused on the places where the streets, often poorly paved, were filled with people moving about and where the children playing in the streets seldom wore shoes.

To me, traveling in these places was more than traveling through their country. I was now traveling through their lives and loving it! I was literally mingling with the people, heart to heart. I often stopped and tried to communicate with them, as my love for Central America and her people was continuing to grow. Her people, who always seemed to have a warm and loving smile to give, quickly found a place in my heart.

As I traveled through Belize and took pictures of the people, I thought about the great disparity in our opportunities. In the U.S., I was just a cement finisher who had scraped together a few bucks and bought a motorcycle and then rode it to their country on a once-in-a-lifetime adventure. I was just a guy who lived in an old ten by fifty-six mobile home in a dusty, dirt field in Chandler, Arizona. I had so little, in comparison to those who lived in the neighborhoods around me. But on this trip, I was *El rico americano.* (The rich American.)

I wore clothes that were more expensive than theirs and my beautiful, fairly new motorcycle with its big engine and chrome everywhere, was a rare sight for them. By American standards, my motorcycle was a less than average road bike. Being new, with bright paint and loaded with chrome and my rumbly *twice-pipes*, the bike was something they had only seen in a magazine. My bike to them was as a Rolls-Royce, to me. It was something totally out of reach and reserved for only the wealthy.

In their faces, I saw and acknowledged that the blessings of prosperity were so abundantly mine. I had been blessed in a way they couldn't even hope for. I was probably their first sighting of a rich American playboy. To them, I owed my time to no one. I had endless funds to just take off on a new, beautiful bike and ride thousands of miles from home and tour their country.

I *am* blessed! I am v*ery blessed* and very aware of it and never forget it! I am indeed ...*El rico americano!*

Wherever we went, Steve and I tried very hard to keep low profiles and avoid contact with the police. Even though, most of the policemen we came across, seemed friendly toward us. But there in Belize, I met a particular officer that I would never be able to forget.

He stood there in his light blue shirt and dark blue pants, with his hands clasped behind his back. He was a black man in his mid-thirties, standing under his hat as he watched the goings-on around him. He had a slim build and a closely trimmed mustache. His stance was very erect. He sported proudly a gentle smile, as he stood and looked about.

When I pulled up next to him, I could see that his uniform was worn out and threadbare by U.S. standards. His collar was frayed and his shirt had a few loose strings. His uniform pants were worn out as well and they would no longer hold a crease. His pockets and cuffs were frayed. His leather shoes were worn too badly, to hold a shine. Around his waist was an old, black, Sam Brown police belt. Strapped to his side was an older model, Smith & Wesson, 38 caliber, Police Special with much of its bluing worn off. The gun was an old, long barreled, Skinny Smithy, just like Elliot Ness and his Untouchables carried.

When he first looked at me, I could see he didn't know how to take me. I was obviously a North American in my mid twenties, sleeves rolled up, wearing a full beard, fairly long hair, shades and no helmet. I was physically larger and I was on a big, expensive, brightly colored motorcycle with loud pipes.

As I began asking him questions, I could see that he was continually sizing me up. He answered in English and sounded like he had lived in England. He never relaxed around me. I could sense a very strong command presence, such as I had seen before in men I knew, who possessed true honor—not arrogance—but true honor! He was not like some of the others I had met, professing honor, but not having it. His tone of voice, his actions, the way he conducted himself, was that of a man who espoused honor without having to say it. It was as if he had a loyalty to the very word itself. I could feel it and I was impressed by it.

As we talked, I noticed one more thing about him. I could tell that those ideals were not something he was forced into believing. Of all that impressed me about him, that was the most impressive. That he was that way, because that's who he chose to be. He could have chosen to be so much less, he could have fit in, instead of stood out. He could have lived by lesser standards and he would have still been a great person, but he didn't. He chose instead to be great. He was one of the *Protectors* and who he was, came from a decision he had made about himself, a long time ago.

It was a lot to perceive in our five minute conversation, but it was so strong with him, it was easy to detect. I knew then that any man could live that way, if they chose to. Their personal honor and integrity can be so strong, that a stranger, who is around them for just a few minutes, can easily and immediately feel it and can recognize that he has it!

This officer reminded me of the two other officers I had met on this trip. I recognized the same type of thing, in each of them. I met the first officer in Mexico City, when I asked him, "Yo nessesito largo distancia telefono." (I need a long distance telephone.) I was impressed by him because he was nothing like the border officers that I had dealt with. He was several cuts above what I expected and I noticed it immediately.

In a small town near the Guatemalan border, I met the second officer near another old church, I had stopped to photograph. I had stopped him to ask directions. He did fairly well in his instructions to me and understood me better than I understood him. As he talked, I noticed what poor condition his brown uniform was in. His uniform was in the worst condition of them all. However, the condition of his uniform seemed to make little difference to the man who wore it. The man inside that far past threadbare uniform, was a man dedicated to being a man of honor and a servant of the people. I could tell that offering him *mordida* (a bribe or *"the bite"*) would have offended him.

It would be three years, before I became an officer myself. Even so, the encounters I had with these three officers, left marks on my character and personality. They actually played a big part in what kind of officer, I became. I lived a whole police career, trying to be like these three men of honor, that I had met along the way, in their raggedy uniforms and dusty shoes, *Sur de la frontera.*

When we left Belize, we headed for the Yucatan, the land of the ancient cities. We rode to Tulum and then followed the coastal road to Cancun, meaning, *The Throne of the Snake* or *The Pot of Snakes* in Mayan culture. Before it was named Cancun, it was called Ekab, meaning *Black Earth.* The place is beautiful and the ruins are by the seashore of the Caribbean Sea.

Today, Cancun is a bustling, thriving city with 600,000 people, 140 hotels, 24,000 rooms, 380 restaurants and 190 flights a day. When Steve and I were there in 73, Cancun was just a little community along the seashore with about a thousand residents.

The very year we were there, 1973, was the beginning of the boom era for Cancun. It began changing from a little sleepy town on the edge of the Caribbean, to a major metropolis and tourist attraction. When I see photos of it now, I cannot believe that back then, it was just another small village we passed through.

Each year more ancient cities are excavated by the government and each year, more of each ruin is excavated. Some were already brightly uncovered and very delicately restored like Tikal, Tulum, Cancun, Chichen Itza, Uxmal and Campeche. Walking among these places, sitting on the stone buildings and monuments, overlooking the vastness and the ancient city, filled my mind with awe. I had a wonderment and interest for these people, I knew little about, yet somehow, felt close to. The Phoenix Valley has very few skyscrapers compared to the amount of people that live here. By that same comparison, these ancient communities must have been huge!

As I visited these places, I often remained quiet, just feeling the sights and sounds of the breezes passing through the jungle. I could almost see the people around me and hear their voices in the wind, as I visualized them, living their lives before me.

Coba was the only ancient city, which was not similar to the others. The road to Coba, was perhaps the worst road I traveled, the entire journey. It was literally a first gear, ten mile an hour, bumpity-bump, Jeep trail, that was filled with pot holes. The ruin was in the early stages of excavation. It was mostly just big, foliage covered lumps in the jungle floor.

Coba was my first look at what an ancient city looks like, before it is excavated. The ruins were heavily covered with dirt, grass, bare roots, vines, trees and plants. Steve and I climbed some of them, but it was quite a task. It was like climbing a steep hillside that was covered with jungle growth.

Climbing the mounds and looking over the jungle below, brought very special and unexpected feelings. It felt similar to being in a graveyard. Visiting a site, where an entire civilization had vanished, who probably felt their extinction would never happen, made me think of the many civilizations throughout time, which had disappeared completely. Each one amazed me, as each one was an entire civilization that had vanished into the unknown. It reminded me of those civilizations, which are being discovered in the layers of the earth and at the bottom of the oceans.

As I stood there looking over the jungle covered mounds, I could not help but wonder what causes an entire city or civilization to vanish? What causes the people in a city like Mesa or Phoenix to disappear, to totally vacate and allow the city, eventually, to be overrun with vines, plants and trees? What causes the earth to just swallow an entire city and then hide it, as if it were never there?

Science has many theories about their disappearances. There are so many ancient cities, whose inhabitants are totally gone! Each city was as if we were looking at a city on the moon. They were not little wooden ghost towns, with a few streets and a few buildings, like the over 8,000 ghost towns, we have here in America. They were massive cities with massive structures and thriving civilizations! The structures took thousands of people to build them and yet now, there is not even a sheepherder or his dog.

I thought of the Scriptural accounts of the cities that were sunk or destroyed when Christ was crucified and left to die a very painful death on the cross. I thought of the troubles that become ours, when we turn away from Him and decide we don't need Him in our lives anymore. As I stood on the top of that steep mound, overlooking the covered mounds around me, my testimony of how much we need Christ in our lives was magnified. From where I stood, Coba looked like endless jungle and as I listened to the sounds of the jungle, I envisioned the ending of their civilization.

While climbing a trail in a nearby location, over the top of the hill above me and heading straight for me, I encountered a Mayan-Guatemalan man and wife. They were less than five feet tall, a little round and were both dressed in bright Guatemalan clothing and blankets. They were carrying baskets. When I saw them, I immediately took out my camera and got ready for the perfect shot as they came toward me. They then paused for their picture to be taken. As I said thank you and began to continue up the path, the man stepped in front of me, blocked my path and took hold of his machete. It didn't take me long to figure out, that this would be a great opportunity to share some of those singles in my pocket. So I gave him a few and he smiled and stepped out of my path. "Who knows?" I said. "Maybe he thought I was a reporter or something and doing a great story and that he should be fairly compensated for his part!" Whatever his reason, I was glad for the shot and glad to share a few bucks, that I am sure helped him and his family. I smiled as I turned and walked away.

After I climbed back on my bike and started riding back down that bumpy, dirt road we came in on, I remember thinking that I was thousands of miles from home. I was in a place where there were no phones, no help, no medical assistance, no tourists I could ask for help, no mechanics or even anyone that spoke my language. I was just some half-wit, traveling with another half-wit, on motorcycles, through the jungles of the Yucatan. But I also remember that peaceful feeling never leaving me. That prayed for—peaceful feeling that filled my bosom and brought with it the calming assurance that the Lord was with me and that I need not fear and that I would be fine.

After leaving the ruins of the Yucatan, we followed the Gulf Coast to Miramar, Villahermosa, Veracruz, and Madero. All the cities along the Gulf Coast were so very beautiful and very advanced. They were set up for not only the residents, but for the thousands of tourists that visit each year and the coastlines were adorned in massive buildings. These not being what we came to see, we kept moving along.

Soon we were at the U.S. Mexico border at Brownsville, Texas. After going through Customs, we said our goodbyes. Steve headed north to Nebraska and I headed west to Arizona. We both had hopes of making it home before Christmas.

Two days later, I found myself in the middle of long lines, trying to buy gas for my bike. I was in Tucson, trying to get home. Though grateful to be back in America and headed for home, I found the OPEC oil embargo was now in full swing. Gas lines, angry people, tension and often fights were my welcome back.

Station after station, posted big signs that read, "**NO GAS.**" Lines of cars stretched out in front of them, filled with angry drivers. Some were standing in the street arguing and waiting for fuel. In the midst of it all, I was blessed to find a very kind man who gave me two gallons of gas. It would be all I needed to get home. It was another tender mercy from the Lord. It was also another reminder of the promise, I had received, that I would be fine throughout my journey, *sur de la frontera.*

A very special thing happened in my life on this trip. With this being my first real reaching out experience to the Lord, I found that I had never been left alone. It caused my testimony and faith in Him to begin to grow and define. Perhaps most important of all, this trip ...became the launch pad for the rest of my life.

On this trip, I had ridden where few would ever get the opportunity to ride. I had lived experiences and seen things that would create in me a strong foundation of faith and trust in the Lord. This once in a lifetime journey south of the border, would only be the beginning of my many spiritual journeys with Him.

As I was pouring the two gallons of gas into my tank, I thought of the Savior and the story of the blind man, He healed. "I am the good shepherd," said the Lord, "and know my sheep, and am known of mine. As the Father knoweth me, even so know I the Father: and I lay down my life for my sheep." As the last of the gas dripped into the tank, I smiled and thought, He not only lays down His life for His sheep, He watches over them and prepares help for them, long before they are in a crisis and need it.

Though I am sure my personal relationship with Christ, actually began in my youth with my mother and her teachings of Him to me, it was this journey that built the massive footings, where all other experiences in my life would rest. This journey would be the starting point, where having faith and trust in the Lord, would be paramount in my ability to succeed.

It didn't take years of college, a Doctorate in science or a degree in the Ministry, to have such a relationship with the Lord. It came from the simple things. It came from the desire to know about the Lord and the willingness to believe in Him and to follow a feeling inside me, which told me He was there and I could trust Him. My experiences became a priceless foundation for me, that would one day hold the massive structure of faith and miracles, in a guy who was no one special, but now knew that his Savior, Jesus the Christ, lives!

With the two gallons added to my half gallon, I now had enough gas to make the one hundred and ten mile ride home. As I left that very kind man behind and headed north to Chandler, I thought of the Scripture that reads, "Blessed is the man that trusteth in the Lord and whose hope the Lord is."

37) Tragedies or illnesses can actually be great blessings in disguise.
38) Be quick to recognize your blessings, never taking them for granted.
39) Notice the Lord's hand in the Swiss Watch precision in life and nature.
40) True honor and integrity is discernible by others and priceless to the Lord.
41) Let the Spirit teach you by everyone and everything around you.
42) Nurture-nurture-nurture, your half of your Divine relationship.
43) Build a spiritual foundation that could hold a skyscraper.

Chapter Thirteen

The "PCH" Pacific Coast Highway

After having ridden my beloved 1972, 650 Yamaha several thousand trouble free miles, I bought a new 1976 Suzuki GT750, two-stroke, triple. It was faster than anything I had ever ridden. It was nicknamed the *Water-Buffalo*. It was the first successful water cooled, big-bore, production bike. My *Zook* was a screamer! Also, it was Julie's favorite bike. I loved it too, but I was just not a lover of the "Multi's." To me, the bikes were too smooth and the engines didn't make the right sound. Especially mine!! Being a big-bore, two-stroke, triple, though it was fast, the engine sounded like a can full of angry bees.

Almost every year, the Japanese turned out bigger and better bikes. The British bikes, BSA, Triumph and Norton, got to the point they could no longer compete. One by one, Japanese quality and dependability drove them all out of business. Even Harley-Davidson was feeling the impact of the Japanese. The Japanese had something Harley didn't have—low cost, high dependability and trouble free motorcycles *that didn't leak oil!*

Taking the place of the British motorcycles were the innovative, multiple-cylinder bikes from Japan with their three, four and six cylinder engines and never-before-seen horsepower per "cc" ratio. Even today, the Japanese multi's are the fastest bikes on the road. Until the Indian recently reappeared, Japanese bikes, with their over 66 inch wheelbases, were also the largest. Until Triumph reappeared, they also had the biggest engines and they still set the benchmark for dependability and rider confidence.

Because I was a lover of the twins, I sold my GT750 and bought another new, 1980, 650cc, Yamaha. After all, it had the correct number of cylinders a motorcycle should have …*two!!*

In 1982, I threw my leg over my new 650 and took off on my first ride up the PCH. If you have ever been up that road, you know that the Pacific Ocean is to your left, the land is to your right and you literally wander back and forth along the coastline. The ocean is sometimes just a stone's throw away.

My plan was very simple. I would ride west until I hit the ocean and then turn right. Ride and enjoy each day, try to find someplace safe to sleep, and then repeat the process until I finally worked my way back home. "Another great plan!" I said.

Before leaving on that trip, I did the same thing I had done before riding through Mexico, nine years earlier. I prayed and prayed, until I received the feeling that I would be watched over. I would be the *Lone Ranger* this time, riding alone and relying on my Mexico experiences and my police training to be safe. As an officer, I had many scary calls, where I had prayed for that feeling of safety before I arrived on scene. Sometimes the incident would deteriorate right before my eyes into one of my worst nightmares. So as I did in Mexico and in my police career, I prayed. Once I received that feeling of safekeeping, I never worried again.

On the PCH, I would be riding for ten days, sleeping out in the open air as I traveled. As a lone rider, with no companions to help watch over me at night or to help me in an accident or a breakdown, I knew I would be an easy target. Receiving that confirmation, would remove the fear of the unknown.

Looking back, I don't know what I was thinking, doing something so obviously dangerous. Yet, there I was with this dream to ride the PCH. So, remembering that I had called on God before, and remembering the feeling that came with the answer, I prayed until I got it again. It was the whisper, the promise that I would be safe and could enjoy the journey and not worry.

Now, having that feeling again, I felt I was literally wearing the Armor of God. I traveled those ten days, sleeping out wherever I found a place I felt good about, and never worried in the least. Afterwards, I returned home safe and sound, not a scratch on me or my bike. I had entered and left large cities and small communities. I had traveled a couple thousand miles and had slept out for nine nights. And never once, did I doubt the Lord and His promise.

A few years later I wanted to take that ride again. As a police officer for the City of Mesa, I met Stan Peterson. Stan was a paramedic for Southwest Ambulance. Having never been on a ride like this, Stan wanted to come along.

So as before, I prayed for a confirmation that we would be safe. Experience has taught me that if something is worth doing, it is worth praying over and if it is worth praying over, it is worth getting on your knees for. I have also learned to start praying long before I need the help and to put some effort into my prayers. There is something about our prayers meaning a lot to us and being willing to sacrifice a little for them, that seems to make them mean a lot to our Father in Heaven. Sometimes I think that quick and thoughtless prayers cast toward Heaven, receive just about as much attention as the effort we gave them.

This time, like the times before, the feeling of peace and safety finally came. Stan and I loaded our bikes and took off for the California, PCH. But by the third night, Stan was having second thoughts. He wanted to turn around and head for home. I didn't blame him. After all, on night one, we slept behind some bushes in the desert and on day two, we had had some close calls in the heavy L.A. traffic. By the third day, we had had *more* close calls, we were living on junk food and the police had run us out of the alley we had been sleeping in. It was now 2 a.m. and we were sleeping in a city park, when the sprinklers came on and forced us out. We quickly gathered our stuff and ran through the sprinklers. Now, we were wet *and* cold. All this had taken place before we had even made it to San Francisco. And Stan was right. What we were doing was very dangerous with a high possibility of getting hurt. So, as we tried to get back to sleep in wet sleeping bags, south of San Francisco, Stan rolled over and asked if we should turn around and go home and call it a good effort.

I assured him that I had prayed and received a confirmation that we would be okay. If we turned around now and went home, calling it quits, we would never forget that we threw in the towel on ourselves. I promised him more great adventure lay ahead. I told him we would be safe and it would be a trip he would always remember. I told him the Lord was with us and we need not fear. This was the faith and feeling I had inside me and I really believed it. Stan reluctantly agreed. We talked a little longer but soon drifted off to sleep, lying next to our bikes.

We continued on our journey and we were safe throughout. Our bikes never failed us and we ended up having the time of our lives. Stan moved to Missouri, shortly after our trip, but I know he has not forgotten that ride or the lessons in faith, we talked about on the third night. We were just two buddies on bikes, that believed in the Lord and believed He would watch over us as we rode and slept out along the way. …And He did!

The third time I traveled the PCH was in a car. What made this trip enjoyable, as motorcycles are my preferred method of travel, was the fact that I was with my beautiful wife. It was one of our very best vacations and one we still talk about today.

The travel plans were again simple but what really made this trip memorable and so wonderful was the fact that *we were alone with no itinerary*. We didn't start with a list of things we had to do or places we had go. We just took off, headed west with only two things in mind—spend time together and return home in two weeks. Once we turned right at the ocean and then into Santa Barbara, we did whatever we felt like at the moment. We saw what we felt like seeing, got a room when we felt like getting one, woke up when we were done sleeping and moved along when we felt like it. We drove with the radio off and we talked instead. Some days we traveled only fifty miles before getting another room. Sometimes we left a room at 11 a.m. and had another by 1 p.m. At night, we would watch maybe one movie and then turn off the TV and lay in bed talking, sniggling and planning our future until the wee hours of the morning.

Sniggling is our word for giggling and snuggling. This is what we did for two weeks up the PCH. We are best friends and our attention was always toward each other. It was one of the best, most memorable, relationship building vacations we have ever taken together. It was so great, that it set a pattern for us that continues today. Whenever we are in the car together, the radio is off and we talk. At night, we sniggle. We learned that happiness in a marriage has to be created instead of expected. *Creating*, instead of *expecting*, has given us …*a great life together!*

44) Turn the TV and computer games off and go and live real adventures.
45) Once you receive the feeling of peace, ignore the things that go wrong.
46) Being completely true to your spouse, elicits trust from the Lord.
47) *Create* the happiness in life and marriage, instead of foolishly expect it.

Chapter Fourteen

The Storm

"I am a Christian – that is to say, a disciple of the doctrines of Jesus Christ."
Thomas Jefferson

The fourth time I traveled the PCH was again on a bike. It was in 2005 and I was with my brother-in-law, Olin. We were on our Sportsters. This is where my PCH story really begins.

Praying for the feeling of safety on these trips has carried over into praying for safety every time I start a motorcycle and leave my home. Whether to the corner store or on a six-hundred mile day ride or on an adventure filled, ten day ride, I never begin without a prayer first. I even pray at every gas stop.

So here, like all the other times, I prayed until I got that feeling that we would be safe. Like all the other trips I had taken, we would be sleeping out along the way, behind some bush or building or in some vacant lot or field. If not there, we would sleep on a beach or in an alley someplace.

Each time I had one of these motorcycle journeys and praying experiences, my faith and understanding was moved up a few notches. In fact, having this feeling was so important to me, that I would not go on these rides without it. On this particular ride, my experience, faith and understanding would be greatly magnified. This time, instead of my faith in Christ simply moving up to the next step, my faith in Him was literally catapulted up the staircase.

This ride was during an unusually wet June. California was experiencing an El Nino year. Riding in the rain is very miserable, regardless of your gear. It is very uncomfortable and it's like getting hit with millions of spit-wads.

Rain drops sting when they hit your skin and the sound of the rain hitting your helmet, sounds similar to being under a metal awning. Riding in the rain gets everything wet, no matter how hard you try to keep it out. Soon, everything you have is soaking.

The everyday dangers of riding motorcycles in heavy traffic are greatly multiplied by rain. The roads become slick from the oil that breaks lose from the surface. A huge factor when you consider that riding motorcycles is all about balance, leaning and traction. Unless you have to ride, it's best to sit rainstorms out.

Sleeping out in the rain is another miserable experience. I don't think there is any such thing as a rainproof tent. Perhaps the only upside, is that criminals are not as much of a problem during rainstorms, as most are fair weather opportunists. So, having that feeling of safety was paramount.

Receiving that feeling of safety is quite an incredible experience all of its own. To pray and receive a confirmation, that you will be okay on a dangerous journey and then to feel so confident in that feeling, that all will be well, regardless of what happens, is quite addicting! I don't know how else to express it. It is addicting and it is so very precious. It changes your attitude completely and leaves an indelible mark in your mind. It changes your outlook and becomes a hunger. With each new experience, comes the memory of the last experience and the greater need and hunger for that same feeling in the *new* experience. With it, comes the knowledge that your prayers are actually being answered. In your mind forms this realization that you know that the Lord actually lives and that He is reaching out to you!

I have often wondered what brings me the greatest enjoyment—the journey itself or the praying and the receiving of that feeling! Wanting that feeling as a constant feeling, instead of a visiting feeling, has over the years, caused me to change my life. I now try to be worthy of that feeling all the time. For lack of a better explanation, receiving that feeling is like receiving insider information. Though I have a long way to go, I continually go over my life and try to remove the things that block that feeling.

So, in June of 2005, while YouTube was making its debut, Olin and I headed for the California, Pacific Coast Highway. This trip would bring to the forefront just how important having that feeling of peace is. It also showed me how protected we can actually be and how earnest prayer *really does* work!

We headed west out of Phoenix, turned northwest toward Salome, Parker, Twenty-nine Palms, Victorville, Palmdale, Venture, toward the coastline and into Santa Barbara. It was all on secondary roads or rural routes, with very little freeway. We saw parts of southern California that were not only beautiful, but they were the reverse of the stereotypical image of *Southern Cal.*

That night, after riding 618 miles, we slept in a Baptist Church parking lot, southeast of Solvang. It was in the mountains along the 154, nestled among the trees, on a narrow windy road, near a tall highway bridge, just before we got to the beautiful wine country of Santa Ynez. Like all the other camp spots, we picked this one, based on a feeling. Knowing the Baptists to be good people, we rolled out our bedrolls and went to sleep.

Early the next morning, riding through the mountains, we passed a herd of deer to our left and rows of fruit trees to our right. The sights and smells were breathtaking. After breakfast in Solvang, at The Belgian Café, we headed up the coastline. The views were incredible and the smell of the countryside, the early morning air and cool weather, made for a fantastic journey up the PCH. Even more incredible, almost everywhere we stopped, someone would make the comment, "Boy, you're lucky to be here now. Last week it was really raining."

We heard that time after time. We also heard, that rain was in the forecast, for the following week. I chuckled every time I heard that, because I knew that our prayers were being answered. We were literally riding in between storms, because of what the Lord was doing for us. It was as if we were *of the world,* but not *in the world,* as if we were unaffected by the perils around us!

With that simple faith in both of us, at night as we bedded down, we prayed and spoke often of how the Lord was protecting us. We had slept in a Baptist Church parking lot, on the beach twice, just off a dirt road in the forest and alongside the highway, as we went. Each night we would decide on the spot where we would sleep. It was always based on the feeling we got as we surveyed it. About a half hour or so before sundown, the process would begin again …where to bed down.

As we continued north along the coastline on Highway 1, north of San Francisco, the opportunities for stunningly beautiful camp spots were met at each turn of the road. The never ending magnificence of the land and seascape was indescribable!

The hills along the northern half of California were covered with grass and trees. The air was so fresh, I was sure that it had never been breathed before. As we followed the curvy road in front of us, we eventually came to Fort Bragg.

At Fort Bragg, we decided to spend the night, north of town. We ate dinner at a little, no-name roadside diner, sporting a sign that said simply, "Ham and Eggs, Fish and Chips" in big red letters. There was a car, a truck and three motorcycles in the little dirt parking lot. Just as counting the number of trucks at a diner, is a good way to judge the food inside, so is counting the number of motorcycles. Seeing the three bikes, we took the bait.

The meal was nothing to write home about, but the three riders we met there, were a real kick. Two of them were older than Olin and me. They were in their early seventies and were out enjoying the PCH. The oldest guy (old guys rule!) could no longer keep his balance on a bike, but still loved to ride. He was riding a Ural, a Russian made WWI, BMW copy with a side car. The other old guy was riding a 1980, XS1100-4 cylinder Yamaha. The guy in his thirties was riding a new Triumph café racer. He was itching to let it loose on the curves and sweepers along the coastline. But the old guy on the Ural wouldn't do over 50 mph and the other old guy was happy to do the same. So while the older guys were as happy as two pigs in a mud patch, it was all the younger guy could do, to smile. However, the three of them were best friends and they made for great company as we ate our not-so-good hamburgers and greasy fries.

The next morning when we woke up, we packed and headed for Legget, for some hot chocolate. On the way, the sun was trying to break through the ocean fog that had settled along the shoreline and in the trees, along the roadway. The sun through the fog, created incredibly beautiful streaks of light bursting through the trees. For a moment, it was as if we were riding on a road in heaven, as the brilliant white and golden streaked sky changed, with every patch of trees we passed. I stopped and took pictures of the incredible dawn and feasted upon the artwork of the Lord.

We then turned inland to Legget, where we got some hot chocolate at the little store at the fork in the road. Then we began looking for breakfast. We found it at the Eel River Café in Piercy. It was small, but there were two motorcycles out front, so we went inside—our mouths already watering for a great breakfast.

Inside, there was no place to sit, except at the bar, so we sat in the two middle stools of four, which were open. A few minutes later, a couple came in. Seeing there were no seats they could sit together in, we moved over and invited them to sit at the bar.

They were well dressed, too well dressed for this little sleepy town and seemed to be passing through. Judging by their dress and demeanor, I imagined that they had a very nice car outside. Unfortunately, the wife sat next to me. I was very self conscious of my body odor, so I apologized to her for smelling bad and ruining her breakfast. She was very polite and said she could not smell anything, that I was fine. Feeling she was being more polite than honest, I scooted as far away from her as possible and sat on the far edge of my stool.

After breakfast we continued north to the Giant Redwood Forest. Just before Phillipsville, we left the 101 and headed up the Avenue of the Giants. It's about a seventy mile ride of incredible scenery. Because this was Olin's first time here, we stopped often and enjoyed the unbelievably moving experience, which comes as you look at those giant, majestic trees, in quiet reverence. I don't think it is possible to be among those giants and not have a feeling of reverence. You suddenly feel so small. The forest is almost deathly quiet, yet it has a unique echo all its own, as sounds struggle to move through the enormous trees. The trees are ten to fifteen feet thick and they're so tall and so close to each other, they seem to be fighting with each other, for sunlight.

I looked up and noticed that, even the sun was having a difficult time getting through the thick branches overhead and finding its way to the ground, where I stood. In the meadow by *Drive Through Tree* were half a dozen wild turkeys. They had come to greet us or at least suspiciously watch us.

Deciding we were not their type, they moved along. But the scenery, coupled with the sun trying to break through the giants and the sound of the birds and the smell of the cool, clean, damp air, quickly took us a thousand miles away. The feeling of peace and serenity there, was unsurpassed by any place, I had ever been. I am blessed to be able to feel the presence of the Lord and it was as rich *there*, as in any place, I had ever been before.

We left the Giants behind and continued north along the coastline toward the Oregon border. Our northern goal was Brookings, Oregon, to buy some freshly made Oregon cheese.

That part of Oregon is low rolling grasslands with heavy, tall grass. In the air was the scent of rain fresh farmland. After enjoying our freshly made cheese, we turned southeast through Redding to Truckee and Donner Pass, around Lake Tahoe, into Carson City, Nevada and then to Virginia City. Virginia City is where the miracle begins.

After spending a large portion of the day in Virginia City, we headed south, back to Carson City. Our plan was to hit Yosemite National Park, from its east entrance. As we rode, we saw two large storms south and west of us. As we got closer, they merged into one very large storm that was directly in our path. Olin rolled up alongside me and pointed to the huge black storm ahead of us. I nodded my head and said, "I see it, but we'll be fine. I have a confirmation!" He shook his head sideways and rolled back into our staggered formation. I didn't know what the Lord would do for us. Maybe He would part the clouds for us, like He did for Moses, when He parted the Red Sea. Or maybe He would move the storm off the road! But I knew He would do something and that we would be fine. My faith in the Lord is just that simple. I believe all the miracles in the Scriptures with no "yeah-butts." I also believe, that whatever the Lord says in the Scriptures, is true, just as He said it—no questions asked. After all, why read the Scriptures, if you are not going to believe them?

When we turned south on 395 at Carson City, it was very obvious that we were going to hit the middle of the storm. The cloud was huge, dark and ominous, with no way around it.

Still not knowing what the Lord was going to do, we kept pressing forward. At about Indian Hills, we hit the storm. It was only raining moderately, but it had poured just seconds before we got there. The road was still covered with a heavy layer of water, that had not yet drained off and our bikes started throwing huge rooster tails. The rooster tails were soaking us and our luggage. We pulled over underneath a huge tree to bag our stuff. When we did, we saw a little roadside restaurant with a lodge behind it. It was just off the road and behind the big tree we had stopped under.

We left our bikes under the tree, took our bags, dropped them inside the doorway and walked in and ordered steaks. It just seemed like the right thing to do. Through dinner, we were trying to figure out what we should do. I kept watching the sky and it seemed to be letting up. However, it was also close to sundown.

As I contemplated our course of action, I looked further up the road, a little closer to the mountains. I could see that the storm still seemed to be raging. So while eating our steaks, we tried to figure out if it was worth moving on, after dinner.

Even though we didn't want to break our plan of sleeping out, I had this feeling to ask the waitress if they had any rooms in their lodge behind the restaurant. She said they were full, but she would call ahead to the little town of Minden. She said she knew the motels in the area and they helped each other out.

She came back and said, "There is one room left. Everything else in town is booked up because of the motorcycle rally. If you want it, you better take it." Unsure what she meant about a motorcycle rally, I felt to take it, so I got up from the table, got on the phone and reserved the room and then returned to finish my steak—which was pretty good, I might add!

Taking this room brought mixed feelings in me. I worried that I was somehow showing distrust in the Lord, that He would feel that I had lost my faith in Him, in face of the storm. If my faith was as great as I said it was—I would have just pressed on.

After dinner, we rode the three miles to the small motel. After we checked in, I took a hot shower. The hot, steamy water running down my back felt good. I stood there contemplating my decision. The thought to get the room was accompanied with the feeling of peace. The thought to forgo the room and keep pressing on, was not. This time however, the need to be very faithful was extremely important to me and it weighed heavily on my mind. As I continued to sift through my feelings, I was starting to feel upset. Turmoil and uncertainty began building inside me. And the feeling of peace—had now left me.

After my shower, I went outside and checked the sky over the mountains three times before it became too dark to see. Each time I checked, the sky was clear. It made me feel that I had surely betrayed the Lord's trust in me, to trust Him. The clear sky was proof that I should have had more faith and just continued on.

By this time in my life, developing this trust relationship with the Lord was extremely huge with me. I wanted to do my part in this relationship and show Him that I not only *could*, but *would* trust Him. Trust Him, even in the face of what seemed like impossible situations. So for me to show, what I felt was distrust in Him, was a very big disappointment to me—about me.

Later that night, with a broken heart, I went to my knees in prayer. I apologized for not having had greater faith in the Lord to watch over me. I honestly felt that I had let the Lord down.

The next morning at 5 a.m., we had our bikes loaded and were heading south. When we left the motel, it was cool and perfect riding weather. But we had gone no more than five miles up the draw, when we finally had to pull over, to put on warmer clothing. It had gotten very cold and both of us were freezing. As we started up into the mountains, it kept getting colder and colder. The roads were still wet from the storm. Water was along the roadway and the tall grass was laden with heavy beads of water.

At Topaz Lake, the roads were not only wet, but the local parking lots were flooded. We continued on, but by the time we got to the Virginia Creek Settlement Restaurant, it was so cold, we were numb and everything hurt! My knees were aching from the cold and my hands could no longer control the brakes or the clutch. I pulled alongside Olin and said, "I've got to stop. I can't take anymore." The strength in my arms had all but gone and my hands were having a hard time gripping the bars. We were just not dressed for what we hit. I had hypothermia so bad, I couldn't move. We pulled over into the little roadside café parking lot.

As I was putting my kickstand down, I found I could hardly control my legs. My hands were so cold, I could barely straighten my fingers. In fact, it was easier to just slide my hands off the end of the bars, than it was to straighten my fingers out.

We staggered into the café and ordered breakfast. The guy who waited on us said, "You guys are real lucky. It really rained here last night." I didn't think much about his words, then. After breakfast it was a little warmer and we were feeling much better.

The evidence, it had rained all night and rained hard, was everywhere. Luckily for us the day warmed up as we continued on. We rode past Bridgeport and at the Yosemite National Park turn off, we turned into the park. To our astonishment there was a sign across the road that read, "Closed due to storm".

We continued on to Mammoth, where we pulled in for gas. There were bikes and riders everywhere. I asked the attendant, "Where did all the riders come from?" He told me that there was a huge motorcycle rally going on and that last night it rained so hard, that most of the riders spent the night under gas station awnings and under the eaves of buildings.

The attendant went on to say that each year, a rally takes place in Mammoth and it brings riders in from everywhere. He said the weather is usually very nice, except for this year. Then he chuckled as he said, "This year it poured rain all night long and there was no place for them to go. They were everywhere and trying to hide under anything they could find, trying to keep dry."

Only then, did I begin to understand what the Lord had done for us. Through His great love for us, He had saved us a room and saved us from the storm. The feeling I had to take the room was His way of protecting us. If we had pressed on, we would have found no place to sleep in those mountains. It would have been a huge mistake and a very miserable night. Tears of gratitude came to my eyes, as the attendant told me what the other riders had gone through.

Later, just south of Bishop, I saw a small roadside store so we stopped for an ice cream. While there we visited with the store owner who told us much the same thing. He said, "It's a good thing you weren't here last night. Yesterday a whole group of motorcycles passed through, heading north for Mammoth and hit a storm in the mountains. It was so bad, many came back and our pump island was full of riders, trying to stay out of the rain. They were even hugging the building." His words to me had been another witness of just how much the Lord had protected us and kept us safe. It was yet another tender mercy moment for me.

Having that first impression to get the room was right. It was part of His plan, not a failure on my part to have faith. I didn't understand that at first, but I did after it was over.

As I studied this out in my mind, I learned that sometimes bullheadedness can be mistaken for having great faith. As the attendant talked to us, I thought about my experience in the shower. I knew that my own bullheadedness had affected my judgment and my reception of the soft feelings. The feelings to stop were soft and gentle. Because of my stubborn determination, I could have so easily missed them or overpowered them.

I also realized that the feelings of doubt, uncertainty and turmoil I felt in the shower and later on, was the signature of the Adversary. It was the listening to the soft feelings inside, to stop and get a room, which made the difference in our lives that night. It was yielding to the decision, which was accompanied with the feeling of *peace,* which proved to be the right choice after all.

I am sure that if we had chosen to press on, He would have helped us, but I am just as sure, that it would have been in our bullheadedness, and *not in our great faith.* We would have had an extremely miserable night to think about the other choice—the one that was accompanied with the feeling of peace.

The Lord expects us to be calm, to be quiet and to listen to the Spirit. He expects us to take the path that is accompanied with the feelings of peace and not the feeling that is accompanied with stubborn determination or that is accompanied with doubt and uncertainty or turmoil. Both paths can ultimately require great sacrifice and hardship. But one path will be accompanied with that sweet and unmistakable feeling of peace and assurance. *That* path is the best path—and things will somehow work out.

Remember that just as a letter has a signature at the end to tell you who it is from, the feeling of peace inside you, is the signature at the end of the message that you are looking for. That feeling of peace is the signature of the Comforter. The Comforter is the Holy Ghost and *His peace* is the mark of the Lord. That peace means that it is the Lord's will and it is your best choice. The decision is always yours to make, but each decision will always have a best choice and that best choice will always be accompanied with the signature of peace.

The experience and decision at Minden, coupled with the cold 175 mile ride that vacillated between five and eight thousand feet through the rain soaked mountain range to Bishop, has never left my thoughts. The difference between a wonderful experience and what could have been a nightmare—was a mere feeling apart.

Many times since that experience, while traveling my own journey from Faith to Trust in the Lord, I have needed and remembered …*The Lesson of the Motel Room!*

In your own journey from Faith to Trust, remember your own unique experiences and remember to trust and follow the peaceful feelings inside …*regardless of understanding!*

48) Be quick to recognize the Lord's hand in highly unusual events.
49) Don't confuse bullheadedness with having great faith.
50) Choose the path that is accompanied with the signature of peace.
51) Have faith and trust the feeling of peace, regardless of understanding.

Chapter Fifteen

The Baja Peninsula

Two years later, in October of 2007, I would find myself with an opportunity to ride the Baja Peninsula with three other adventurous and experienced riders. They were Fernando, Juan and Cory. Siria, Fernando's wife and Lexi, Juan's wife, would be following in a truck, full of gear. Fernando's parents live in La Paz, Mexico. Thanks to Fernando, our plan was much better laid out than any plan I had ever laid out for myself. He was going to be the lead rider and we were glad. He was very thorough.

The plan was to ride to Ensenada, spend the night and get our Visa's the next morning. We would then continue south, spending the nights in Guerrero Negro, Mulege (Moo-lay-hay) and be in La Paz on day four. We would spend two days in La Paz, head for Cabo San Lucas for three days, back to La Paz for two more days, then work our way back up the Baja. It was the perfect plan and the perfect opportunity for me to ride the Baja and fulfill another dream I had since high school.

Because the criminal environment had changed so much, since my first Mexico ride, once again, praying for that feeling I would be safe, was critical. News about drugs, cartel kingpins and wannabe cartel kingpins, was frequently in the headlines from south of the border. Stories of tourists being high-jacked and held for ransom, seizures of vehicles, shootouts between the police and the cartels were also beginning to surface. There was beginning to be a lot of risk associated with traveling south. The only problem was—I still had the dream of *riding the Baja!*

As the excitement about the possibility of going, continued to build, finally my prayer was answered and the confirmation came that the Lord would be with me. Now, I knew I would be safe. So, long before the deadline came to make up my mind if I was going or not, I called Fernando and said, *"I'm in!"*

In mid October, we met on the far west side of Phoenix, at 5 a.m. and headed for the border town of Tecate. We chose Tecate for several reasons, but mostly because it was a closer entrance into Mexico. Secondly, it was far less crowded and a lot cleaner than Tijuana …*and* it was more *real* Mexico!

I have always been for less traveled roads and small towns along the way and for leaving the big, snarly cities, with their four lane highways, mega intersections and heavy traffic, for someone else. So crossing at Tecate, was a wonderful treat for me.

The Mexican Border Agents were busy moving some boxes, so they just waved us through. I was instantly aware that I was now entering Mexico, when I crossed that little border station. The scenery immediately changed. The big, wide streets and well planned communities, I was used to in the U.S., were not to be found. The evidence of poverty was everywhere.

At the crossing, the rocky, jagged hillsides of Tecate are covered with little homes. Many of them are very rundown, with varying colors and some are interestingly painted and rather bright. There is also, what seems to be, an unusually large amount of out-side storage items in their yards. Sometimes you even see some very amusing things. Like for instance, the four older guys I saw, crammed inside an old, beat-up, white Datsun pickup truck, going down the road …with no windshield.

Traveling in Mexico is different than in the U.S. There are differences in their traffic laws, driving conditions and their roads. Compared to the norm in the U.S., Mexico's roads are in average to poor condition. Most often, their roadways are more like the original sections of Route 66, with its eleven foot lanes.

The speed limits are usually between 75 and 90 kilometers an hour (about 40 to 55 mph.) Watching semi's pass each other and seeing if they can make it, without striking their left side, rear view mirrors on the curves, is sometimes a show. Because of cost, another unusual thing is that the roads in Mexico seldom have any shoulders. Sometimes, I would find a broken down vehicle in the traffic lane with its hood up and people repairing it.

They can't pull off the road because oftentimes, the shoulders have rapidly sloped, one to three foot drop offs. One time I had to stop because two guys had their tools out and were trying to fix their vehicle in the lane in front of me.

In the U.S., we punch holes in mountains, to make tunnels or create big crevices through mountains. We fill in deep, smaller canyons and we lengthen out our curves. We use bridges and lessen our grades, to create a road that feels smooth with fast and fairly consistent driving conditions. Mexico's roads are narrower, have less visibility and they tend to follow the landscape. Mexico 1, the Baja road, is very similar to the old Route 66. It's a narrow, often winding two-laner, with risky passing opportunities.

The Mexican people have a solution for their visibility problem and it is in the use of their left turn signal. If the driver in front of you turns on his left turn signal, he is either going to make a left hand turn, or he is telling you that it is safe to pass him. It is your decision and it is your neck. Watching for his brake lights is the only way you can really tell. It is a risk and a gamble you have to get a feel for, as he may not have functioning brake lights.

However, on this ride, I once again found myself among people that I loved. It was a unique feeling, almost as if they were distant family to me. I have ridden to the town of Puerto Penasco (Rocky Point) twice, and the feelings there were the same.

Though the Mexican people in Puerto Penasco, and on the Baja, were more Americanized than those on the Mexican mainland, they were still a humble, friendly people and their smiles were genuine and from their hearts.

Though there are evil people in every country, the warmth I felt in the eyes and smiles of the Mexican people on the Baja, was the same as it was when I was deep in the interior. I have never been snubbed by the Mexican people. I have never been where I could not get a warm smile and an "Hola" (O-la, Hello.) The people there have good hearts. To the Lord, a good heart always trumps talent, education, ability or financial success.

I was quite amazed to find that the streets and gutters in the Mexican towns, along the Baja, were often covered with a layer of blow-sand. Of the towns that had curbs, sometimes the gutters were completely filled with sand from street level to curb height. The town of Guerrero Negro was the worst I saw. I could only suppose they get a lot of wind that crosses the peninsula.

Another great thing about the Baja, is that it is so easy to stay on the right road. You see, from Ensenada south, if the road is paved as you leave town, then you are on the right road!

The only other thing I had to watch out for was the *Topes* (tow-pays.) Mexico doesn't have a lot of money for traffic control and for police officers to run radar. Their solution is the use of six foot wide, by six inch high, speed bumps in their roadways. I missed my first *Topes* sign. After going airborne over the large speed bump and managing to keep the bike upright, I never missed another *Topes* sign. The same was true with Fernando, Juan and Cory—each of us, only missed one …the first one!

One thing, I dearly loved about the Baja, was the fresh ocean air that continually blows over the peninsula. We slept out along the way, but chose to sleep at small motels that had RV parking. In each place, we slept on the ground in their parking lots, feeling safer than just sleeping out alongside the road, except in Mulege. There, we chose to sleep on the beach.

It was a beautiful beach, with incredible scenery and sunsets. However, this choice turned out to be a little too risky. There were two-legged predators in the area. In the middle of the night, one such predator came into our camp. But when Fernando met him with axe in hand, he quickly decided to leave. Fortunately, that was the only incident of that kind, throughout the journey.

Getting to La Paz took some planning. There are several stretches of the Baja, where no fuel is available. The longest stretch is between El Rosario and Guerrero Negro. We had to haul gas to make the approximate two-hundred thirty mile section of desert road. Very little is there, except for the rocky scenery.

However, there were two enterprising men, at about the halfway point, selling fuel from a fifty-five gallon drum in the back of their pickup. Luckily, we didn't need it, because we had been warned to bring extra fuel.

The next longest strip is from Loreto to Centenario, outside of La Paz. That distance is about two hundred miles. When I got to the Pemex (their gas stations) on the outskirts of Centenario, I was on my last quart of fuel and had been praying for a station.

Mexico is rural and everything is remote, even on the Baja! There just isn't much there and you need to come prepared to solve your own problems. Luckily, the *Green Angels*, a government sponsored road service for tourists, is available on the Baja.

The Green Angels carry water and extra gas and a few odds and ends that may come in handy. They are a great help, but I only saw two Green Angel trucks, during our entire journey.

After the long, almost nonstop ride, I was glad to get off the bike at the Pemex Station. The female attendant looked at me, rather suspiciously, as I slowly peeled myself off the bike. I was dirty, unshaven and on a bike loaded with gear. By the look she gave me, I am sure, she thought I was an American outlaw biker.

While there, a woman in her fifties approached me and asked if I was with three other riders from Arizona. I told her I was and she asked me if one of them was Fernando. I smiled and said, "Yes, he's just a few minutes behind me." Fernando, Juan and Cory, had stopped for a break about twenty miles back.

Her face lit up with a huge smile and big beaming eyes. She was Fernando's mother. Like a typical mother who never stops being a mom and loving her child, she was now bubbling with joy and excitement. She knew that her son was only minutes away from her loving embrace. At that very moment, I could instantly feel the love my mother had for me, as I looked into this mother's eyes. Her countenance was filled with extreme joy, for a son she had not seen for a long time. When Fernando pulled up, I watched as his mother threw her arms around her beloved son. It reminded me of one of my most cherished police experiences I ever had as a cop. It had occurred about twenty years before, but was still vividly fresh in my mind.

One afternoon a *suspicious person* call came over the air where the complainant said that a black male adult about thirty-five, was hanging around the eastbound on-ramp of Ellsworth and U.S. 60. I found him, just off the embankment, in some waist high weeds. His coat and pants were old, ragged and dirty. He was obviously just a transient. Next to him was a little, black duffle bag that contained everything he owned. I gave Radio a Code 4, cancelled my backup and waved off the helicopter.

As I walked up, I noticed that he was reading from Second Corinthians. I smiled and said, "Hey partner!" But he didn't say anything. He just kept reading. I said it again, a little more sternly and again he just kept reading. After the third time, with the same response, I was now a little angry. I was sure I had a wise guy. So, I bent down, next to his ear and said, "You don't have to talk to me, but you do have to get up and get off the right-of-way!"

At that, he closed his Bible, rose to his feet and then slowly turned and looked at me. When he did, my heart melted. Instead of a wise guy, I could see in his face, that I had a young boy, in a middle aged, man's body. I could see he had been told to move along, a thousand times before. As we faced each other, neither of us said anything for a while and then he reached into his right front pocket and pulled out a wrinkled piece of paper. From his left front pocket, he pulled a pen and then wrote the words, "I don't have any place to go." My heart went out to him. I had always been afraid of the kind of loneliness, I knew he was living.

I asked, "Where's your family?" He just shook his head and shrugged his shoulders. I asked, "Where's your mom?" He wrote, "Dead." I asked, "Where's your dad?" He shook his head and looked away. I asked, "Where's your brothers and sisters?" He wrote, "I don't have any." After a pause, I asked, "Who takes care of you?" He smiled and wrote, "God." I smiled back. There was another pause and then his eyes began to fill with tears and he wrote, "I wish I could be with my mom again."

I became filled with emotion and empathy for this young boy, in a man's body, who was facing the world all alone. However I had been a cop for over fifteen years and I managed to keep my feelings from showing. I knew the Gospel plan and I knew of the love my mom has for me. I wanted to tell him that there is a way. Christ has already taken care of this for him and families can be families forever. But I was a cop and I was there on police business. So I kept my feelings and desires to myself and merely replied, "Well pal, I don't know what to tell ya!"

He looked at me for a few moments and then wrote, "Yes you do!" I looked back up at him and asked, "I know what to tell you?" He shook his head, yes, and beckoned an answer with his hands. My heart went out to him and a rush of emotions came over me. I told him the things that I felt in my heart to say. To this day, I remember them, as if I just said them, minutes ago.

I said to him, "I know that Jesus Christ lives! I know that Jesus loves you! I know that He watches over you! And I know that He allows your mother to watch over you, even still. So on those nights when you're cold and all alone and there is no friend for you—remember that your mother loves you! That she watches over you! And that she does her best to protect you and comfort you ...even still."

I really don't know who was more surprised at those words, me or him. But they were just there for me and they came out of my mouth. His eyes immediately began to fill with tears. He took a step forward, threw his arms around me and began to hug me. He then laid his head on my shoulder and began to cry. Even in uniform, I was very touched and speechless at what just occurred.

We became friends and we talked in the same manner for a few more minutes and then I asked him, "What's your name?" A big grin came across his face as he wrote, "My mom called me Mikey." I smiled back and told him, "My name is Sam." We then shook hands and I told him I had to go. I wished him well and as I turned to walk away, he reached out, grabbed my arm and stopped me. With a smile on his face and with tears running down his cheeks he wrote, *"Tell me again about my mom."*

I don't know where he went or how he lived, but I know I will never forget my moment in time, alongside the road, with Mikey. I will never forget his terrible loneliness or his love for and faith in God to protect him. Somehow deep inside me, I believe that Mikey's mother was there that day, with the two of us. And somehow, through the grace of God, I believe she was allowed to share her love for him, through those words, I was given to say.

Now, about twenty years later, I stood alongside the road again and watched Fernando's mother, as Fernando pulled up and peeled himself off his bike. She instantly began kissing and embracing her son and pouring out her love for him, in the way, I imagined Mikey's mom, will one day embrace and kiss Mikey. All made possible because of what Christ has done for us.

Fernando's parents and family were extremely gracious to us. Fernando's father was building a small motel onto his home. They live on the outskirts of Centenario, directly across the Bahia De La Paz (Bay of La Paz.) from La Paz, itself. Their home is on the west side of the bay, on the shoreline.

The rooms were small with shared showers and the project was about eighty percent complete. Each of us were given a room with running water—most of the day anyway. It all depended on how things were going in La Paz, if we had any water pressure in Centenario. At certain times of the day, all we had was a trickle of water and taking a shower was an impossibility. Our rooms were without doors, but that was okay, because the windows didn't have any glass in them either.

However, compared to where we had been sleeping, it was the Hilton. It was new, nice and it was clean. I was happy. Fernando's parents couldn't do enough for us. They fed us breakfast and lunch. We even ate shrimp and prawns, in a skillet over an open fire. We talked and laughed. During the day, we walked on the beach and let our toes sink into the sand as the cool, ocean water ran over our feet and lapped against our legs.

In the morning, Fernando's father woke us up at 4:45 a.m., to see one of the most beautiful sunrises, I had ever seen. The sun was bursting over the mountains, behind La Paz, across the bay. The ocean water and the sky was a mixture of different golds and blues. The bay shined as if it were a glass mirror.

Later on during the day, we toured La Paz with Fernando's parents and ate ice cream. Two days later, we left La Paz and rode the last one-hundred seventy-five mile journey, to Cabo San Lucas.

In Cabo, we toured the city. On the day Cory, Juan and Fernando went on sea excursions, I went riding around to see the city. Like most big cities, it is divided into sections with those who have money and those who don't. Cabo San Lucas is also very commercialized and caters heavily to the tourist industry. Everything along the beach is beautifully built. That said, if you take a walk inland, it is a different story. Within blocks, it begins to change and what you encounter is a very poor city.

I then decided to investigate a beach, I had seen about fifty kilometers north of Cabo. As I kept making my way down the dirt road toward the beach, I suddenly felt this very strong feeling to turn around and leave immediately. That feeling matched the feeling I had felt at 3rd Street and LeSueur, when that guy shot through the door at me. I don't know what danger awaited me, but I yielded to the Spirit, turned around and quickly rode away.

My favorite experience in Cabo, was the excursion to see *El dragon* (draw-goon) *de bebidas*, *The Dragon that drinks* or the Drinking Dragon as we would say it. It is the giant rock formation at the very tip end of the Baja. The water on the east side of the Dragon is clean, clear, fairly calm and green. When I walked across the sandy beach from the Sea of Cortez to the Pacific Ocean, the water changed. There, the water was blue and seemed angry. The waves were smashing against the beach and pulling back into the ocean. They were dropping as much as twelve to fifteen feet, and rushing back to smash against the beach again.

Too near the water's edge, a woman stood watching the angry, crashing waves. Suddenly, that one really big one came, that ran up the beach, knocked her off her feet and drug her into the ocean. Two men ran after her and grabbed her and struggled to pull her to safety. Before they could make it to high ground, the ocean came back, with another huge wave and knocked them all down and pulled them back toward the sea. I was surprised any of them lived through that. The distance between the angry west side and the calm east side of the Dragon is only about a seventy-five yard walk. But the drastic contrast is astonishing.

On day three in Cabo, we packed up and headed back up to La Paz to spend our next two days with Fernando's family. It was on the eve of our trip back up the Baja from La Paz, where this story of a magnificent miracle began.

On our last day in La Paz, Fernando, Siria, Juan, Cory and Lexi went sightseeing with Fernando's parents, in Fernando's truck. I chose instead to ride alone through the streets of La Paz. I rode toward the northeastern hillsides of town, where the town climbs up the mountainside. I came to an area of high-density apartment housing for the poor. The condition of the housing made me stop and stare. I noticed that more than half of the windows were broken. Many had drapes that were hanging out and blowing in the breeze. There were no lawns or playgrounds, for the children. The little children were playing in the streets and the streets seemed barren of cars. It reminded me of what, I imagined, the Projects in Chicago must have looked like in the sixties, minus the gangs and the graffiti. These were extremely poor people. As I looked at them, I felt a feeling of hopelessness for them. They seemed to be forgotten about. As I sat on my bike and watched them, I felt an extreme gratitude toward the Lord for all He had given me. As they looked at me, I felt again that I was *El rico americano*.

After awhile, I turned around and headed back. At first, I decided to return home the way I came. Changing my mind, I chose to skirt the edge of the city, instead of passing through it. So I slowed to make a U-turn in the middle of the street. The street was steep, narrow, highly crowned and had a shadow halfway through it. I tried making a U-turn without putting my feet down. But with the totality of the circumstances, it was a mistake. I didn't have the talent or the training I needed …and I fell over.

I saw people watching me and I didn't want any trouble. I didn't hurt anyone or anything, I just fell over. In Arizona, this would be a motor vehicle incident, not a motor vehicle accident. So pulling my left leg out from under the bike, with embarrassment, anger and adrenaline as my companions, I reached down, grabbed the handle bars and literally jerked the 550lb bike up and off the ground. I then got on and restarted it to ride away.

Instantly, I felt an incredible burning pain in both of my shoulders and my arms felt weak. I knew I had torn something in both of my shoulders! The pain got worse by the minute. By the time I got to Fernando's parents home, my shoulders were literally on fire. They felt as if someone was holding torches to them, literally trying to burn holes through them. I don't know how to better describe it and it was all I could do to handle the pain.

When the others returned, I said nothing to them about my shoulders. I was hoping they wouldn't notice and that the pain would go away. The pain was almost overwhelming, especially in my circumstance. I was on a motorcycle, over 800 miles south of the U.S. Border, in Mexico. I had severely injured both arms—the main controlling mechanisms of the motorcycle. And tomorrow morning, we were beginning our long trek northward.

Though the others stayed up and visited, I retired early that evening, in hopes that my shoulders would be better by morning. Every move I made, intensified the burning pain. They hung almost as dead weights at my side. When I went to bed, I had to sit down, fall backwards and squirm, until I got myself onto the mattress. I had honestly never felt this kind of pain in my body before. As I lay on the mattress, I said my prayers, pleading for relief and the ability to ride out in the morning.

Sleeping was a difficult thing. At 5 a.m., I awoke with my shoulders hurting much worse than when I went to bed. Now, I could not move them at all. I tried to raise my arms, to see if I could hold onto my handlebars, but I was powerless to move them. They were on fire and the pain was incredible. I am blessed with a very high tolerance for pain and with a little effort, I can usually mentally block it. In 1984, I hurt myself and thought I could take care of it by going to bed. I ended up staying in bed for four days. I was unable to move. My younger sister, Rebekah, finally called the paramedics. They came and took me by ambulance to Mesa General Hospital, where I spent the next six days in the ICU.

This time, at 5 a.m., the pain was so intense, that it was all I could do, to keep from crying. I slid off the side of the mattress, knelt by the bed, my arms hanging at my side and prayed with all my might. I asked my dear Heavenly Father to heal my shoulders, so I could ride home. We were to get up by 6 a.m. and leave, just one hour from then.

I poured out my heart in that prayer, pleading for help. It was during that prayer that I again felt that confirmation, that feeling that said, "I told you everything would be alright." As I remembered that earlier confirmation, I smiled a deep loving smile and my heart was once again filled with joy and peace. I said, "Thanks Heavenly Father. Thanks!" and ended my prayer.

I knew at that point, that I would be alright. I lay down on the mattress by falling forward. I began pushing myself onto the mattress with my legs and laid face down, half on and half off the bed. I then fell back asleep. At 6 a.m., just one hour later, the alarm went off and I woke up. I lay there, face down and slowly rolled over to my back. I began moving my hands and lower arms to check for pain. I then sat up in bed and tried moving my arms. To my great joy and expectation, though my arms were very sore, the intense burning was gone. The pain was one tenth of what it had been, just an hour ago. I knew I'd be just fine. I then fell to my knees in prayer with great, heartfelt gratitude, I uttered the words, "Thank you, Heavenly Father ...thank you!"

52) Pray always ...dare to believe in Christ ...*expect* miracles.

The Shortest Prayer…

It was finally over. It had been a very trying day.
Upon his return home, he felt he needed to pray.
The need to get things done had stressed and worn him out.
Leaving him beat down with worried thoughts of self doubt.
He felt to pray for help. To ask that he not falter.
So he knelt at the couch and used it's pillow as an alter.

Now, many things are asked for, when one begins to pray,
with troubles abounding, there's always plenty to say.
But as he began, he thought of all the Lord had done,
all that had been given him, from the Father and His Son.
So he offered the shortest prayer he ever offered before.
These are the words he uttered as he knelt upon the floor.

"Oh God the Eternal Father, of all I'd like to ask of you,
all I feel to say ...is to tell you ...that I love you."
He then uttered the same verse. Slowly and one more time,
came the simple, humble, words, sounding as a child's rhyme.
He expected no answer, just wanting to express his love
for the Father of the Christ Child, who lives so far above.

But then a beautiful and wondrous feeling, slowly fell upon him.
One that engulfed his being, from his head to his furthest limb.
The feeling brought such joy, that suddenly he burst into tears.
And he heard a voice from above, but not with his earthly ears.
It came to his heart and soul, piercing him through and through.
The words were sweet and simple. He heard, "I love you too."

Officer Samuel Jeppsen, #3751

Chapter Sixteen

Miracles, Gratitude and Common Sense

When I stood up from my prayer, I was wearing a huge smile. The feelings that were flowing freely inside me, were feelings of overwhelming joy, mixed with a feeling of electricity. I knew I had just received a miracle—and no small one. I started moving my arms back and forth, up and down, to see how much movement I actually had. On my first try, I was able to raise both arms to just below my chest. With just a few more tries, I was able to raise them to shoulder height. I knew I would be able to hold onto the handlebars and operate the motorcycle. I then slowly packed my bag, carefully carried my gear to the bike and loaded and tied everything on. Fernando's parent's home is about three-hundred yards from the roadway and is on a small road, which has never been bladed. I knew if I could negotiate the rutted trail, dodge the bushes, the big puddle of water and navigate the sandy washes, until I got to the road, I would be okay.

I contemplated all those things, while still praying for help as I sat there, waiting for the others to saddle up. Finally it was time to leave. I began my ride through the desert, dodging the obstacles until I finally made it to the roadway. I looked to my left and then made my northbound turn onto Mexico 1. I then started hitting my throttle and gears. My shoulders were sore, but the pain was manageable. It was nothing compared to what it had been. I could hardly control myself, because of the joy I felt inside. As I rode, I was so filled with gratitude, that I could not stop repeating the words in a prayer, "Thank you, Heavenly Father, thank you!"

On the way up, we stayed at the exact same camping spots, we did on the way down. Our first night was back on the beach at Mulege and I was able to lie on my side in the sand, and sleep without pain. The next day, I had very few reminders that I had ever hurt my shoulders, at all. That night, we slept on the same concrete parking lot in Guerrero Negro and as before, I slept just fine. When I got up, nothing hurt. As I rode, I couldn't help but ponder the fact, that I had my very own Biblical type miracle.

Just prior to Ensenada, I found myself, a good half hour ahead of Fernando, Juan and Cory, so I pulled over. I rode a lot slower than they did. I kept my speed at around 60 to 65mph and they usually rode around 70 to 80mph. Because they were riding so much faster than I was, they felt they had plenty of time to keep pulling over and so they did. I love to ride and just kept riding. So in typical *Tortoise and the Hare* fashion, I often arrived at our destinations sooner than they did. For safety reasons, we made a pact with each other to never enter a major city, alone. The reason was, that reuniting with each other, after entering a major city, was several times harder and much more risky. So we agreed to stop outside of town and reunite along the highway. As I was entering the outskirts of Ensenada, I pulled over and parked on the dirt shoulder. I then got off my bike, stretched and waited.

While waiting for the others and looking over the southern fringe of Ensenada, I again pondered the miracle that had taken place. It had started with a promise that everything would be fine. The test of faith came in La Paz, when I hurt myself and could not move my arms. Yet, after prayer and in *just one hour,* I was able to load my bags and ride out. Now, three days later, here I stood alongside my bike, outside Ensenada, as if nothing had happened. I was just hours from the U.S Border and a day's ride to home.

As I stood there, next to my bike, I began to longingly look around. I knew that soon I would be crossing the U.S. Border and leaving this beautiful country, with its very simple ways and warm hearted people. I looked south, from where I was standing, to look at the town, against the sunset. I noticed the shoulders of the road were poorly maintained and the dirt shoulder was a six inch drop off from the road. The entrances and parking areas, to the little businesses along the way, were mostly dirt. Most of the buildings needed paint and there were no sidewalks. But to me, because of my love for these people, it was all so very beautiful.

Up the road, a hundred yards or so, was a Mexican man in his mid to late sixties. He was walking along the shoulder and heading in my direction. He had every appearance of returning home, after a hard day's work. He was also carrying a little plastic shopping bag. I watched him, for about sixty yards, as he came toward me. His worn out khaki-colored pants, his old shirt, faded green jacket and beat up old straw hat and worn, brown, dust covered shoes, told me he was, by every definition of the word, a poor, humble, hard working man. As I leaned against my bike and watched him getting closer, I found myself intrigued by him.

Though slightly bent forward, from years of hard work, he walked straight. He had his shirt tucked into his pants and he appeared to be a very old-school and highly principled man. I was impressed, as I studied his face. But it was the deep wrinkles, the tan of his skin and the heavy, tired look in his eyes that captivated me, as he walked along. Though looking tired, he seemed resolved to doing what it took, to take care of his family, which I supposed he had at home. He had every look of a kind and gentle grandfather who espoused old-fashioned character.

He noticed that I was watching him and when I smiled, he smiled back. When he got about forty feet from me, I stepped out in front of him. I wanted to take his picture, with the town in the background. He, thinking I didn't want him in the picture, tried to move out of my way. I stepped in front of him again. He paused for a second and I took my shot.

In just those one-hundred yards, I developed a love for this humble and tired man, who I believed was a father and grandfather and who was still contributing to the needs of his family. Though there was no pile of straw on his back, no steep hill in front of him to climb, he was doing what it took, to take care of the family, that I imagined he had, someplace up the road. As I watched him, my mind reflected on the many that leave their families behind and flee to easier pastures. My mind also reflected on the many, many more that were just like this guy, here. Still there, still making a difference, still loving and taking care of his family. …Still!

He reminded me, in every way of my own father and my father-in-law. Two men that I love, respect and admire. Two men who are very old-school and have worked so hard physically, that they literally wore themselves out, while trying to take care of their precious, little families.

After I took the picture I smiled at him again and gave him a nod and said, "Hola." He smiled back and said, "Hola." and kept walking along the shoulder of the road. My Spanish is poor but I am learning and if the Mexican people will work with me, *y hablar despacio* (and speak slowly), because of my love for them, I can usually communicate with them.

As he was walking along, he was looking at my new, chrome covered and beautifully painted motorcycle. About ten feet away, he stopped and said, "Esta muy bonito. (It is very beautiful)" I replied, "Muchas gracias. (Thank you very much)" He said, "El motocicleta esta suyo? (The motorcycle is yours?)" I replied, "Si. (Yes)" He then said, "Quantos denero por suyo motocicleta? (How much money for your motorcycle?)".

I was on my new Suzuki, 800cc Boulevard and other than a little dusty, it was in mint condition. His question deeply hurt me, because I knew what he was *really* asking. His *real* question was not, "How much did you pay for your motorcycle?" It was, "*How much does a motorcycle like that cost?*"

Here was a man, who had probably walked most everywhere he had ever been in his entire life. He probably lived in a very small one or two room home that was very crowded. He probably lived with his wife, children and grandchildren, perhaps even some in-laws. His home may or may not have had running water or electricity. He probably didn't have any lawn out front and his children probably played in the street or in a dirt lot.

I, on the other hand, live in America, in a very beautifully landscaped, beautifully decorated, 5000 square foot home with a three car garage. In the garage are two new cars and a Harley.

The chances of him ever owning, what I own, was someplace between slim and none. And while he walked to and from work every day, on a dirt shoulder along the highway, I was down here in his country, basically goofing off on a great motorcycle adventure, while enjoying paid vacation time from work.

At home, I have wonderful medical and dental insurance, a home with three air conditioning units, heating and running water. The home is new and is in a beautiful neighborhood. The streets are lined with trees and bushes and there are several large greenbelts, many with playgrounds. The disparity between the two of us was almost choking me. I fumbled for my words, as I tried to answer his question.

I had about 9,500 dollars into my Boulevard, but the base price was about 7,000 dollars. So I answered simply, "Siete. (Seven)" His eyes got wide and on his face suddenly appeared an astonished look. He lifted his voice an octave and said, "Siete mil? (Seven thousand?)" I humbly nodded and replied, "Si, siete mil." He looked for a few moments and then slowly began moving his head from side to side, as if to say, "It must be nice." He then turned away and kept walking along the shoulder of the road, saying nothing more as he continued on his journey. As he walked away I said, "Adios mi hermano. (Goodbye my brother)" Without turning around, he nodded his head, raised his right arm halfway up and with the slight movement of his hand, waved goodbye.

I watched him until he was out of sight, as I continued to wait for the others to catch up. While waiting, I said a prayer of thanksgiving and gratitude for all I had been given and for all I took for granted. I had been blessed so richly and yet I was not any better than this man, who struggled to try to understand how anyone could ever have 7,000 dollars—*much less an extra* 7,000 dollars, for a new motorcycle. Now out of sight, I thought of the exchange of feelings that had taken place between us. I am indeed blessed and the few moments I spent with him, gave me a chance to look and see, just *how* blessed. Like Mikey, I would never forget him and I prayed that life for him, would be easier.

Pondering the moment, I glanced up the road and could see Fernando, on his black and red Aprilia 1000 racing bike and Juan, on his black R-1000 Yamaha. They were moving quickly. Cory was picking up the rear on his white 750 Honda Shadow. I threw my leg over my bike, started it, took off and bounced over the six inch lip on the edge of the road to join them. We rode to the same RV Park as before, near the center of Ensenada. It was just east of the giant Mexican flag, that so beautifully waves over the city.

That night, as I lay on my sleeping bag, my leather jacket for a blanket, I found myself unable to sleep, for thinking about the many spiritual experiences, I had received on bikes. Each ride I had taken had brought with it, some kind of major building block to my testimony. Each journey seemed very specific in what I was to learn and seemed to target, what needed to be added to my faith and character. As if the experiences were tailor-made, inch by inch, step by step, personalized training programs. I lay there and thought about how, in each experience, I was added upon.

Each experience brought a few more pieces of a greater puzzle. Each piece increased my understanding and faith. With each increase of my faith, my faith started turning into trust. With trust, I began drawing nearer and nearer to my Lord and Savior. As my trust grew, fear and worry fled. I was amazed at the changes I could feel taking place inside me.

As I lay there staring at the stars, unable to drift off, my mind went back to the miracle in La Paz and the confirmation that came to my mind, when I prayed. I had experienced that kind of miracle only one other time in my life. It was about a year earlier when I gave a kidney to my brother, Harvey. I had taken off work, traveled to Utah and because of one setback after another, I lost two full weeks of recovery time. I was worried, I could no longer have the operation and keep my job. My brother said, "Sam, if you can no longer do this, it's okay. I understand." I went upstairs and poured out my heart in prayer. During that prayer, the same feeling came to me that came in La Paz. It was an overwhelming, peaceful and reassuring feeling that said, "I told you everything would be alright," and it was. The success of the operation, speed of the recovery and medical results even surprised the doctors.

That miracle in Utah was almost the magnitude of the one in La Paz. Like so many other times in my life, both answers occurred during prayer and the results of each, defied logic. I thought of the many other times in my life, where I had wagered so much on just a feeling inside, that was in itself—illogical. With the sky filled with stars and the moon now almost straight overhead and sleep unable to come, I pondered a truth, I had learned long ago. It was the use of common sense, in conjunction with the use of faith.

Experts say the use of common sense is the least used of the human senses. Hundreds of books have been written about exercising good, common sense. Not arguing the point, I had also learned that the use of common sense *...can ...cancel out faith.* Common sense, though a great tool in the problem solving process, doesn't have much need of faith. After all, it's not common sense to have faith. And in a panel discussion, common sense will always trump faith! But I also know that those who are ruled by common sense alone, will probably never experience a miracle. While those of sound judgment, who also have faith and can override common sense ...will witness many miracles in their lifetime.

No, one cannot throw caution to the wind and run off in a blind, passionate, unreasonable and illogical quest, believing and hoping in foolish things. However, not one of Christ's miracles was logical! Not one!! No recipient of any of His miracles would have expected anything, while exercising good common sense!

Using logic and common sense, there is simply no way to explain the ten plagues of Egypt, the animals that filed two by two into the ark or the man that was able to see, after Christ anointed his eyes with clay and spittle. There is no way to explain the raising of Lazarus. Elijah never would have gone to the widow, who was making her last meal for her and her son and said, "Thus saith the Lord God of Israel. The barrel of meal shall not waste, neither shall the cruse of oil fail…" as he asked for her last bit of food. And if the widow had exercised good common sense, she never would have believed him. Moses would never have stood on the shore of the Red Sea and told the Israelites not to worry, as they stood and watched the approaching Egyptian army. Today, no young single adult would get married and no young married couple would have children. No man looking at the heavens, could understand how a God could have created them or hold them in place. Nor could he understand how a God could create life on earth, or how there could be life after death.

Common sense is important, but I have learned to be very careful with it, because it can be *a robber of miracles*. To the man who lives solely by common sense, illnesses will only be cured by doctors. Mountains will only be moved by machinery and water will only be parted by dams. But, to the guy who has faith in Christ, throughout his life, he will see many mountains moved and many Red Seas parted. He will see many illnesses and injuries mysteriously cured and he will have many experiences that logic cannot explain. He will have feelings inside him, that assure him that God lives and that God is no myth and no figment of the imagination of the uneducated. He will also receive an incredible knowledge that God loves him, that he himself is a child of God and that everything in life has a purpose. He will also gain an uncommon peace within, where fear and trembling do not exist.

When I attended the Phoenix Police Academy, Captain Benny Click told us the definition of courage. He said, "Courage is the ability to move, when all around you are frozen in fear and no one would blame you, if you did nothing at all!"

Faith and Trust in Christ can be measured with the same measure. Many times, the facts won't add up—yet inside you, is a feeling that says, "Everything is in place and waiting for you." You'll find that in those moments, Christ won't nudge you either way. Instead, He will wait and watch for which decision you make. He will observe your faith in Him. In those moments, your only clue may be the signature of peace accompanying the decision you make. It can be a really self confronting experience.

Will you take the road of great faith? Or will you take the road of surety and common sense? Either way you choose, you will find that He will have everything already worked out. The details will already be in place and waiting for you.

When Peter said, "…the trial of your faith, being much more precious than gold that perisheth…" he gave more than the value of gaining faith in Christ, he gave the secret to the pathway of finding Christ and knowing for yourself, that He actually lives and we need not fear. When James said, "…the friendship of the world is enmity with God," he not only taught that God's ways are different than the world's ways, he gave the clue that there is more to life than what the world believes, teaches and understands. There is! There are higher laws of truth that bring much greater knowledge and happiness, than what we currently know or comprehend. But those higher laws require faith in Christ—to be able to tap into them. If we follow Christ, piece by piece, inch by inch, we will find them. And with finding them, we find Him and when we find Him, we will find an eternal happiness.

Try your faith! Let it grow! If you do, in time, you will find that your faith will transition into trust. With this transition, comes a faith so strong, that believing and hoping, will sound and feel, like learning your ABC's all over again. In moments of great trial, when the hearts of others around you are in despair, inside you will be an unusual peace and courage. Having trust in Christ, is the ability to move, when all around you are frozen in fear and no one would blame you …if you did nothing at all!

53) Cling to your miracles and experiences and don't let time diminish them.
54) Use the miracles to reach out to the Lord and grow your faith in Him.
55) Go ahead, try your faith in Christ and watch as it transitions into trust.
56) Exercise common sense …but be careful it doesn't rob your faith.

Chapter Seventeen

The Ride of a Lifetime

In early December of 2009, I heard about a ride—more of a race—where one thousand Harley-Davidson riders would take off from Key West, Florida. They would be winding through America, into Canada, up the ALCAN (Alaska-Canada) Highway, into Alaska and down the Kenai Peninsula to Homer.

After the one hundred and ten mile ride from Key West to the mainland, it would be every man for himself, to Alaska. The riders would receive a new map about every fifteen hundred miles and the route would be wandering. There would be no freeways and the ride would be on secondary roads and rural routes.

It was called the *Hoka Hey.* The words are Sioux. They are the words Chief Crazy Horse used for his war cry that he yelled at the beginning of battle. There is no direct translation and many of the Sioux will tell you it means, *"It's a good day to die."* Other meanings could be, Let's do it, Let's go, Let's fight, On to victory or *CHARGE!!* To the organizers of this motorcycle challenge, it meant, *"It's a good day to ride."*

The organizers of the Hoka Hey were three Sioux men, from the Lakota Tribe, in South Dakota. They had a dream of one day seeing a thousand riders, riding their *iron horses* across America. They were Arlin and Elijah Whirlwindhorse and James Durham Red Cloud. With a half-million in gold waiting for the winner, the rules of engagement were simple. We would leave Key West, Florida on Father's Day, June 20th, 2010. There would be specific routes, seven check points and we had to be in Homer, by July 3rd. It meant riding eighteen to twenty hours a day.

Motel rooms were not permitted and because the Indians of old, slept on the ground, next to their horses, we had to sleep on the ground, next to our bikes. Tents were optional. We had to follow the map and, oh yes, the entry fee. It was $1000.00, due six weeks in advance and it was non-refundable.

Well, I never had a dream of seeing one thousand Harleys ride across America, but I *did* have a dream of riding to Alaska on a Sportster. The magic of being able to be part of such an event as this, made my dream begin to percolate inside me. It was the chance to participate in a great adventure, the kind that comes only once in a lifetime. Only the first one thousand applicants would be accepted. No matter what, there would never be another *First* event of this kind ever again. It was the first, biggest, longest, most grueling and demanding, organized ride in the world. The feelings of excitement and adventure grew like a wildfire inside me. My dream, my o*ne day*, was now right in front of me and it was larger than I could ever have imagined or hoped it to be. However, there were a few minor roadblocks in my path.

First, this year was my fortieth wedding anniversary. How in the world, would I ever talk my sweet wife, into letting me trade our fortieth anniversary celebration together—for a solo ride to Alaska for me! We had planned to celebrate on a cruise and had been talking about it for the past year.

The ride and the cruise were to take place at about the same time and we didn't have enough money or available time off work to do both. So, if I could talk her into letting me go, it meant that she had to stay home and forgo her cruise. One dream had to give way to the other. Either she or I had to let go of what we wanted. Personally, I don't think there are many women that would have given in and I would not have forced the issue with her. Nor would I have blamed her if she said, "*Absolutely Not.*" And if her *Absolutely Not*, was ***ABSOLUTELY NOT,*** I would have let go of my dream to participate in this ride.

The second minor problem was that we didn't have the money *at all!* The cruise was going to cost us about $1,500 and we were really squeaking to put that together. This ride was at the very least a $5,000 bill. If the $1,500 was a stretch, then the $5,000 was an impossibility!! Hmmm, I discouragingly thought.

Third, we were struggling with an investment property with four others that was losing money—like crazy.

There was another minor issue or concern and that was that I didn't have the time available from work to take a month off. A month was the minimum time needed for this event. If I didn't use any of my vacation time, until the ride, six months from now, I would still be a week short of the time needed to participate.

Another factor was that I was on probation at work. In January of 2009, I had been part of a three hundred and eighteen person RIWF (Reduction in Work Force) layoff. I was fortunate to be rehired six months later as an At-Will Employee. So I would be asking for a week of *leave without pay* while on probation in a tough economy and as an At-Will Employee ... *for a bike ride.*

And then there was the issue of my age. I am no longer a spring chicken. In my younger years, I had done a lot of this type of riding and sleeping out. But at fifty-eight, turning fifty-nine, a month long grueling trip, could be pretty taxing! And oh yes—my fifty-ninth birthday would also be taking place on some long lonely road, as I worked my way back home from Alaska.

Next, was the fact that, like me, my bike was no spring chicken, either. It was a seven year old, 100th year, Anniversary Special, black and silver Harley-Davidson, Custom Sportster with over forty-two thousand miles on it. It's a great running machine, but it has never been in the shop for anything—even a checkup. The estimated thirteen to fourteen thousand mile journey could be pretty taxing on my little friend. Besides that, Sportsters are not bikes for those who are creatures of comfort. I love them, but at very best, they are small, uncomfortable and ride bad.

Fuel was also a concern. The new Sportsters have four gallon gas tanks. Mine has a three gallon tank and carrying extra gas was prohibited. The danger of running out of fuel, someplace along the ALCAN, was a real worry and a real possibility for me. And a breakdown, thousands of miles from home in either the remote parts of British Columbia, the Yukon Territory or Alaska, meant I was totally on my own to solve a very difficult problem.

Last but not least, was the issue that I was in the Ocotillo Ward Bishopric. Not only would my duties have to be shifted to the other two bishopric members, but all my scout duties for the boy's Scout Camp would have to be shifted as well. Scout camp was taking place right in the middle of the ride. Shifting that much responsibility for a month, so I could go on a motorcycle ride, was a lot to ask of Brother Cardon and Bishop Beckstead!

These were the *not so minor* issues in my way! The fact was, I didn't know what to do or where to start. I was at a total loss and could only think of one thing. It was to follow the words of my mother. She had always taught me that I could pray to my Heavenly Father and trust in the Lord, His Son, Jesus Christ.

Believing and exercising faith does not replace the use of common sense, good judgment or wise decision making. But this much I do know; faith is the invisible key in the invisible door that turns the lock and brings the blessings from Heaven.

To this day, I can tell you that I never got a *Yes* or a *No* or an *I should* or *I should not*. I prayed a lot over this question and took this question to my Heavenly Father several times. But as important as it was to me, the answer I was given was that I would have to decide for myself if I should or should not go. That He would not say.

Though He would never give me an *I should* or *should not*, He did give me this two part promise and it was given to me every time I prayed. The two part promise He gave me was:

"The way is open and you will be safe."

With that feeling coming time after time, each time I prayed, I felt certain about two additional things. One, other than the fact that it was a dream of mine, it was otherwise not important to Him. The second thing, I felt certain about, was that what *was* important to Him was, *would I follow the step by step feelings the Lord gave me.* The feelings were always, *the way is open.* However, *the how to* ...was nowhere in sight.

As I continued to pray for understanding, it became clear to me that the object lesson of this motorcycle ride was going to be in following the path the Lord laid out. "Well," I said, "if the way is open, then the how to, is someplace in front of me!"

It took me about three months to tell Julie about my desire to ride in this event. There was a lot going on in my mind and I had lots of planning and thinking to do, before I told her. Honestly, I saw no way to hurdle the obstacles, blocking my path.

When I finally told her about the ride, well, let's just say she thought it was less than a good idea. When I finally got her to listen just a little, I told her about my idea to fund it. Find a way to charge it and figure out how to pay it off later.

With that idea failing miserably, my next idea was to find a Harley-Davidson dealer who would sponsor me for $1000 and sell my other motorcycle, my 06, 800 Suzuki Boulevard. I thought that was a great idea. Well, that wasn't a big hit with Julie, either. Her reply was, "Sell the only bike we can ride on together!! If you want to go, get sponsors for the whole trip. *That* would be a great idea!!" "Hmmm," I admitted to myself, "she's right."

So the question was how? As I pondered the answer, I started adding up what I needed to go. I needed at very least $5000 cash. What I had available was a few hundred. In finding sponsors, I was sure that I could find two or three that would be willing to donate $200 or $300 dollars, but would I be able to find twenty or thirty of them? As I kept pondering this idea, I got the feeling that the Lord could find five or six that would donate $1000 each. So I chose to follow the Lord, by following the feeling.

First, I realized that if I needed sponsors, the sponsors would need a reason. Their reason would be publicity in exchange for their money. So the new question was what could I do to create publicity for them? As I kept mulling this question over in my mind, the idea of creating a fundraiser began to form.

I realized, to have a good and successful fundraiser, I would have to have a good and needy cause. I chose four. I chose the *Phoenix Children's Hospital* because they had helped save the life of my granddaughter, Bella, and *The Child Crisis Center* of the East Valley, because I had worked with them a lot when I was a police officer. I chose *Sunshine Acres Children's Home* because I had done a lot of tractor work for them in the past and they do so much good for local children in need. I also chose *Make A Wish Foundation of Central Arizona* because that organization was started by a police officer who wanted to make a wish come true for Chris. Chris was a young boy who was dying from Leukemia.

Friends of the Lost Dutchman was later added. The park is perhaps the most beautiful park we have in the east valley. It was also a hot topic at the time, because it was slated for closure. The reason for the closure was Arizona's crumbling economy.

Then the idea came to include weight—political weight! I felt directed to those I should go to. I received the endorsement of Arizona State Senator Charles (Chuck) Gray, Arizona State Senator Larry (Lucky) Chesley, who is also a former POW and the author of *Seven Years in Hanoi.*

Later on, I felt to seek the endorsement of all the East Valley Mayors. They were Mayor Scott Smith of Mesa, Mayor Art Sanders of Queen Creek, Mayor John Lewis of Gilbert and Mayor John Insalaco of Apache Junction. They all graciously accepted and willingly endorsed the fundraiser.

At first, my children and siblings felt certain I was out to lunch—*way out to lunch!* But one by one, as time went along, they began rallying around me and began helping. My daughter-in-law, Lindsey, came up with a beautiful and dramatic poster. It became the official Phoenix Valley Fundraiser poster and it tripled the enthusiasm behind the Valley event. I also had two siblings, quietly slip me a couple hundred dollars here and a hundred there. My dream was little by little, coming to pass!

After the poster and receiving the political endorsements, I felt to go to the news media. I worked very hard and had to be very patient. The news media gets asked quite often to give free coverage to *worthy causes*. So they have to pick and choose.

My efforts were blessed. I received ten minutes of air time on Camel (KMLE) Country Radio with *Becky, Tim and Willy in the Morning*. I also received news coverage from Channel 15, news coverage and photos from AZ Central of The Arizona Republic. I received a five minute air interview on Mesa Talking on Channel 11, news coverage from KPHO Channel 5 and news coverage from the Apache Junction Newspaper.

With my political weight, my official poster, my up and coming promissory news coverage, I went after my sponsors. It took me more than a month to obtain them. They were busy. They too, get asked a lot to donate to charities. So, finding sponsors was not a simple thing. It was turning out to be a lot of work!

Many I went to, said no, but before I went to thirty prospective sponsors, the Lord made good on that feeling inside me. That feeling that said He could find five or six, that would say yes. I was happy with five, but He knew I needed one more. So at the midnight hour, He provided me with number six.

Who sponsored me was another huge blessing from the Lord. Who they were, was as important to me, as the money itself. Yes, I needed money, but I wanted to be sponsored by those who were known for honesty and service and were known for being good people. Though I went to about thirty to find my six, the six were the actual six that I was hoping and praying for.

I had bought my Harley at Superstition HD and I do most of my business there, because I really like the owners. I also like Dennis, who sold me my Sportster six years ago and who is now a friend. But, JD at Skunk Motorsports, is the only one I let touch my Sportster, because he treats customer bikes, as if they are his own and that is really important to me. He also grows his hair long and then cuts it off and gives it to cancer patients.

I buy my leathers and gear from Joeta at Joeta's Leathers. She is a cancer survivor, a cancer activist and an all around incredible woman who believes in Karma. The law of Karma is, if you do good things to others, good things will happen to you!

Bob at Santan Ford is a rider himself. He is a huge fellow as well as a hugely liked fellow. He and the San Tan dealership have great reputations among Valley customers.

Keith Salyer at American Family Insurance has been our agent for years. He is very kind. He is a very family oriented man, who also serves as a Christian Motorcycle Association Chaplain. He told me that he relies a lot on feelings and felt to sponsor me, even though it was so expensive to do so.

The leaders at Infusionsoft are a group of very unusual thinkers. An *Inc. 500* company, they spend their time working with business owners, helping them to become more successful. My son, Clay, who works there, not only worked the sponsorship detail, he used his talents to help advertise and to keep the world posted of my fundraiser and ride. A year afterwards, I ran into an old friend from Hawaii, who said he followed me on the ride, via the coverage and promotion I was getting here.

I hand selected each sponsor, because of their high standards and great reputations. Each one fit exactly the criteria for which I had hoped and prayed. I wanted my name associated with people who were far above the norm and I received it. The same can be said for all who chose to help promote the Valley event. Some of my sponsors gave me money, but most gave a combination of goods *and* money. When I was done, I had about $3,500 in cash and about $2,500 in goods and services.

My brother-in-law and best friend since the ninth grade, Olin, and his nephew Andy, agreed to transport my bike and me to Florida and then bring my truck back home to Arizona. Also, my dear Julie, who now had become excited for me, gave me what would have been her fortieth anniversary cruise money, the $1,500.

Oh, and as for work? My Director, Christine Zielonka and my Deputy Director, Tammy Albright, agreed to give me the dock time I needed. They even allowed me to work with Lesley Davis and Veronica Gonzalez who helped organize a department fundraiser that coexisted with the valley wide fundraiser.

Little by little, the impossible was being made possible. One by one, every roadblock was systematically being removed and door after door was being opened. I knew not where to go and had merely kept moving forward, on feelings and faith. I realized I had experienced the exact thing, Nephi had talked about when he said, "I was led by the Spirit, not knowing beforehand the things I should do." Like him, I never had the opportunity to see the entire picture. I was given only small pieces at a time that required moving forward on faith …instead of knowledge!

It was the repeat of a pattern, I had seen in times past, where I had struggled through a problem, while following a feeling and then watching, as it ended in a miracle. It was in those moments, that I noticed the miracle matched the feeling, I had from the beginning that said, "The way is open." The events had unfolded one at a time and a little at a time! I had succeeded, by following the promptings and exercising faith, without knowledge. The greatest blessing of this experience had been *the same blessing* of every experience! It was the knowledge that the Lord lives, that He loves me, cares about me and I can trust Him to help me!

Just before Shadrach, Meshach and Abednego were to be cast into the fiery furnace and everything they held dear was only seconds away from being brutally taken from them, even their own lives, the only thing they focused on, was the Lord. Daniel was the same way. All these men, in the face of extreme danger and with no one else to turn to, their focus and their faith was on the Savior.

Though, the consequences of me not finding sponsors that were willing to donate a thousand dollars, was not life threatening, the principle was exactly the same. The situation was impossible for me to solve. I had no one to turn to and no place to go for help, but to Him. It required the exact same thing of me, that it required of Shadrach, Meshach and Abednego …*focusing on the Savior!*

57) Focus on the Savior and don't be afraid of impossible situations.

Chapter Eighteen

The Money Trail

While on the trail for the money, I had received countless blessings at the hand of the Savior. He had reduced the money problems, to where they were now my size. As I pondered what He had done for me, my mind went to our family Easter egg hunts.

Julie and I have eighteen grandchildren. On Easter each year we have an Easter egg hunt, usually at our home. We first let the toddlers outside and give them five minutes. Throughout the backyard we place many gifts in easy to find places. We generally walk with them and let them pick up their own gifts. If they are not doing well, we guide them to one prize after another, until they have plenty in their basket. As long as they keep following the promptings we give them, they will continue to find prizes. Prizes we have set out for them that match their ability and talent.

Next we send out the three to four year olds and let them find prizes we have placed just for them. We guide and direct and prompt them too. However, we never fill their baskets for them. It is important that they walk along through the tall grass and around the bushes, to find the prizes that we have placed for them. The ones that are a little more difficult to find.

Then we send out the older grandchildren who find the ones we have placed for them that require more thinking, more effort and more skill. Throughout the backyard, we always place plenty of gifts for everyone to find—and more gifts than are found by anyone. This trail for the money was my very own Easter egg hunt. Though it was a lot of work, the gifts were there, He was there, and I am sure I found less gifts than He had placed for me.

Though obtaining the funds was a constant challenge, I didn't have to force my way through any of it. The trial was not to solve the problem, it was to keep following the feeling. It was to keep moving forward and because I didn't know where to go or how to accomplish this, *need* was as a hunger to me. Need made prayer my continuous practice. Continuous prayer brought me the companionship of the Lord. As this trial began to unfold into a journey of its own, the *ride* became the *reward* for following the feeling and *following the feeling* became the *reward* of the ride.

Through this experience, I learned another powerful truth. I learned the secret of how the Ancients in the Scriptures had gotten their faith. They gained it by trial and error.

The *faith* the Ancients had *in* Christ came to them by experimenting on the words *of* Christ. Then, they were willing to continue the experiment by following the feelings inside them. Those two things, coupled with trying to live worthily of the gifts, led them all the way from Faith to Trust. The Ancients that performed those miracles in the Bible *didn't have stronger impressions* that we have—they just *understood more about those impressions* than we understand.

Mind exploding concept isn't it?! To actually tap into the powers of heaven, by trying to live worthily, experimenting on the words of Christ—then following the feelings to their destination!

Life and history, has many heroes, many inspiring people for me. All those I choose as heroes, as role models, have at least these four common denominators. 1) They are dreamers. They are visionaries, who can see what *could* be, instead of what *can't* be. 2) They have a strong need to chase their dream and to do good with it. 3) It is their nature to be honest, fair and to have charity. 4) Regardless of what they understand *about* God, they believe *in* God. The son of a wool weaver, is one such hero to me. His name is Christopher Columbus.

Christopher Columbus had many interests and one of them was the Bible. Known for having discovered America and for naming the indigenous people of America, Indians, Columbus is also known for this statement. He said, "You can never cross the ocean unless you have the courage to lose sight of the shore."

Life with Christ is that same way. You can never get to know Him unless you have the courage to venture forth and leave where you now stand …regardless of where that is.

Columbus also said, "Following the light of the sun, we left the Old World." Therein lies the answer!! How do you find this new path? It's easy. You follow the Light of the Son and leave the old ways behind. Leaving the old world, the old ways, means stepping away from who you used to be. It means stepping outside of your comfort zone and following a new path, the path of faith.

Following the Light of the Son was exactly what I had to do in following the money trail. Following the money trail was an exercise in faith. The money was never the object. Receiving the feelings and finding the courage to follow those feelings …was!!

Not long ago, in a stake conference, my son-in-law, Jay, was called to serve as Second Counselor in his Stake Presidency. During that conference, my daughter, Katina, was asked to speak. She told of an experience with her neighbor. She said he came home one day, pulling a trailer and in conversation told her that things were not going well for his family.

Seeing that he was depressed, she asked him, "How's your faith?" He told her that he did not have much and that he didn't grow up with much religion in his life. He also said that he did not believe in a God who sat back and counted our mistakes and then held them against us at Judgment Day.

Katina said, "I don't believe in a God like that, either." She then related the story of the woman taken in adultery and brought before Christ. The woman's accusers demanded an answer of Him to see if He would follow the Law of Moses and stone her. Katina told her neighbor how Christ used love, wisdom and mercy to solve the problem.

The neighbor told Katina that he was not familiar with that story. She went on to tell him that, though there are many things to learn from that story, the most important is that through following Christ and having faith in Christ, all of our problems will be solved. So maybe the *real* question is: *"How's your faith?"*

58) Trust the impressions of the Spirit. Step forth …be willing to be led.
59) Use your feelings more than your eyes and follow the Hansel and Gretel breadcrumb paths to the prizes the Lord has awaiting you.

"But behold, if ye will awake and arouse your faculties,
even to an experiment upon my words, and exercise a particle
of faith, yea, even if ye can no more than desire to believe,
let this desire work in you, even until ye believe in a manner
that ye can give place for a portion of my words."

Jesus Christ.

The Bridge…

It happened one cloudy day in my darkest hour,
as I was walking along.
I was in the hills, following a creek,
when I came to a small pond.
It was quiet and peaceful so I sat on a rock,
near the water's edge,
near a big oak tree and a walking bridge,
that spanned the canyon ledge.
As I sat there I just stared into the water,
for what seemed a long time.
Mulling over solutions to problems,
that were so unfortunately mine.
It was then that I noticed the old man,
sitting under the big oak tree.
He hadn't moved or made a sound.
He just looked and smiled at me.
I could tell he wasn't a man of means.
His clothes and boots were worn.
And I noticed that the old hat that he wore,
was frayed, ragged and torn.

His hair was a little long and it was so white,
it looked like the driven snow.
But there was something about this old man,
I could feel an inner glow.
I smiled back and said, "Hello."
as I sat and thought of what to do.
After a few moments he asked,
"Are you lost or just passing through?"
I was depressed and didn't feel like talking,
so I didn't answer back.
That's when he said,
"Your life is out of control and sliding off track."
Somewhat annoyed, I gazed over the water and said,
"Who are you old man?"
He said, "I'm a bridge builder,
and I've built many bridges across the land"
"I don't need a bridge!" I said.
"I need solutions to problems that are troubling me."
He said, "What you need is a bridge indeed!
Have you sought help on bended knee?"

"I pray." I said. "But I need more than that!
I need these problems to come to an end!"
He said, "That's the easy part!
The Lord will help you if you let Him, my friend!
You see, solving problems in life,
is like learning to build a series of bridges.
You don't have to stumble and fall in the canyons,
learn to live on the ridges!
When you pray and ask for help,
if you listen, you'll feel the way to go.
And if you feel the Holy Ghost in your heart,
by this sign you'll surely know!
Following the guidance of the Lord,
is like building a one sided bridge.
You start from one side of the canyon,
and try to build to the other ridge!
There will be times when you will wonder,
if you're making a big mistake!
You'll feel alone, won't see the other side,
may even worry, quiver or shake!

But then one day something will happen,
and you'll realize you have been wrong.
Where once you felt He'd left you alone,
you'll see He was there all along!
You'll also see He was there helping to build
and support your side when you fell.
And with the turn of a single event,
you'll see He's built the other side, as well.
And now the bridge to your new life is complete,
and off into the future you will go.
The darkness that surrounded your life,
now gone, because of a God who loves you so!"
At first I was stunned by the things I'd just heard.
Who was this man indeed?
Though I knew him not, I somehow felt,
he'd come to help in my hour of need!
As I thought about the things the old man said,
I quickly realized he was right.
So I turned to thank him ...but he was gone
...and the Son was now shining bright.

Ofcr. Samuel Jeppsen #3751

Chapter Nineteen

Get Your Motor Runnin

"If I have learned anything from this and all the other rides I have taken, it is to trust my feelings more than I trust my eyes and my ears."
My last email to my friends, June 14th, 2010

With everything in order, all that was left was to load the bike into the truck, pack my new saddlebags and ditty-bag and head to Florida. It was time to enjoy the fruits of my labors. The reward for following the feeling the Lord had placed in my mind.

The excitement in me at that point was almost overwhelming. It was a feeling that I had already ran the hardest part of a twenty-five mile marathon and was staring at the last half mile in front of me. Now, all I had to do was cross the finish line. "I love riding." I said. "Riding long days are no challenge to me. It's a treat! I have already received my teaching moments. It's time to kick back and ride!" ...Or so I thought!

One of the things I have come to learn about the Lord is that each teaching moment is merely a step on a staircase that will prepare you for the next step. He will cause things to happen in your life. If you are mentally awake and perceptive, you will see that He is leading you closer and closer *to* Him and farther and farther down the path of faith *in* Him. It's an interesting journey. As your testimony of Him grows and your faith in Him increases, the experiences not only become more frequent, they begin to become more meaningful in your life. Those experiences begin to create a change within you. You begin to thirst for the experiences and you begin tracking the outcome. The thirst for another such experience becomes a powerful driver in your decision making process. You realize that life *with* Him is a path of continual learning. It is like making your way from kindergarten to college and then into a career. And so it was with this journey as well.

The trip to Florida was basically two, twenty-four hour, round the clock drives, with a welcomed twelve hour layover in De Ridder, Louisiana, to visit family. After a good night's sleep, Olin, Andy and I got in the truck and once again headed east.

When we hit the tip of Florida, we worked our way through the heavy traffic until we saw the sign, "U.S. 1 Florida Keys." As we made that last left turn onto the Florida Keys Highway and began island hopping across the forty-two bridges, including the historic, *7-Mile Bridge* to Key West, the reality of the adventure began to unfold, as never before. The one hundred ten mile drive from the coastline, through Key Largo and the Florida Keys, was the unfolding of a lifelong dream. Now, my long awaited dream, my *one day*, was just hours away from becoming a reality.

The drive took four hours to complete. Traffic was fairly heavy and traveling was slow. However, the scenery was beautiful and it was worth going slow to be able to see it. The closer we got to Key West, the more the excitement built inside me. As we drove along, I kept saying, "It's here!!! My dream, my great adventure, is finally here!!!"

With each passing mile the crescendo of excitement built as if I were living Tchaikovsky's 1812 Overture. As I made that right turn onto N. Roosevelt Boulevard in Key West, the pounding of the drums and the firing of the cannons in the Overture, was taking place in my heart and mind.

When we pulled into the Marriott Hotel in Key West, there was a big welcome banner. There were bikes and riders everywhere. After we off-loaded my bike, Olin and Andy said their goodbyes and took off for the mainland. I was now alone with just my dream and hundreds of other riders and their bikes. I started looking around for friendly faces. It wasn't long before I ran into Travis Metcalf, a retired police detective from Mesa, PD. I also ran into Mike Martinelli. Mike was a friend and a professional Harley-Davidson test rider.

My plans for the next two nights in Key West, was to sleep in the parking lot, next to my bike, in the Marriott parking garage. Why not? I thought. But when Mike found out, he and Doug Hines, another professional test rider for Harley-Davidson, out of friendship and professional courtesy, invited me to sleep on the floor of their room. So I traded my two nights, in the concrete parking garage, for two nights on the floor and a shower.

Key West is beautiful, but very humid. This was my first time to Florida. I took off on my bike a couple times, to just cruise the island and see it firsthand. The beautiful, clean, little town is surrounded by water on all sides.

Except for the forty-two bridges that connect it to the world, Key West is literally, a small city, in the middle of the ocean. The people there seemed to be in a slower, more relaxed pace than what I deemed as normal. The town of Key West is beautifully taken care of. The lawns and yards are green and well-manicured. The businesses are quaint and there was no *beep, beep, get out of my way,* going on. There were lots of cars and a lot of traffic, but everyone seemed to take it in stride and calmly go about their business.

Key West reminded me of the many times I had ridden through San Francisco, as you come into town on the Oceanside Cabrillo Highway. San Francisco, the town that invented Denim jeans during the 1849 Gold Rush, has that same quaint feeling.

Like the landscape, the skies in Key West are gorgeous and change by the half hour. They went from sunny skies, to overcast with looming clouds, to someplace in between. Being an island, quite a ways from the mainland, the skies and salt air never let me forget that I was a hundred and ten miles out in the ocean.

There are no hills or mountains in Key West. The highest elevation on the two by four mile island is eighteen feet above sea level. As beautiful and quaint as it is, the little town that has more bars and more churches per capita than any other city in the U.S., is just a little too small, too close to sea level and too far out in the ocean, for this Arizona boy. I prefer the vast mountain ranges and huge rolling valleys and endless land with no borders.

As I rode back to the Marriott, I noticed that riders were now everywhere. The parking lot was now full of bikes. The electricity, created by the excitement, was building as more and more riders showed up. It was creating a feeling of adventure in me that I would never forget. The excitement and the electricity were literally everywhere and in every conversation. Contributing to this surge of energy and excitement, that was now flowing in all our veins, was all the non-contestant riders that were showing up, as well. The vast majority of them had come from the mainland, ridden the one hundred ten mile ride and were now cruising the streets and parking lots, wanting to be part of the Hoka Hey.

The non-contestants were *Curious Georges* on clean bikes with no luggage or on stretched-customs or sport bikes. Many were racing back and forth in front of the Marriott on North Roosevelt Blvd., continually cracking their throttles.

In every rider there is a kinship toward other riders and a shared dream of a great adventure. This was no different and there were *Curious Georges* of all sorts. They were a welcome sight as they only added to the excitement and upped the worth of what was taking place in the event and in the hearts and minds of us all.

I had never been a part of anything like this before. Watching them ride back and forth, made me realize, just how blessed I was, to be a participant in this first, longest, craziest Harley-Davidson ride in the world. The event and the feelings I felt, were greater than I could have ever imagined or hoped for. I felt like someone important and very special. I felt like an Olympian before the crowd, like a champion in an arena, standing in the center of the field, slowly turning in a circle and facing the stands and listening to the roar and applause of the crowd.

The Hoka Hey contestants were just as I imagined they would be. There were no outlaw bikers, no colors, gangs or no wannabes. There were no rowdies, yahoos, drugs or lawlessness. The riders were respectful of each other, of the Marriott and of the other Marriott patrons. They were there as challengers from every walk of life. Each person was a hardcore, long distance rider who loved the open road, loved bikes and loved adventure. They were dreamers, here to fulfill their own dream. There was no common age. Ages ranged from twenty-five to seventy years old. Most of the bikes were FLs, many were Dynas and Softtails. There were about half a dozen Sportsters. Mine was one of the half dozen.

I didn't know how many riders came to finish, but I knew that I did. Dropping out, a few hundred miles after the start or a few states away, was not even a consideration. I had come to go the distance, to experience each mile and then ride back home to Arizona. Short of an accident or engine failure, I was finishing.

The two days in Key West went quickly. Soon it was the morning of the 20th, Father's Day. We were to be in line by 6 a.m. By 3:30 a.m., we could hear bikes firing up and getting into position. By 4:30 a.m., Mike, Doug and I were in position. The Key West Police Department was already on scene. Their top-lights were blinking brightly against the calm, black sky.

We were to take off at 6:45 a.m. This had something to do with an Indian tradition about leaving at sunrise. At 5 a.m. most all the riders were in position, lined up four abreast all throughout the Marriott parking lots. I was fifty yards from the start banner.

As I looked ahead of me and behind me, there were bikes as far as I could see. They went from the starting line, to me, to around the corner and out of sight as the parking lot continued around the building. All of us wanted to take off. Finally James Red Cloud decided to give the okay to start. The Key West PD began blocking off the intersections and let us leave as a group.

The dream had begun for all of us. The sound of hundreds of Harleys starting up and rumbling, as they were trying to warm up, broke the peace and quiet of the morning. I am sure that sound was annoying to some and I am sure that there were many patrons in the Marriott that were glad to see us go. But to me, it was music to my ears and it came as a shot of adrenalin to my heart.

The riders were finally let onto the street two by two and the rush of emotions that filled us all could hardly be contained. When the bikes hit the street, the throttles were cracked open and I am sure that the roar of hundreds of Harleys, against the calm of the morning, could be heard throughout Key West.

To my great surprise, the streets were lined with Key West citizens, who had come to wave us on. I had not expected that at all, but there they were, waving and cheering us on. We were about thirty minutes ahead of the announced start time, yet there they were. This added to the feeling that we were Olympians or knights, crossing the drawbridge in search of the dragon.

There were also scattered groups of cheering people all along the Keys to the mainland. This type of experience was a first for me. I had never experienced the feeling that builds in the soul, when you see people alongside the road, cheering you on. I wanted to stop and take pictures of the riders as they passed by, but I could not let go of that powerful, escalating, euphoric feeling inside, that came from being an actual rider and not a spectator.

Watching the people cheering and waving us on, was creating such a rush of emotions inside me, that I broke out into an almost hysterical laugh as I rode. I felt as if I were pumped full of some sort of happy drug and I couldn't control my response to it. I began waving back, almost out of control with excitement. I could feel the sensation of adrenaline, now filling my laughter.

In my eyes, I was a hero, leaving the townspeople behind and riding my trusty steed off into the light of day. The men, alongside the road, were looking at me in adoration. The women were looking at me, as if I were the *Duke* himself, proudly riding his horse, *Lexington,* in *How The West Was Won.*

When we hit the mainland it was every man for himself. The large group that started out together was now fragmenting into smaller groups. Speeds increased as riders began positioning for the lead. Some were there for the gold and it was evident. To others, like me, the gold was in the journey. It was in the day to day ride, the spree décor and the fulfilling of a dream coming to pass. It was all here and I was savoring every moment of it.

Sadly, it wasn't long before I came upon our first, serious accident. As I rode across the everglades, Alligator Alley and into the interior of Florida, I saw that two guys on FLs, had failed to negotiate a sweeper. It was at Oil Well Road and SR-29.

Before noon, four riders, Joseph Johnson of New York, Michael Rodger of British Columbia, Charles Marble and Jerry James both from Alaska, were involved in accidents. I remember at the scene of the fourth accident, many of the riders began to sober up to the need to ride safe. Those four accidents would not be the last of the accidents. There were an estimated twenty-three, with two, ending in fatalities. But it was at this accident, we all began to realize, that getting there was much more important, than hurrying and not getting there at all.

Our first destination was Daytona Beach Harley-Davidson. It was only about four-hundred miles away. But because of the maps we had to follow, many of us were riding well over six-hundred and fifty miles that first day. And like me, several riders got there at 1:30 in the morning. My friend Dave, the only other City of Mesa employee in the ride, ended up riding seven-hundred and fifty miles that day. We were all getting lost and were making lots of U-turns as no GPS guidance systems were allowed.

As a result, frustrations were running high. I found several other lost riders that night who, like me, were tired and were trying to follow the directions, in the middle of the night, in a strange town. I made a wrong turn and ended up on an on-ramp. I rode about twenty-five miles southeast on Interstate 4 before my first opportunity came to turn around. I then rode the twenty-five miles back and tried again to find the right street.

Finally making it to Daytona Beach Harley-Davidson, I checked in. I visited with Doc, then found a place in the parking lot and just laid down and went to sleep. No sleeping bag, no taking anything off the bike, no getting ready for bed, no taking my boots off, just laying down on the pavement and going fast asleep.

I had ridden through four swamps, two storms, gotten lost a dozen times and rode nineteen and a half hours and I had been awake for twenty-two. In the few seconds it took me to fall asleep, I could hear more riders coming in. Their bikes had no effect on the dozen riders, which were fast asleep on the parking lot.

At Daytona, many riders decided that this kind of riding was not for them and some were talking about going home. I was sad that they had let their mind's eye, focus on the things that were going wrong, more difficult than planned or not as easy as they thought they would be. Instead of seeing the great adventure, they were seeing the issues. Truth is, we were all experiencing the same experiences. The difference was in where we kept our focus. Some were laden with complaints while others were having the time of their life. How true of life itself, I thought, as I bent down, first to my knees, then onto my hands and then stretching out on the asphalt parking lot. "How true of life itself, to focus on the things that are going wrong," I muttered, as I stretched my arms above my head. I was sore and the parking lot was hard, but to my body, it felt like a wonderfully soft mattress. The night air was muggy and the bugs were buzzing, but I was just too tired to care about any of it. With one more huge stretch, I let out a sigh and said, "Whata ride!" Within seconds, I was sound asleep.

60) The difference in being miserable …or happy …is your outlook. Don't believe it's complicated or out of your control. It's a decision of the will.
61) Live the Dream. Don't let anyone take it from you. Even yourself.

If on Me…

"Ohhh, the long, lonely, road ahead,
Seems so dark and scary," I said.
"You'll be fine," came His reply,
If on Me, you'll keep your eye." sj

"The future is as bright as your faith."
Thomas S. Monson

Chapter Twenty

Lone Rider

At about 5 a.m., I woke up, as the rising sun began to announce daybreak. After sleeping on the parking lot for three and a half hours, I stumbled to my feet and struggled to feel awake. I looked around, as riders mounted up and prepared to leave. My eyes felt like someone had tossed dirt into them during the night. As I stood there and held onto my bike, trying to gain my balance, I looked for my helmet and my gloves. Still holding onto the bike, I thought again of the riders that were leaving and heading for home. My friend Dave, was one of them. I felt sorrow for all who left, but especially for those who quit because of frustration. Why would you quit a dream just because it was hard? Why would you work so hard to get here, spend so much time and money to prepare, only to get mad and pack it in? Sadly, each day was like that. More and more riders quit. Because it was harder than they first thought and the grass wasn't as green as they first imagined, they got mad and quit. When they quit, they not only became quitters, they left their prize behind.

It was then, as I was holding onto the bike, that I made the decision to ride alone the rest of the ride. Day one was filled with hard riding and a lot of competition. The bikes had taken a lot of abuse, while trying to keep the pace, the gold-seekers were setting. Also, too many riders, including myself, were getting caught up in the excitement of being in a pack. They were running hard and they were pushing past the speed limits and were riding to win. It was a dangerous decision they were making and I chose not to make it. I decided instead, from then on, I was going to be what I like being the most ...*a lone rider*.

When I left Daytona, I rode north toward Jacksonville on Florida's rural roads. I was amazed at how green that state is. The trees were sixty to eighty feet tall and lined the roads. The only downside was that there were no mountains to look at. I often felt I was riding in a green trench. Luckily there were those occasional breaks in the tree line. Through the breaks I often saw a beautiful little homestead, nestled into a green and lush meadow.

As I rode up the Florida peninsula from Daytona, I passed the turn-off to the historical site of Rosewood. Rosewood is off SR-24 on the Gulf Coast side of the peninsula. Loving history as I do, I remembered the very sad story of the three-hundred and fifty people of Rosewood and what had occurred there in 1923. The town was predominately black and over an unsupported accusation by a local white community, violence broke out. A lot of blood was shed and many people were hurt or killed. After which, the town was burned to the ground and left abandoned. It happened merely because of the hatred people can have for someone else, who is not like them. The only crime, the people of Rosewood committed, was *being different*.

The local and Federal government at the time turned a blind eye to the incident. A federal investigation began in 1933, but no action was taken and the incident remained quiet until the 1980's. The movie, *Rosewood* is what brought it to national attention and Rosewood became a historical site in 2004. The brutality the people of Rosewood went through, has never left my mind.

As I continued north and crossed into Georgia, my mind shifted to the five peaceful Indian Tribes that used to live there. As I rode along, I tried to imagine them to my right and left. Many of them lived in houses, had farms, owned businesses, spoke, read and wrote English and wore the same kind of clothing, their white counterparts wore. When they were forced off their land for *being different*, they were marched to the plains of the Oklahoma territory at gunpoint. Seven-thousand, armed soldiers, forced over twenty-thousand unarmed Indians to leave their homes and march cross country. The largest of the five tribes and last tribe to be forced off at gunpoint was the Cherokee Nation in 1838. It is the biggest forced march in American history. Of the twenty-thousand Indians that were forced to move to Oklahoma, over four-thousand never made it. They died along the way. The incredible true story became known as the *Trail of Tears* and I was riding that trail.

Being able to ride through this country was humbling for me and it was also an honor. I was riding on sacred ground. I imagined them walking along the road, as I passed by. I could see the old men, the old women and the children and the braves who were trying to understand what was happening. In the thumping of my motor, I could hear their drums reaching out to my soul.

I love history, because so much can be learned, if the lessons are not forgotten. As I rode, I thought of all the other great injustices I knew about in history and all the injustices I had seen as a police officer, where victims had suffered so terribly. It made me wonder how the Lord could make everything right. What is it He can do to heal their horrific scars and erase their terrible memories and remove their awful pain? I have pondered that question a lot. As a police officer and as an ecclesiastical leader, I have tried to help people through major crises and then help them understand that the Lord will make it right. He always does.

I have come to realize that because I don't fully understand the big scheme of things, I don't know how the Lord is going to do it! I only know that He can and He will do it, if we let Him! In thinking of the many people I have tried to help, I have come to realize that it was not me that helped them, at all. When the Lord left His apostles, He said He would send the Comforter to be with them. It was the Comforter who gave me the words to say and supplied the feelings that caused the peace and strength within them. The peace that came to them, comes through trust in the Lord. *Trusting* the Lord, means you don't need to understand *the how!* You just need to understand …*He will!*

I have also watched those who cannot seem to trust Him with their hurt and will not turn it over to Him and release it. To them, their hurt becomes a cancer, one that eventually eats them up. It has been said that letting go of the hurt and trusting the Lord to solve it in His own way and time, is like taking a key and letting a prisoner loose—only to find out that *you* were the prisoner!

As I rode along, I noticed that Georgia and Alabama were more rolling and more my taste, because I could see farther in every direction. Julie and I have often dreamed of coming to this area and walking the sacred grounds of the Civil War battlefields. We want to see the beautiful mansions, the plantations and get to know more about our southern neighbors! I looked for that southern hospitality everywhere I went and never failed to find it.

In love with the ride, I finally found my way to Southaven, Mississippi, the second checkpoint. It was another really nice Harley-Davidson dealership, asphalt parking lot, which became my bed. I again arrived at about 1:30 in the morning.

The people at Southaven HD were extremely kind. True to the ideology of southern hospitality, they literally opened their doors, all night long, to let us use their restrooms and get in out of the heat and the humidity. The south in late June is hot and very humid. Our clothing was damp and sticking to us. Making it worse, was the road grime that comes from traveling on bikes. This was day two without a shower and in the same underwear. With the long, humid days of sitting on a small Sportster seat, I now, not only had a very sore backside, I also had a very bad rash!

I walked as if I was straddling a horse, but most everyone else did too. This was our second, twenty hour day of riding and it was beginning to show in the attitudes of many of the riders. However, there were those, like me, who were having the time of their life and wouldn't rather be anywhere else. As much as my rear-end hurt from the rash and all the riding on a Sportster seat, I loved every minute of it. To me, it was a dream unfolding before my eyes. Who cares if I hurt!

So I took my mummy bag off the bike and used it as a pillow and laid down on the parking lot. I shared that area of the parking lot with Geoff Trenin. He told me he was from New Zealand and was the only New Zealander in the event. He had a strong accent and was excited to be here. Both of us just laid down on the pavement, without using sleeping bags or tents.

Before falling asleep, I looked toward heaven. With a big smile, I began to pray. "Thanks, Heavenly Father," I said, "for a wonderful time and for loving me." As I lay there, I looked at the clear, star filled sky in amazement and thought about the Only Begotten Son of God who had created everything I was looking at.

As I tried to get comfortable on the pavement, I saw two police cruisers, slowly drive past. I wasn't worried about foul play from local criminals. I felt they would avoid us, because most criminals are not brave. For them to strike, there has to be a big chance they won't get hurt. They would probably look at this motley crew and think we were meaner and crazier than they were, and stay away. But I smiled, as I imagined what the police officers must have been thinking as *they* looked us over.

I was so sore when I laid down, that the parking lot actually felt good. So, with a big stretch, a big heartfelt thanks to God and a chuckle in my heart, I closed my eyes and drifted off to sleep.

The next thing I knew, it was three hours later. Daybreak was just beginning. I staggered to my feet, waited till I could see and think clearly, bungee-corded my sleeping bag onto the bike and left at sunrise. I crossed into Tennessee and soon found myself right in front of Graceland. I had heard about this place many times, but never imagined I would ever see it. Now, here I was!

As I stopped in front of the grounds and sat there on my bike, I looked over the beautiful rolling grass hill. I saw the walkway and the old fashioned white rail fence that led up to the home, which had once belonged to the great musical legend, Elvis Presley. The perimeter wall was rock and mortar and it literally had thousands and thousands of inscriptions on it.

I thought about Elvis and how I admired him. He made his share of mistakes, but he did a lot of good too. I admired him, not just because he was a great artist, but because to me, he was a true patriot. As I sat there, leaning back on my luggage, I began remembering how I had felt, during the Vietnam War.

I graduated from high school in 1969, when resentment for the Vietnam War was near its worst. I thought of the riots and the anti-war demonstrations. I thought of the Tet Offensive, the My Lai Massacre, and the battle of Hue. All were big events that left lasting marks in my memory. They all took place during my junior year, the same year Martin Luther King and Robert Kennedy were assassinated. 1968 was also the year Mayor Richard Daley of Chicago, ordered his officers to crack down on the rioters. I remembered the TV coverage of the police with their night sticks, the police dogs and the water cannons. I remembered the news coverage and the twenty-eight city blocks that were destroyed and the thirty-nine people, who were killed. It was a time of great turmoil and uncertainty.

Many young men were trying everything they could think of, to avoid the draft. Some were changing their names, claiming religious objections or mental illness or faking injuries or even committing self-inflicted injuries. Some were showing up at induction centers in dresses or even fleeing the country. Everyone seemed to be coming up with some kind of shenanigan or reason why they didn't have to serve, but not Elvis!

I remembered when Elvis was drafted by the US Army. The US Navy and Air Force offered him sweet deals if he would join them instead. But he wouldn't do it. He wanted to be a regular GI. He was a singer, a movie star, a national celebrity and heart throb. But even so, he answered the call of duty.

Every time I think of Elvis, it is that memory that comes to mind. He answered the call of duty. How can you not deeply respect someone like that, I thought, as I gazed upon Graceland.

He reminded me of Arizona's Pat Tillman, linebacker for ASU and the Arizona Cardinals. Pat turned down a contract worth over three and a half million dollars, to join the US Army and support his country. He became a decorated Army Ranger. Sadly, in 2004, he was killed in Afghanistan. We all die. However, from now until the end of eternity, he will always be a hero.

After a few pictures and about ten minutes of reflection, I fired up the bike and headed toward Arkansas. I think Arkansas is in the running, for one of the most beautiful states, I have ever been in. Also, it is the home of one of the most colorful judges in history, Judge Isaac Parker, the Hanging Judge. It is also the only state in the union where it is illegal to mispronounce the name of the state. By law, it must be pronounced, Ark-an-saw.

When I got near the east border of Oklahoma, I was so tired, I had to pull over and sleep. I don't remember the actual place, but next to the road was a little brown home with a large front yard. In that yard were two ladies visiting with each other. Near the road about fifty feet from where they stood, was a wooden picnic table.

I stopped and asked if the table was a public table. One of the ladies turned and said, "No, it's mine, but you can use it." I pulled over, got off my bike, laid down on her picnic table and fell asleep. When I woke up, they were gone. I can only imagine what they thought. However, I will be forever thankful to that nice lady, who let me sleep on her picnic table in her front yard.

I mounted up and headed toward the west Texas border. At about 1 a.m., I pulled over again for some much needed sleep. As I left the south behind and hit the Midwest, the humidity was now gone, but my rash was still there. It was now in full bloom. In fact it was so painful, I had to get a room and take a shower. I had been on the road for four days, without a shower or change of underwear and I could hardly walk or sit.

When I took my shower, I noticed that I had a huge bruise on my derrière about twelve inches around. It was the exact size of my Sportster seat. Along with the big bruise was a huge and painful rash. A shower, *a lot* of talcum powder and some clean underwear, made it where I could ride by morning. The pain was still there, but it was manageable and I was smiling again.

The next day I crossed into New Mexico. At almost Sunset, I ran into a huge storm. It was storm number three and it was the worst storm of the entire journey. It looked like a dark blue-black wall of water coming right at me. But the Lord, as He always does, led me to shelter. Before hitting the storm, to my right about a quarter mile off the road was an old, abandoned gas station. Every window was broken out, the ground was covered with old tires and the building was all but totally destroyed. But it had a roof and a place to park my bike out of the rain.

Later, the sun having gone down and thinking the worst was over, I tried to ride on. However, less than five miles later, I was forced over under another roadside shelter, which the Lord had provided for me as well. There I found two other Hoka Hey riders from Australia. Their names were Marc Storey and Lyn Les. The three of us huddled against the building, trying to keep dry under the eaves and awning of a small, roadside gift shop.

Lyn was a pit-driver in a huge mine and Marc was the owner of a Harley-Davidson dealership. Lyn's accent was so strong, I could hardly understand her. She gave me a memento from Australia. It was a little koala bear holding a boomerang. I still have it. It is sitting on a shelf in my bedroom. The three of us talked for a while, as we huddled under the awning in the pouring, blowing rain and tried to keep dry. The rain came off the roof and splattered on the pavement with such force, it sounded like a dozen garden hoses pouring off the roof.

Alongside us was another rider, a young guy on a sport bike. He waited for the worst to stop and then he headed out to face the stormy night alone. He was wearing only a t-shirt and Levis. Knowing the dangers he was facing, I said a prayer for him as he mounted his bike and began riding away. I then watched as he slowly disappeared into the pouring blackness.

62) Plant for tomorrow, but smell the roses of today.

“And it came to pass that Jesus spake unto them,
and bade them arise. And they arose from the earth,
and he said unto them: Blessed are ye because of your faith.
And now behold, my joy is full”
Jesus Christ

Chapter Twenty-One

The Slender, Bearded, Navy Seal

> "While zealously performing the duties of good citizens and soldiers, we certainly ought not to be inattentive to the higher duties of religion. To the distinguished character of Patriot, it should be our highest glory to add the more distinguished character of Christian."
>
> *George Washington*

When the last flicker of his red taillight disappeared, I turned my attention back to Mark and Lyn. It was just the three of us now. Our conversation was of the experiences of the journey we each had faced. Despite the rain, we were having the time of our lives. Marc and Lyn had shipped their bikes over here from Australia. It took them a month to get them here and when they flew in, their bikes had not been off-loaded yet. They had ridden hard to make it to Florida in time to start the ride. I chuckled as they told me their story. I supposed that every rider had sacrificed and struggled greatly, just to be able to participate.

As the rain died down, we looked for places to sleep. I lay down on the concrete, between the wall and my bike. My mind went to the young rider on the sport bike. I said another prayer for him and imagined a beautiful girl, praying for his safe arrival.

On day five, at about 6:30 p.m., I pulled into Globe, Arizona, the most southern point in our western journey. Julie had asked me to call her with an ETA for Globe. To my great surprise, most of my family met me, as I came through. Larry had my name on a piece of cardboard alongside the road. The look on the faces of my grandchildren was one I will never forget. In their eyes, I saw the look I had given that old man on the Cushman, years ago.

Family is where it's at!! When this life is over and all the toys and money are gone, it is family, friends and relationships! Relationships are all we get to keep. If you haven't built them here, you will have very little there!

I spent about an hour with them and then headed northwest across Roosevelt Dam and up to Payson, Arizona. In Payson, I met another rider and we spent the night on the stone covered front yard of my mother and father-in-law's home. They were gone so we made the granite, a bed. We even had the police come by and check on us. Someone must have called. After telling the officer who we were and what we were doing, sleeping in the front yard, we were bid a good night and allowed to go to sleep.

At daybreak I headed north, finished crossing Arizona and worked my way across Utah. At Vernal, Utah, I pulled into the Chevron Station in the middle of town. When I gassed up, the female attendant, about the age of one of my daughters, asked, "Are you one of those guys riding to Alaska?" Trying to keep from beaming, yet proud to be on the Hoka Hey, I smiled and said simply, "Yeah!" She smiled back and said, "I thought so!" She then began asking me several questions. I have to admit, I felt like a celebrity and it felt good. When I left Vernal, it was about an hour before dark and I headed for Rock Springs, Wyoming.

Crossing Flaming Gorge at night was scary. It was dark and there were lots of deer and they were on the road. From where I started my climb through the mountains, it took me over five hours to travel that last one-hundred ten miles to Rock Springs. Flaming Gorge is high, very mountainous and loaded with game. I was in second and third gear most of the time. I was riding slow and straining my eyes, trying to spot the deer, before they ran in front of me. Though I wanted to see this crossing during the daytime, this nighttime ride was incredibly beautiful and made riding at twenty to thirty miles an hour, enjoyable.

The night sky was completely clear and filled with millions of brilliant stars. Looking at the stars from these high mountain tops, gave me a celestial feeling. I felt I could almost reach out and touch heaven.

In most places the contour of the road and the bright, clear night, allowed me to see fairly well. However, the shoulders rolled off and I struggled to see them. The deep canyons along the way were brilliantly lit up from the full moon and stars. But because I had a hard time seeing the shoulders, the road seemed unattached to the earth. The curvy, rolling road and the deep canyon walls in the distance, reminded me of a ribbon in the breeze. The beauty of it all made me feel as if I was riding on a ribbon in the sky.'

After signing in at Rock Springs, I had the chance to visit with Chuck, who was one of the organizers. He was also an old Navy Seal from Vietnam and he became our guardian angel.

It was cold in Rock Springs, really cold for an Arizona boy. Even Chuck was bundled up in a heavy coat. There were over a dozen of us, sleeping in the parking lot. Chuck stayed awake all night and all alone, to watch over us. He treated us and watched over us, as if we were members of his Seal team.

Chuck had a bad limp because he was missing a piece of his backside. During the Vietnam War, he had been standing too close to an incoming mortar. After visiting with him for about a half hour, I decided it was time for bed. I had signed in at 1 a.m. Chuck gave me some food and after I ate, I found a place to sleep between two other riders, on the sidewalk. I was grateful that the Lord had protected me, as I came through Flaming Gorge.

In the morning I asked Chuck for a photo with him. It was then, that I noticed on the right side of his vest was a little, old, red and white patch. I looked closer and was even more impressed with our guardian angel. Chuck, the slender, bearded Navy Seal from Vietnam with a bad limp …was an Eagle Scout.

Very few men become eagle scouts, and yet, we had been watched over all night long by an eagle scout that had become a Navy Seal. Though this guy was quite rough around the edges, in the times I had heard him speak, I noticed some very unique things about him. He clung to the principles of honor and loyalty to God, country and friends. He reminded me of an old car, all dented and banged up, but always dependable and trustworthy. This old Navy Seal with a bad limp, inspired me to become a better man and to live at a higher level as a human being.

At just past daybreak, I got up and decided I wanted to see what I had missed, crossing Flaming Gorge at night. So I headed back down to see it in the daylight. It was an eighty mile back-track. "Why not!?" I said! "After all, I came to ride!"

I rode all the way back to Dutch John, where I had some peanuts and hot chocolate, before turning around. The detour was an extra hundred and sixty miles, but worth every mile.

After hitting Rock Springs again, I crossed Wyoming and headed for the Pine Ridge Indian Reservation in South Dakota. I was heading for one of the highlights of my entire journey—one I had anticipated and looked forward to since I heard about this ride.

For whatever reason, I have always had a deep love for the American Indian. Like the Mexican people, the American Indians are simple in their faith and they are great believers in God, whom they call *The Great Spirit*.

Perhaps, because of what I knew about them as a people, their closeness to nature and to the Great Spirit, I was very excited for this part of the journey. How good can it get?

There are twenty-one tribes in Arizona, over five-hundred and sixty tribes in the U.S. and I was riding toward one of the most famous tribes in American Indian history! "I'm going to get to see the Chief of the Sioux Nation!" I said. I remembered most of what I had learned about Chief Sitting Bull and his vision of a great victory in battle over the soldiers. His vision had taken place just two weeks before the Battle of the Little Bighorn, which became the major turning point for the American Indian.

What took place during the aftermath of that battle, had not caused me to take the Indians' side, but it did affect me and cause me to ponder. I have never been able to forget the words spoken by Chief Crazy Horse. He said, "They said we massacred them! But we did to them what they came to do to us."

Chief Sitting Bull is also a big favorite of mine. Besides being a great Sioux leader, he was a very religious man with high ideals. He was quoted as saying, "What white man has ever seen me drunk? Who has ever come to me hungry and left unfed? Who has seen me beat my wives or abuse my children? What law have I broken?" He also said, "I am here by the will of the Great Spirit, and by His will, I am Chief." To me, Chief Sitting Bull bore the marks of a truly great leader and a truly great man.

One of the other great Sioux Chiefs that left an impression on me was Chief Red Cloud. He said something that I quite often think about. He said, "They made us many promises, more than I can remember, but they never kept but one. They promised to take our land, and they took it."

To me, the most powerful thing Chief Red Cloud ever said, the thing that told me who he actually was inside, was when he said, "I am poor and naked, but I am the Chief of the nation. We do not want riches, but we do want to train our children right. Riches would do us no good. We could not take them with us to the other world. We do not want riches. We want peace and love." Where are those leaders today?

Now, over one-hundred and thirty years after that great battle, here I was, riding toward those sacred battle grounds and riding into the heart of the great Sioux Nation. With each passing mile I anticipated my arrival. I prepared myself to meet with the Chief of that people, a people I had great interest in and empathy, love and respect for. Today, I was going to be able to meet the actual descendant of Chief Red Cloud, Chief Oliver Red Cloud.

Arriving on the reservation at about 11 p.m., I met four other riders, who were also looking for the Chief's home. We were all lost. The road signs were either poor or nonexistent. Again, as He always does, the good Lord came to my rescue. We were stopped on the side of the road, in almost total darkness. We had no idea where to go or where we were. It was about the fourth time we had stopped to refigure things. Then, a couple in their early fifties, in a late model Bronco, stopped and asked if they could help. I told them we were looking for the Chief's home. They tried two or three times to give us directions, but seeing that deer-in-the-headlight look in our faces, they decided to just take us there, instead. So we followed them for seventeen miles, right to the dirt driveway of the Chief's home.

There I had the great honor of being invited into the home of Chief Oliver Red Cloud of the Lakota Sioux Tribe. It was now 2 a.m. and the Chief had gone to bed. But Beth, wife of James Red Cloud, had been waiting up for the riders as they straggled in. So here we were, sitting at the table with her, in the home of Chief Oliver Red Cloud. In the kitchen were two local Indians, a man and his wife, making Buffalo stew and fresh, hot Indian fry bread. From the big pot on the stove, they dipped a bowl of hot stew and from the oven they gave me homemade fry bread. They had been cooking all day, making food for the riders. Now, at 2 a.m., here they were, still cooking, cleaning and inviting riders inside. Beth, though very tired and exhausted from the long day, was still wearing a smile, as she sat at the table and asked how we were doing. Though I don't know Doc's real name, wherever Beth and Doc were, like loving parents, they were always checking on our welfare and seeing if there was anything they could do for us.

The kitchen and home were very small. They reminded me of some of the poorer homes, I had been in, as a police officer. Yet, what I often found in those poorer homes, I also found here. There was love and respect for one another. There was faith in

God and true humility of heart and soul. They didn't know me and in all probability, our paths would never cross again. Yet even so, I felt as if I was a dignitary, from a foreign land. A Prince of a King and I felt welcomed from the bottom of their hearts. What a humbling feeling and an absolute highlight, this experience was for me. Soon, I would be able to meet the Chief, himself. But now, it was about 2:30 a.m. and I had been riding since sunup.

To make my visit to the home of the leader of the great Sioux Nation even better, I was told that I could sleep on his front lawn. Wow …look at me now! Sleeping on the front lawn of the Chief of the Sioux Nation! A night in the Hilton on clean sheets, wouldn't have been better!

After eating, I walked outside a little clumsily from fatigue. I remember realizing that every part of my body seemed to hurt and what didn't hurt seemed to be numb. The prospect of sleeping on lawn, instead of pavement, was now really inviting.

"Ahhhhhhh!" I said, as my back hit the grass and I stretched my arms and legs out. Grass never felt so good. I had gone from sleeping in the open bed of my truck, next to my bike while Olin and Andy drove, to sleeping on a motel room floor, to vacant parking lots, a picnic table, a granite stone front yard, a sidewalk and now sleeping on the Chief's front lawn, in the middle of the Lakota Indian Nation. *What a life,* I thought as I smiled and gave a sigh! As that sigh left my lungs, I could feel some of the pain and soreness easing out of my body.

As I lay on the grass looking like a homeless person in a city park, I listened to the stillness of the night and gazed upon the beauty of the starlit sky. With no streetlights, I could see a million miles. The sky was filled with more stars than I had ever before seen and I was again in awe that Christ had created them all. As I looked into the Heavens above, I began to thank my Heavenly Father in prayer for this incredible opportunity and for loving all of us so much that He was willing to give His Only Begotten Son, so we could return to Him someday. I also thanked Him for the feelings of love from Him that were now coursing my veins.

Suddenly…

63) See the good in others, see who they *could* be. Focus on their strengths instead of their faults. Reach out *and build them*, as you build yourself.

Chapter Twenty-Two

"Red"

I awoke three hours later and knocked on the door. Though I didn't know exactly what to expect, I did know from listening to organizer, James Durham Red Cloud, that the Sioux Nation is the poorest tribe in the U.S. The Lakota Tribe has an unemployment rate of over eighty percent and the average yearly income per family is $3,700. About forty percent of the homes don't have electricity or running water. James is an interesting fellow. He has a great passion and strong love for the Lakota people. His goal in organizing the Hoka Hey competition, was to try and bring attention to the needs of this nation, within a nation.

Throughout the entire journey, though rough around the edges, James Red Cloud was always trying to make things better and more memorable for all. I was impressed with that. In Key West, he rented the Marriott Convention Center and always asked how we were doing. I was also impressed with his desire to help the Lakota tribe. He always spoke so reverently of Chief Red Cloud. And now I was just minutes away from meeting him.

As the door opened and I was invited inside, I again sat at the kitchen table. I was introduced to Chief Oliver Red Cloud. He is a man with a very powerful and positive spirit. At ninety-one years of age, he is still mentally sharp and has a passion for his people. He told me of their needs and of his hopes and dreams for them. He was like any other loving father or grandfather, who had a family for whom he wanted to make things better. He was everything I saw in my father and father-in-law and everything I had seen in the eyes of that old man, alongside the road in Ensenada.

Chief Oliver Red Cloud is the fourth generation Sioux Chief to bear the name of Chief Red Cloud. After visiting with him personally for about ten minutes, I met Jesse Sonez(?). Jesse was the medicine man that had performed an Indian ritual smoke dance at Key West. It was a warrior's dance and prayer to the Great Spirit for safety over the riders.

Having spent twenty-five years as a cop and two years as a prison minister, I noticed that Jesse had every earmark of having *been to camp,* himself. With Chief Red Cloud, he stood back and was quiet. I thanked him for his smoke dance and prayer over us. We started talking and when I told him I was a retired cop, he stopped for a moment. Then he turned around and lifted his shirt to show me a scar on his back. He didn't have to explain what the scar was from, I recognized it immediately. It was a bullet hole. He said a cop had shot him, when he was twelve years old.

Never knowing the other side of the story, I usually don't apologize for another cop's actions. I didn't here, either. But I did have a lot of empathy for a young boy, who had been shot by the police. Though he appeared to have been an outlaw at one time, he now had a kind, gentleness about him. He said he had forgiven the officer that shot him. I thanked him for that. I also told him that I respected him, because I recognized him from a police video about gangs and where he was reaching out to troubled youth. He was surprised I recognized him and said he does reach out to troubled youth. I thanked him for using his background and his influence to make a difference in the lives of young men, who were heading down the wrong path. We shook hands and parted as friends.

Before saying goodbye to the Chief, I noticed a picture on the wall in the living room, of him and President Clinton. The Chief was in full Indian headdress. This leader of a nation lived very modestly, but it was never *things* he had talked about. It was always his people, his love for them and his desires to help them. I wanted to be like him. I wanted to be ninety-one years old, still living with a purpose and making life better for someone else!

When I left the Chief's home, I headed east on BIA-32, into Pine Ridge and then toward Rapid City. At a little corner store along the way, I met a tall, handsome gentleman, atop his black stallion. His name was Oscar. Oscar was sixty-five years old, a Hoka Hey rider and Vietnam vet with severe heart problems. With a saddened look, he told me, "This was my last great ride."

Oscar was trying to fulfill his dream of riding to Alaska. His friends had helped him, by collecting $3800, so he could go. But this was as far as he could make it. His heart was giving him too many problems. He was heading to the Chief's home to present him with a commemorative knife. Then, he was heading back to his own home in Natchez, Mississippi. Though he was sad to have to quit, he was proud that he had made it this far.

After our visit, I mounted up and headed out. Just outside of Sturgis, I ran into an interesting fellow by the name of Red. When Red saw my Blue Knights' patch, he asked me if I was a cop or if I was wearing the patch, out of sympathy. I told him I am a retired police officer and a member of the Blue Knights.

When I looked at his vest, I saw that he was a member of the Bandits, an outlaw motorcycle gang. He wore the 1% patch. It meant that he was a *One-Percenter*, the percent of motorcycle riders, which are outlaws. The patch, itself, has to be earned! Red was a very big fellow and very strong. Thank goodness he was also kind and very friendly …at least then. As I visited with him and his girl, I noticed that he didn't use any foul language. Red seemed like a decent fellow. I was impressed with him. He was unlike, what I had expected an outlaw motorcycle rider to be. As we visited, I thought of the *Hell's Angels.*

When one hears the name, Hell's Angels, most likely they think of the outlaw motorcycle gang, which began in 1948 in San Bernardino, California, at the end of WWII. When one hears the name, *Memphis Belle,* those who are old enough, will think of the famous WWII, B-17 bomber. This was the first plane recognized for flying twenty-five missions in the European Theatre, without being shot down. It was quite a feat, as the average life span of a B-17 in that theatre, was only six missions. It became a hero's story and the plane was sent back to the U.S. It toured many cities. The pilot, Robert Morgan, and his crew became famous.

The interesting thing is that the Memphis Belle was not the first B-17, to fly twenty-five missions over the European Theatre, without being shot down. The B-17, named Hell's Angels, was the first to do it. It was flown by Captain Irl Baldwin, of the 303rd bomber group, of the 8th Air force. The Memphis Belle was the *second* B-17 to do it. The Memphis Belle was chosen to be the hero plane and to tell the hero story, because of what the name, *Hell's Angels,* depicted.

Because the captain and crew had chosen a name that did not lend to honor, glory and goodness, the plane named Hell's Angels, was left in the European Theatre. It flew twenty-three more missions, before it was unceremoniously scrapped.

There is an often perpetuated story, that the crew of the Hell's Angels were misfits, drunkards and malcontents. After WWII, unable to make the adjustment to peacetime, they started the outlaw motorcycle gang, now known as the Hell's Angels. That is a myth. The crew of the Hell's Angels were very dedicated and disciplined professionals. They were highly decorated for their heroic acts of bravery. They were every bit as disciplined and professional as the crew of the Memphis Belle. But because of the image they chose to portray themselves as being, they were held back and brought down. It cost them all the great things the crew of the Memphis Belle enjoyed so richly.

The crew of the Hell's Angels could have been the heroes that the world recognized, celebrated and remembered. The movie, *The Memphis Belle,* could have been about them! They could have been the ones found in the history books! But all that credit and glory went to the crew of the Memphis Belle, instead. It is a graphic example of what happens to people, who allow themselves to be influenced in the least by Satan—thinking that what they are doing, makes very little difference.

As a chaplain with one of the largest law enforcement agencies in the state, I attended the ICPC (International Conference of Police Chaplains) 2010 Conference that was held in Scottsdale, Arizona. One of our speakers was Judge William J. O'Neil.

The judge spoke of the little flaws in our character, that allow us to make decisions, that often backfire on us and turn our world upside down—often ruining our life for good! He said there is no one in prison who struggled and worked, so they could be in prison. There is no broken marriage, which began with the dream of getting a divorce. There isn't any sports star or public official who wants to be in the paper for cheating on his wife or proving himself untrustworthy. He said it is always their *SUD's* that ruined their life for them—their *Seemingly Unimportant Decisions* that were made during seemingly unimportant moments! He said that people seldom fail because of their big decisions. It is usually the simple decisions that *seemed* to be acceptable at the moment. The decisions that begin with, "*Well, everyone else is doing it!*"

Judge O'Neal said, "The answer for every situation is not a question of whether or not it's legal—for many things that are legal are wrong." He said that the safeguard answer in any situation is in the two words—*should* and *ought!* What *should* you do, what *ought* you do? His words made me think of my police career and all the tragic stories of officers *and* citizens, who had made *seemingly unimportant decisions*. They had followed Satan, either by word or deed and were brought down, regardless of their original intent, talent, gifts or achievements! He who seemed to support them, to progress them and make the bounties of life plentiful for them—in the end, *always* brought them down!

As I looked at Red, I could see a very good person inside. As we talked, I was surprised at how opposite, he seemed to be from the stereo-typical profile of an outlaw biker. If I had not seen his outlaw motorcycle jacket and his 1% patch, I never would have pegged him for an outlaw motorcycle gang member. He was kind, respectful and loving to his girl, whom I believed may have been his wife. That was my impression anyway, as they said they had been together for several years.

As Red talked and I listened, I smiled as I realized that here we were, two guys on total opposite sides of the law. Even so, we spoke with respect for each other and as friends. The situation made me think of an old classic song by Lorne Greene. The song is called *Ringo* and it's one of my favorites. The song is a ballad, like the many ballads sung by Marty Robbins.

Ringo is an outlaw, who was found shot and left for dead. The singer finds him and nurses him back to health. He then watches as Ringo practices day after day, with his gun. Then, after Ringo is in full health, the song says, "And then one day, I went east and he went west. I took to law and wore a star, while he spread terror near and far. With lead and blood he gained such fame, all through the west, they feared the name, *Ringo*." The story continues to develop and one day the two men meet. As the singer goes for his gun, Ringo is so fast, that he shoots the gun from the singer's hand. Then the singer says, "They say, that was the only time that anyone had seen him smile. He slowly lowered his gun—then he said to me, 'We're even, friend.' So at last I understood that there was still a spark of good …in *Ringo*."

As I visited with this outlaw biker, those same words came to me, "That there was still a spark of good …in Red."

Red said that recently, he had lost his job, after his employer found out he was a member of the Bandits. He said he was very good at what he did and had done an outstanding job for them. He had been there for eight years. He was even well liked by his employer. Even so, because of his affiliation with the Bandits, they let him go. There was a deep sadness in his eyes, his voice and in his countenance, as he spoke.

As I listened to his story, I thought of the things that we hold up in front of us. Things, which in reality bring us down, simple things we think are so important or so harmless for us. Maybe it is the way we think, talk, dress or act! Maybe it is the big things we choose to do, that holds us back and keeps us from being who we could have been. But most likely, the things that hold us back are the little things we do or think that we know are wrong. Whatever they are, each has a price and a consequence! If it is wrong, regardless of our talent, like the B-17 named the *Hell's Angels*, it holds us back and robs us of our glory.

After a most interesting visit with Red and his girl, he let me take their picture. He placed his arm around her and pulled her tight, as she did him. We then shook hands and his 1% patch was now eyelevel. It made me think of a very special group of One-Percenters that are in the Scriptures. It is the story of Gideon.

Gideon, a simple man of simple means, is called by the Lord to do a mighty work for his people. Gideon's reply is, "Oh my Lord, wherewith shall I save Israel? Behold, my family is poor in Manasseh, and I am the least in my father's house." After Gideon is convinced the Lord is with him, he assembles his troops, thirty-two thousand strong. The Lord then tells him that his troops are too many. He must reduce the size of the Israelite army that is to fight the Midianites. The reason is to prevent the Israelites from saying, "Mine own hand hath saved me."

The Lord tells Gideon to tell everyone, who is afraid to fight, to return to their homes and families. *Twenty-two thousand* soldiers leave and only ten thousand courageous men remain.

The Lord tells Gideon the army is still too large. The Lord tells him how to divide the remaining ten thousand and tells him that He will choose the soldiers, Himself. The ten thousand are reduced to three hundred fighting men. The Lord has just reduced the Israelite army from thirty-two thousand men to just three hundred—less than one percent of the original army.

I don't know who these men were, but I do know who they were not. They were not just a bunch of highly skilled, tactical soldiers, who happened to drink water, using their hands. To be part of a strike force of three hundred men, against an army that even their modes of transportation, could not be numbered …*was insane!* They were either complete lunatics, totally insane with a death wish, or they were great men of valor, who possessed an unshakable faith in the Lord. There was no in-between, as every man, afraid or not, was free to leave the battlefield.

The three hundred Spartans that fought the numberless Persians, in a similar battle at Thermopylae, were different. Because of their fighting culture and brutal training, they were some of the fiercest, hand to hand combat soldiers, the world has ever known. From their youth, they knew of nothing, but discipline, orders and combat. There was no regard for family, personal relationships or even self-preservation. They were so extremely disciplined, that even today, some twenty-five hundred years later, armies still study them. Yet as fierce, heroic and disciplined as they were, they all died in one conflict, which was no worse than what the Israelites faced. The three hundred Israelites, on the other hand, *all lived.* Not one was lost or even hurt. They were in fact, the One-Percenters, in the Israelite army. They were men who possessed great trust in the Lord and that the Lord knew He could count on …to count on Him!

Since I was a young boy, the thought of being a One-Percenter in the Lord's army has thrilled me. If I could be one of His One-Percenters, it would not be based on how physically strong I was, how fast I could run or on my IQ. Being one of His One-Percenters would depend on my faith, my trust in Him and my ability to surrender my will to His. It would depend on *how great a relationship* I could create with Him …by following Him.

We all come to earth with different abilities and strengths, but the one thing we are all equal in, is our willingness to commit to the Lord. It is here that we have complete control and it is here that *every man is totally and completely equal!!* Though I am plagued with many shortcomings and have to keep trying, being one of His One-Percenters, is a dream that still rages inside me. His One-Percenters, stand among the greatest warriors, who ever stood. They are they who are willing to stand alone, or in small groups and are willing to put everything on the line for His cause.

The possibility of being one of those brave-hearts, who are willing to face impossible odds and impossible situations, reminds me of one of my favorite scenes in all the movies I have ever watched. The scene is that of the elves at Helm's Deep!

In *The Lord of the Rings* series, when the people of Rohan had no place to go and death was coming for them, they gathered into the Fort of Helm's Deep. They were a weak group of people, with only about three hundred warriors among them. The much more powerful Orcs and the Urak-hai, numbering well over ten thousand, were on their way to destroy them. With no one to turn to, Arwen, the daughter of King Elrond, king of the elves, asks her father to help the people, inside Helm's Deep. The human looking elves that are blessed with immortality and eternal life, *if* they don't get involved, must flee or they will be killed. Their only chance to remain alive forever, is to leave Middle-earth before the battle begins. Elrond tells his daughter, Arwen, that they must leave. Her reply is, "Do we elves leave Middle-earth to its fate? Do we abandon the fight and leave them to stand alone?" Her heroic words to her father, pierce his heart. The word is passed. About two hundred brave, elf archers respond to the call and march to Helm's Deep, to help defend the people against Mordor.

It's just a story. But in life, it is always only a small group, who are willing to make the big sacrifice, to often stand alone or in small numbers and do the brave and right thing. The chance to be a coward comes a thousand times, yet, so does the chance to be a hero. In each of us, there is a small part that wants to be counted in that number and wants to let the hero inside of us—out! There is a part of all of us, which wants to be brave, when others are afraid and to do the right thing, regardless of the consequences it may bring. We all want to be able to face fear and not run!

Being a hero has nothing to do with our intelligence, size or strength. It comes down to the choices that we make, that either make it a reality—or keep it inside us ...*as only a dream.*

64) Decide you are in charge of your life and overpower your weaknesses. That decision, is the most powerful self-help decision, that you can make.
65) Now ...trust in the Lord to help the One-Percenter in you ...*break out!!*

The Wrestler…

"I've heard a lot about him. They say he's terribly strong and mean.
They say his strength will fool you. At first glance he appears lean.
He wants you to think you can take him, that he's no threat at all.
So he smiles a friendly smile at you, while planning for your fall.
They say that he will toy with you as you wrestle upon his mat,
letting you think you're stronger, while looking to pin you flat.

I don't worry about him, though. I know my own strength. I'm stout!
I've wrestled him many times before. This will prove an easy bout.
I believe I'm in better shape than he, for I win more often than I lose.
And so things don't get out of hand, I'll quit whenever I choose.
Yes, I'm sure I'll be all right and I've come with the intent to win!
He'll be sorry he wrestled me, he'll see that soon after we begin!"

"I heard that." said the Wrestler! "But you forget I know you well!
I'll wrestle you, tire you and lead you, until I drag you down to Hell.
This time I'll use a new tactic. It will be one you haven't seen before.
Maybe this time I'll get you quick and drive you right to the floor!
You believe I care when I lose a match? You think and act so foolishly!
All I care is you keep coming back ...to take another chance with me."

We all think we can wrestle with the Devil, believing we can win.
We do that each time we cross the line and enter the world of sin.
Satan doesn't care if he wins or loses. He's not keeping score.
He is only glad we keep coming back and opening up his door.
Sadly, many like to think they can wrestle him and do quite well,
Only to one day realize that he's made their life ...a living hell.

Ofcr. Samuel Jeppsen, #3751

"No man can enter into a strong man's house and spoil his goods,
except he will first bind the strong man; and then he will spoil his house."
Jesus Christ

Come
Follow Me

The Savior said!
Twenty times in the New Testament,
He said:

Come Follow
Me

"For the Lord God will fulfil his covenants which he has made unto his children…And they shall know that the Lord is God, the Holy One of Israel."

Chapter Twenty-Three

The ALCAN Highway

As Red and I parted company, I headed for Sturgis. My mind was beginning to shift to the great adventure that lay ahead of me. Sturgis is a town I always wanted to visit. I had heard much about this little town. In 1938, it started the tradition of having a motorcycle rally each year. That first year, nine riders showed up. Now, there are about half a million riders that come, each year. It begins the first week of August and riders from all around the U.S. and even the world come to Sturgis. The riders spend so much money, that the townspeople earn ninety-five percent of their yearly income, just during that week. And the state of South Dakota collects over a million dollars in taxes ...*wow!!*

The town of Sturgis is very pretty and peaceful, with a view of the Black Hills, surrounding it. This is the way to enjoy Sturgis—for me anyway! I have never been a partier and I don't like being stuck on clogged streets with long, endless lines of countless motorcycle engines thumping away. I don't like feeling the heat from my engine come upward and knowing that it's over-heating. That's never been my idea of a great ride. But seeing Sturgis, now, was fantastic! It was quaint and reminded me of old town Tempe or old town Gilbert, where the past has been pains-takingly preserved and tradition has been kept alive.

Leaving Sturgis, I crossed Wyoming again and headed for Missoula, Montana. In Billings, I ran into two outlaws by the name of Lizard and Smilin' Bob. They were two other Hoka Hey riders. And to my great surprise, they were traveling slow, like me. To my greater surprise, like me, they were both former cops.

When Smilin' Bob Nesson saw my rider's jacket, with my Blue Knights patch on it, he said, "Are you a Blue Knight?" Blue Knights are the largest law enforcement motorcycle club in the world. I replied, "Yeah." He smiled and said, "Massachusetts 1st." I smiled back and said, "Arizona 6th." As we shook hands, to me it was another sign that the Lord was again, watching over me.

I had met Smilin' Bob in Key West, but he didn't remember me, until I refreshed his memory. As I passed by one of the taverns, inside the Marriott, Travis pulled me in, to say hello to some other riders, he knew. At the bar was this guy, about my age, with a full, gray beard. It was Smilin' Bob. When everyone started laughing, because I was riding the Sportster, the one with the wooden sign on it, saying I was going to Alaska, Bob laughed the loudest. He said, "Yeah, you hope anyway!" The bar was crowded and noisy and he made some other remark about me falling out a few hundred miles after the start. I let him have his laugh before replying, *"No ...I'm going to Alaska!!"*

Actually, I thought Smilin' Bob had a lot of gall, laughing at me, for riding a seven year old, Anniversary Special Sportster. After all, he was riding a 1984, EVO, with over 200,000 miles on it. It had never been cracked open and was still working on its original motor. And he's laughing at me? He's riding a twenty-six year old, tired horse, all the way to Alaska!? Also, I had my stuff bagged in typical rider fashion, with a bag behind me on the seat and one on the luggage rack. Smilin' Bob had his stuff in one *large* bag, which was tied to the rear of his bike. With his white beard, he looked like Santa Claus on a Harley.

Smilin' Bob had been taking pictures throughout the event and had been emailing them home to his wife. She started a blog. There were lots of people who were following his blog online. My brother-in-law, Ted, was one of them.

The other rider, Scott Gillard, aka Lizard, was a boot-wearing Texas cowboy, with a new FL bagger. Lizard was a former Marine. So, to help with the cost of the Hoka Hey, he advertised as a former Marine, needing help. Soon, Lizard received word, that the father of a U.S. Marine anonymously paid his one thousand dollar entry fee. This father's story was such a tragic one. His son was a marine, stationed in Afghanistan. The son was coming home from his tour of duty and was going to ride in the Hoka Hey. But just before his tour ended, he was killed.

Lizard tried to find out who he was, because he wanted to have his son's name painted on his bike. But all he could find out was that his son had been a sergeant in the U.S. Marines. So, to honor him, he painted the word *Sergeant* on his rear fender.

Lizard, referred to me as Stray-dog, because he had picked me up in Billings, along the wayside. He and Smilin' Bob, both, became good friends to me. Since this was our last night in the U.S., we decided to cross into Canada and ride together.

At daybreak, we packed up and crossed over the border, into British Columbia. I was glad for the company, because I was a little troubled about entering and crossing Canada, by myself. You just don't know what problems, you can run into, when you are in a foreign country, even a great one, like Canada. Having been riding alone since Daytona, I now felt the need to ride with a partner. My Dear Friend, the Lord, is watching out for me again, I smilingly thought! In His great love for me, He sent me two riders, who were just like me. They were two old cops, that were taking their time as they rode! To me, it was no coincidence. I have found that to those who believe, He is quick to remember and He is quick to manifest Himself. He still watches over those who don't believe, He's just not as quick with His blessings.

The three of us called ourselves *The Posse*. We had left our guns at home, but we rode in staggered, motor officer fashion and had each other's back, as officers do. About thirty miles past Calgary, we found a closed gas station and coffee shop. We pulled around back at about 1 a.m. and bedded down on their parking lot.

About four hours later, we woke to the sound of semi's pulling into the parking lot. A garbage truck was picking up the ten yard dumpster, about forty feet from where we lay. The coffee shop and gas station were now open.

The customers in the drive-thru were watching us, as they waited in line for their early morning coffee. The employees and the truckers were also watching us. No one had called the police yet. "Well," we said, "it's a good time to get up!!"

We started crawling out of our sleeping bags and packing up. With the several onlookers watching us, I smiled, as I thought about what they must be thinking. This was beginning to be a pattern and I have to admit, I was really enjoying it. There we were, three motorcycle bums from America, sleeping on the parking lot, behind the coffee shop, like a bunch of vagrants.

Since the coffee shop was open, we decided to get a good breakfast. We then rode steady, hit another big storm, but made Dawson Creek by 9:30 that night. Dawson Creek is Mile Zero or the beginning of the Alaska-Canada Highway—more commonly known as the ALCAN!

The road was started three months after the bombing of Pearl Harbor. It took ten thousand engineer soldiers and six thousand private contractors, nine months to complete it.

This was my second time up the ALCAN. As I was riding into Dawson Creek, that same excitement that was with me in Florida, was with me again. I remembered being here in 1972 and standing under the same sign that read, "You Are Now Entering the World Famous Alaska Highway." Finally, here I was again! I couldn't believe I had ridden a bike to the beginning of the famous ALCAN and yet here I was! I was grinning from ear to ear. I felt my heart would burst with the pride and joy, I had inside. I was feeling the same excitement, I felt twenty-eight years ago. Now, twenty-eight years later, I was able to couple those old feelings with the new feelings of being on the Hoka Hey.

It was cold and breezy. It was 9:30 p.m. and the sun was still shining. I was very saddle sore. Despite it all, I felt like a champion and I was bubbling inside with joy. My joy had overridden the cold of the evening and the pain in my rear.

There are few people who have ever traveled this famous road. If I had only made it this far, I would have been happy. But getting to travel it again, this time on a bike, was the beginning of another dream come true and an adventure all it's own.

After spending the night in Dawson Creek, we headed out the next morning, bright and early. Because of a poor decision on my part, an hour later, I was separated from Lizard and Smilin' Bob. I ended up riding alone, the rest of the journey. Even so, the journey had now taken on a whole different meaning for me. I literally existed on sheer excitement and was savoring every mile.

The road is spotted with little settlements, many too small to call a town. Most of them are just a building or two, a gas pump or two and usually a little mom and pop general store. Scattered around the settlement are the homes of the few that live there.

Except for the gas pumps, the stores and the little settlements, I felt like I was living a hundred years ago. It was so quaint and old fashioned and it was quiet.

On the ALCAN, there are no sounds of the city and only an occasional car or truck on the road, would break the silence. I felt like I was living during a time, which had wagon trains and settlers crossing the plains. I could almost imagine bearded trappers, clothed in hides, walking out of the woods, as they headed toward the little general stores. I even imagined one looking at my Harley, scratching his chin and saying, "What kind of contraption is that?"

Here, there were no jeep trails, ATV trails or even distant houses, off the roadway. It was just open land, looking like it had never been walked on before. The beauty of the mountains, the valleys and the greenery stretched forever. I often got off my bike and stood and looked at the countryside. I knew I was seeing the same things as those who had lived a hundred years ago. It was just raw, endless land, opportunity and magnificent beauty mixed with the incredible sights and sounds of nature!

The ALCAN is similar to the road down the Baja, which weaves back and forth following the natural contour of the landscape. Like on the road down the Baja, there is no way to get lost on the ALCAN. If you leave town and are on pavement, you are on the right road. If you leave town and it turns into dirt, turn around and go back, because you're on the wrong road.

There were several times, I was just too sleepy to carry on. So, I would find a wide shoulder of the road or a rest area and stop. I would then lie down next to my bike and sleep for a while, but never more than a few hours. I remember one time, in particular. There was a large semi, a motor home and a fifth wheel travel trailer, in the rest area. I figured I would be safe enough. So, I pulled off, lay down on the ground and fell fast asleep. When I awoke a couple hours later, everyone was gone. I had not heard them leave. I didn't know what time it was, because the days, nights and the hours were now running together.

Thankful that I had been protected during my nap, I got up, stretched and prepared to ride away. As I rode, I remembered from being in Alaska, before, that you lose track of time, because the sun never seems to set. I was losing track of time again and getting less and less sleep, with each passing day.

I wondered what the travelers, from the rest area, thought about seeing some Harley rider, lying on the ground, sleeping next to his bike. Twice on the journey, I had people stop, wake me up and ask me if I was okay. I guess I *was* a little unusual looking.

I arrived in Watson Lake, the gateway to the Yukon Territory, at dusk. In the center of town is a huge collection of homemade road signs, giving directions and distances to cities everywhere. It's quite amusing to read some of them.

Ever since Rock Springs, the nights were cold, but now in the Yukon, they were getting much colder. At 11:00 p.m. that night, I rolled out my sleeping bag on a concrete slab, next to the Watson Lake Post Office, alongside four other Hoka Hey riders. At about 4:00 a.m. in the morning, I awoke. It was raining—again and now I was freezing.

For the very first time on this ride, I woke up and started murmuring. I did not want to get out of my sleeping bag. I was cold and miserable and began complaining and asking myself, "What in the world was I thinking—going on this stupid ride?!!" I just laid there and watched the other riders take off. I guess it was just my day, to have a bad day. I had averaged riding in the rain about every third day. Now, my first day in the Yukon and it was not only raining, I was freezing—*in July!!!*

Thankfully that feeling and my complaining only lasted for about ten minutes. I finally shook it off and changed my attitude. I forced myself to stop my sniveling and then forced myself out of my bag. I put on my long-johns, two long sleeve t-shirts, two short sleeve t-shirts, my long sleeve denim shirt, my pants, chaps, fleece vest, heaviest leather jacket and covered it all with my rain suit. Then, I put on my warmest leather insulated gantlet gloves. When I finally stopped shivering, I fired up my bike, threw my leg over the saddle …and rode across the street for breakfast.

66) Be positive. It is a decision you make. …Inspire yourself.

Chapter Twenty-Four

"Yeah, I'm one of them"

After breakfast, I started looking for Lizard and Smilin' Bob. We had gotten separated on day two of the ALCAN. I happened to find them, in the center of town. At Watson Lake we decided to take different routes. They wanted to save a couple hundred miles and take the alternative and shorter route down the Tok cutoff. I wanted to stay on the ALCAN to Fairbanks, make the last check point and then head for North Pole, to visit family. They were still packing up, so after some goodbyes, I continued on up the ALCAN and headed for Fairbanks.

From the time I had left Calgary, I noticed the longer days and the shorter and shorter nights. Watson Lake is much farther north than Calgary. The dusk-type nighttime in the Yukon was now, very obvious. It was no longer getting completely dark at night. Instead, the nights were just a little darker than dusk.

The sun circles around the sky, fairly close to the horizon and after making almost a full circle, dips under the horizon for a few hours and then comes back up, repeating the same pattern. It's as if it were morning or evening all day long, with no crossing sun or noonday. The sun is just in a different place, along the horizon.

The upside to the longer days, was that it made riding conditions safer. So I rode and rode, feasting on the incredible scenery. It never became dull, typical or monotonous. Around each bend, began a new adventure. Trying to take it all in, was like feasting at a king's table and never getting full.

The Southwest, where I live, is a different kind of beauty. We have lots of browns with jagged, rocky mountains, deserts, cactus, plains and prairies. We have clear skies and some of the most beautiful sunrises and sunsets in the world! On the ALCAN, the scenery is mostly green and the skies are often overcast. In fact, it is lots and lots of green with beautiful and majestic blue-gray mountains that often pierce the clouds above!

At Haines Junction, staring at the incredibly beautiful snowcapped mountains, just south of town, I almost missed my turn. Haynes Junction is small. If you pass through there, make sure you watch the signs, stay on "Highway 1" and make sure you turn right at the Shell station. It will seem like you're making a wrong turn, but if you don't turn, it could be several miles before you realize you're going the wrong way. Much of the Haines Road is paved and the invitation from the mountains to keep coming straight ahead is very luring.

About fifty-five miles later, I came out of the mountains to Kluane Lake and hit one of the many road construction projects, along the ALCAN. I was about ten miles, outside of Destruction Bay. At a road repair site, I asked the flagman, why it was called Destruction Bay. He didn't know. Destruction Bay is one of the larger of the small communities, dotting the ALCAN. It has a gas station, a coffee shop, a motel and an RV resort. Their population in 2005 was fifty-nine and it looked to be the same now.

At the little gas station and coffee shop, I asked the waitress, why it was called Destruction Bay and she didn't know, either. I picked up a post card in the coffee shop and read that the community got its name given to it, by the U.S. Army, in 1942. The place was the command post for the U.S. Army Corp of Engineers, during the ALCAN construction project.

Kluane Lake is a very large lake. The Army used it to fly in equipment and supplies. In 1942, a hundred mile per hour wind destroyed their camp. Thus the Army dubbed the location, Destruction Bay. Interestingly, the nickname became permanent.

For approximately one hundred miles, from Destruction Bay to about ten miles past the Alaskan border, the ALCAN was in extremely bad condition, due to the frost heave. According to the people in Destruction Bay, the damage was the worst in forty-two years. There were holes, ruts, trenches and fallen sections all along the way. I rode much slower and missed as much as I could, but still bottomed out my shocks, no less than several dozen times, during that one hundred mile journey. The last time I had seen roads this bad, was when I was in Guatemala.

Despite the extremely bad road and the tremendous jarring, the beauty was worth every bump and jag. As I rode, dodging this one and that one, I noticed that everyone I saw was using both sides of the road to dodge the worst of the damage. There was just so much of it and even at best, you could only miss most of it. I was told that there were about a half dozen Hoka Hey riders that lost control and went down on that stretch between Destruction Bay and the Alaskan border.

I kept pushing and made Tok, Alaska, by 11:30 that night. While gassing up, I watched the sun, still on the horizon. I was amazed that the sun was just now setting. I took a picture of it, still shining over the town and then looked for a place to sleep. Though very sore and really tired, I was also excited, because this had been my longest mile day. If I continue on, I thought, I can have a 1000 mile day to my credit. *It's a motorcycle thing*. But I was so tired that I needed some sleep, before I moved on. I looked around and found an empty picnic table, in the city park, across from the Chevron. So I climbed on top of the table, laid down and fell fast asleep. I had been riding for about twenty hours and with the jarring and all the bumps ...everything hurt.

Over an hour later, I woke up very damp. I had forgotten about the heavy, settling dew. I hadn't experienced it in Watson Lake, because I had slept under the awning. Now, everything felt wet and my leather jacket and chaps were damp and gummy. So I got up, put on my rain gear once more and continued toward Fairbanks. I actually needed to get to Fairbanks, within the remaining three hours, to have my 1000 mile day.

At Fairbanks, I made the final checkpoint. I also ran into Eden, a nurse from Tucson, Arizona. Eden was a Hoka Hey rider that I had met in Key West and once again, in Watson Lake. She was amazing. She was also sleeping in a small ditch along the dirt road, alongside her bike. Nearby was a rider with a flat tire.

After signing in, I headed for the town of North Pole to visit my family. I was excited on two accounts. First, that I had made my 1000 mile day and second, because I was able to visit Steve and Alisa, whom I had not seen in years. Alisa is Julie's sister. I had known both of them, since their teens.

I spent the day and night with Steve and Alisa, in their beautiful home by the lake, before continuing on my journey and heading for Homer. *Ahhhh* ...a hot shower, good food and a bed!

Fairbanks doesn't get dark at that time of the summer, instead, it has almost twenty-four hours of light. Headlights can hardly be seen on the roadway in front of you and you can actually see just fine without them.

The next morning, about 4 a.m., with the sun close to the horizon, but shining bright, I awoke and headed south across the Alaskan Range to Anchorage. Though feeling much better physically, I was still very tired and groggy.

Leaving North Pole, heading for Fairbanks and then toward the Alaska Range for Anchorage, I stopped to top off my gas tank, before climbing the mountains. Within just a few minutes after I had filled up, the bike started running terrible and started smoking. With every shift, came a puff of smoke out the pipes. At first, I thought my little friend was giving out on me. Fearing she was tired from the long, hard journey, I thought she must have broken a ring or blew a seal inside the engine. There was a noticeable drop in horsepower too. So I prayed and kept riding. I was afraid to turn off the engine, for fear it would not start again.

Approximately a hundred miles later, I stopped for more fuel. It was then, that I realized what had happened. South of Fairbanks, I had grabbed the wrong handle and topped off my two gallons of gasoline with a gallon of diesel fuel. When I filled the tank with gasoline, she quickly began running better and within a few tanks, was running perfect again. My little friend was just fine but that experience made me realize, just how mentally fatigued I was getting. It was a real wake up call for me.

As I rode the Alaskan Range, I saw only one other rider. He was a Hoka Hey rider by the name of Greg. I had noticed his unusual bike in Key West. It was a homemade looking Hardtail. A Hardtail is a bike that has no rear suspension.

I had seen Greg in Rock Springs, Wyoming. Being an interesting looking fellow, I went over to meet him. When I asked him what year his bike was, he said, "Take your pick! I made it from parts from almost every year." When I said, "It's a Hardtail! It doesn't have any suspension!!" He smiled and pushed on his seat with his hand and showed me that his seat gave a little. He then said, "See…, it has suspension!" I smiled back. His gas tank had been a 6.5 gallon tank. Because we were not allowed tanks larger than 6.25 gallons, Greg knocked two dents in his, to make it a 6.25. …Hmmm! …Very creative!

While crossing the Alaskan Range, I saw Greg's bike alongside the road at a gas station and country store. I stopped because I was freezing. Greg had also stopped because of the cold. This gave me a chance to learn more about this interesting fellow.

Greg had every appearance of being the stereotypical auto mechanic, you would have seen in the late forties. The exact kind you would occasionally see on *Happy Days* or *Gomer Pile USMC* or the *Andy Griffith Show*. He was about forty years old, wore a greasy baseball cap, with the bill rolled up and full overalls. He had a full beard, at least three inches long. He also had black grease packed under his fingernails. He had grease in the cracks of his skin and his overalls were spotted with grease stains.

I could tell he was pretty much a loner and was for the most part, very quiet. He was also very well mannered, soft spoken and very kind. Greg had an interestingly calm demeanor. He didn't use foul language, was very polite and didn't smoke or drink coffee. I learned he was from Idaho. Like me, he loved bikes and was here to fulfill a dream. He had also once lived in Alaska.

Through the little I had learned about him, I had the distinct feeling that someplace there were some very loving parents who had taught him well and now spend a lot of hours on their knees praying for their son. I didn't think he was a bad fellow or outlaw of any sort, only that he had taken a different path, perhaps a wayward one. I felt that, though Greg was probably a wanderer, he was blessed to have parents that wanted so very much for him. I felt a feeling of watch-care over him and that angels were with him, even in his waywardness. Inside me, was a feeling I was talking to a prodigal son.

That opportunity to visit with Greg, made me realize that one of the great prizes of this journey was meeting all the different people from all different walks of life. They were not wealthy people or even well to do people. They were not gang members or outlaws or even competitors for the half million dollars. Most of them seemed to be everyday, kind hearted people, trying to make it through life the best they could and were here living out a dream. Simply said, they were just good people with good hearts.

After leaving Greg and continuing south for about fifty miles, I pulled over to use a roadside J-Jon. Greg who had been behind, pulled over with me to check on my welfare. By now, checking on each other was common with Hoka Hey riders.

The time he pulled over to check on me, was the last time, I ever saw Greg. I know he made it, because I saw his name on the roster. He will be a fellow I will always remember, because of his unique personality and very kind, quiet manner. Most of all, I will remember the feeling I felt, when I was around him, that loving parents were praying over him and angels were with him.

Within minutes after climbing back on my bike, it began to rain. It rained for the next one hundred miles. Just before Wasilla, I pulled over at a convenience store to stop, eat and dry out a little. A fellow in the store started talking to me. After realizing that I was one of the Hoka Hey riders, he said I should stop in at the local Harley Shop and meet the people. He said, "They would love to meet you." I smiled and said I would love to, but I was getting close to my deadline and had to move along.

When I pulled into Wasilla, I saw a rider and his girl on a clean, bright blue, late model, FL. I noticed that they were riding alongside and looking me over. After about a mile, he pulled closer and asked if I was going to continue to ride or if I was going to stop and get something to eat. I was surprised at the question and said, "I'm a Hoka Hey Rider enroute to Homer." He replied, "I know, I just wanted to know if you were going to stop and get something to eat?" I smiled and told him that because of my deadline, I had to keep moving.

I was surprised he knew I was a Hoka Hey rider. But maybe at this point it was obvious. By now, we were all looking terribly battered and road worn. Our bikes were extremely filthy and over loaded with bags that were bungee-corded on. We all looked like *Then Came Bronson* on his very worst day. It also made me realize, that the Alaskans knew we were there. From then on, it was one similar experience after another.

In Anchorage, a group of local riders pulled in behind me and followed me for a while. On the Seward Highway a trucker pulled up alongside me, beeped his horn and gave me a big smile and a thumbs-up. When I stopped for gas, people seemed to be watching me. A few miles later, a local rider on a clean, red FL, pulled alongside me, beeped and gave me the same sign. At the gas station at the Portage Glacier turn off, I was pumping fuel and the young lady in the next island smiled and said, "You're one of them, aren't you?!" Having already had a similar question in Vernal, I smiled back and said simply, "Yeah, I'm one of them."

The feeling of being *One of Them* cannot be explained. To be part of the Hoka Hey, a group of adventurers that rode across America, Canada and then Alaska and went through all we went through, was thrilling. To be part of the biggest, longest and most grueling ride in the world and now to stand there and hear her say, "You're one of them, aren't you?!" was a rush! There is just no other way to say it. It was a rush! The feeling of pride, of being a part of something, of having done something, never having been done before, was incredible. I could almost feel my leather jacket ripping open, from the swelling of my chest. I was dirty. I stunk. I was tired and sore, but …*yeah …I'm one of them!!*

All the way down the Kenai Peninsula, the reactions of the people were the same. One person after another, in each of the little stops along the way, would come up and talk to me. I even had some want to buy me food or offer me something to drink. Each wanted to talk with me. I was also running into other Hoka Hey riders, who like me, were heading down the last two hundred mile leg of the journey. It was like Victory Lane, with people all along the way, waving, cheering us on and wanting to talk.

As I traveled the lower end of the Peninsula, where the road runs near the shoreline for miles, I often looked across the huge, Cook Inlet on my right. It was big and beautiful. On the other side, miles away, were majestic, blue, snowcapped mountains. I wondered what Captain James Cook must have thought, as he floated into this huge bay. I was impressed that he had been the first European to have contact with the people of Alaska, Hawaii, eastern Australia and much of New Zealand. I thought about what an adventurer he was and how in my own way, I too, was an adventurer who had done what had not been done before. The sleepy, little settlements along the way, seemed to whisper to me that I was still very much an adventurer …in a wilderness.

As I rounded that last, left-hand curve that drops down into Homer, I was able to see almost the entire town below. The little town lay nestled into the mountainside, as it faced the bay. I knew that even if my bike broke down now, I could push it across the finish line. I had made it! I had actually made it!! So many things had to happen for me to be able to be here! So many things had to work out! Yet, they all did and here I was riding down the hill and into Homer! I had left the town of North Pole, just after 4:30 a.m. and pulled into Homer at about 8:30 p.m.

I had ridden a little over six hundred miles that day, with about one hundred miles of it in the rain. From Anchorage on, I experienced the mixed feelings and emotions of bringing the journey to an end. "I'm just a few miles away!" I said. "It's almost over!" The big dream was now just a few miles away from being complete. I had waited years for this moment, I had even dreamed of it and now here it was.

Suddenly, as I realized that it was almost over, a strange feeling came over me and I wasn't sure how to handle it. It was almost a feeling of remorse and apprehension. I slowed my pace and almost stopped. I wanted to turn around. I did not want to let my journey end. Feeling similar to a buyer's remorse, I shook it off, began smiling again and then rolled on the throttle.

As I rode through Homer, looking at the little shops and businesses and homes along the way, I was impressed with its calm feeling and beauty. The town of Homer gets its name from Homer Pennock, a gold-seeker, who came to Alaska during the Alaskan Gold Rush. He later went north to join the Klondike Gold Rush. Homer claims to be just over twenty-two square miles, but almost half of that is ocean. …Interesting claim!

Homer, nick-named *The End of The Road* is just two and a half square miles bigger than Key West. But where Key West has a population of over twenty-five thousand, Homer has a little over five thousand.

Throughout the last two hundred miles of the trip, I could not suppress the overwhelming feelings of love and gratitude I had for the Lord. He had remembered my boyhood dreams and He had opened door after door for me. One by one, He had created opportunities that allowed me to go. I had been watched over as I rode along and slept at night alongside the highway! The Lord had been my Shepherd and my Guiding Light! The angels of darkness had been kept at bay! I had no mechanical failures of any kind, no problems with people and no accidents or near misses. I had been allowed to live the dream, I had for over forty-five years. It was my very own tender mercy moment with the Lord and I was basking in every bit of it.

My soul flooded with these emotions as I now rode through the streets of Homer. Gratitude! Extreme gratitude to the Lord was now coursing my veins for Him allowing me to experience what I was now feeling inside.

I felt like the victor of a great battle. I felt as if I were General Douglas MacArthur on his slow ride down Pennsylvania Avenue, in 1932. Though there were no marching bands or parades to meet him, the streets and sidewalks were filled with cheering crowds as he passed by. They were crowds that came specifically, just to see him. Leaning out the windows of the buildings along the way were even more onlookers. All of them wanted to welcome their gallant, war hero, home.

Now, coming in on the Sterling Highway, turning down Ocean Drive, passing homes, businesses and intersections on my *own* slow-ride, I was the one that they were standing along the street and sidewalks and leaning out the windows to watch ride by. I was astonished at what I was seeing. It was *me* who was the great warrior and it was *me* they were looking at! I was dirty and tired from battle, but gleaming with pride. I was accompanied by the sight and smell of victory that adorns every soldier, as he ceremoniously walks off the battlefield.

As I rode the last few miles, I could hear the cheers and applause of those I passed by. I watched as several of the local community members ran into the street to take my picture. Me!! They were wanting to take a picture of me!! The old guy on the Sportster from Queen Creek, Arizona!!

There were newscasters with microphones, wanting to ask me questions, but I continued on, slowly pressing forward, ever forward! I continued slowly making my way past the women, which were waving and throwing kisses and the men that were looking at me in envy, as if I were a great victor! Then there were the little children. The ever abundant children, who smiled and waved and looked at me, as if I were a live action hero! I smiled and waved back as I rode along.

There had been seven checkpoints and seven maps. The maps were like treasure maps, where we needed to decipher clues, watch for landmarks and follow the dotted line. There had been long days and sleepless nights, rainstorms, dirt and destroyed roads and extreme fatigue, all to find the treasure. And I had finally found it. It was right here, right now, as I rode down this stretch of the journey through Homer. The cheers, the smiles and the waves, I was getting from the crowds, were worth everything it cost me, to get here. It was my moment on stage and the townspeople I passed by, was the cheering audience in an overcrowded auditorium.

Well …kinda anyway.

In reality, there was not much going on. The streets were bare. People were inside their homes, probably eating and watching television. No one looked or smiled or seemed to care as I rode down the streets, all alone. But it didn't matter. It was my dream come true and my Best Friend the Lord was with me. He had been with me every step of the way! I had never been left alone and I could feel my trust in Him had moved up to the next level! I felt that I had been on a long and arduous journey toward my own Promised Land. As I rode along, savoring every mile, I couldn't help but wonder if I was feeling what they in the Scriptures had felt, who had been led to *their* Promised Land.

Wondering about the feelings they must have felt, I thought of the Scripture that says, "After ye have arrived in the promised land, ye shall know that I, the Lord, am God; and that I, the Lord, did deliver you from destruction." I then reflected upon the very words that were given me when I began this event. They were, "The way is open and you will be safe." And every bit of that promise had come to pass.

As my thoughts began to turn back to my own entrance into my own Promised Land, I realized I was smiling and inside I was jumping with sheer excitement. I began laughing out loud as I rode and I raised my visor to feel the cool breeze in my face. As I was laughing, I thought, it's true! Only a motorcycle rider can understand why a dog sticks his head out the car window! The thought made me laugh even more. As I continued riding, as the dream continued to unfold in front of me, it was all I could do to not begin yelling, *"…YAAA-HOOO!! …YAAA-HOOO!!"* I had been victorious and the moment was mine! In my mind, there *were* crowds and they *were* waving and cheering me on. I was beaming from ear to ear as I rode along and looked into their faces. I then began looking for Spit Road. Then finally …I saw it.

First Spit Road, and then almost 8,500 miles after leaving Key West, there it was. The banner that read,

"Finish"

67) Love God, take Him at His word, go after life …and see the adventure in everything you dream and do.

Chapter Twenty-Five

The Journey of a Thousand Miles

If it is true to say that the journey of a thousand miles begins with the first step, it is just as true to say that the first step must be the dream. The dream is that formulation of an idea that starts as a hope, becomes a burning desire and never goes away.

Riding in this 8500 mile motorcycle challenge didn't begin on Fathers Day, in Key West. It began when I was fourteen years old. Crossing the finish line on July 3rd, 2010 at about 8:45 in the evening, was the culmination of years of hopes and dreams. When I stood under the banner and had my picture taken, all those years of feelings were still with me. I don't know if I have words to express the feelings, I felt at that moment. I can only suppose that the rush of emotions inside me then, were as anyone else's, who has experienced a long awaited dream come to pass.

My first thought, as I stood under the banner, was again one of deep gratitude to the Lord, for remembering my dream and for taking the time and effort, to help fulfill a dream, which was only important to Him, because it was important to me. I have learned that if we make His passion, our passion, He will make our passion, His passion. He's truly that way!

I was grateful for all the gifts and special moments, He gave me along the way. Most importantly, I was grateful for the lessons in listening and following the Spirit, which began in December of 2009. At that time, all I had in one hand, was an impossible dream and in the other hand, a little feeling that said, *"The way is open and you will be safe."*

When I arrived in Homer, my celebration party was getting to talk with the fifty or so riders, there. My celebration meal was a poor quality hot dog, fresh off the grill, handed to me with love.

The actual celebration party was taking place the following night, on Sunday. After checking in, taking some pictures and visiting with others, I rode around until about midnight. I was engulfed in all the beauty of this little town that lay nestled against the green, rolling hills, on the edge of the ocean.

The town was calm. The streets were almost bare and the thumping of my motorcycle (or someone else's) was all I could hear. The shops were closed, the sidewalks were empty and I had to remind myself that it was late. At 11:30 at night, I stopped to take some photos of the strikingly gorgeous, blue sunset over the distant blue-colored mountains, eastward up Kachemak Bay. I knew that sunrise would be starting in a couple of hours. I needed to stop riding and find a place to sleep.

As I began looking for a spot to bed down, I thought, when would I ever again be able to sleep on the Spit? So I found a good place on the beach, on the west side of Spit Road and set up my tent. I crawled inside, listened to the water lap against the shore and was soon sound asleep.

Just before 6 a.m., I awoke and began making plans for the day. One of the things I so enjoyed, about this trip was the ability to plan each day as it came. In my *real* life, everything has to be preplanned. I have to live by calendars, cell phones, projects and deadlines. Here, I was living week by week, day by day and hour by hour. I did what I felt like doing, went where I felt like going, slept when I was sleepy and woke up when I was done sleeping. I was enjoying my new freedom, as I lay there in my tent.

Not really excited about a party, I decided to return to North Pole and spend the extra time with my family, rather than stay for the celebration. Staying for the party would have cost me a whole extra day, unless I was willing to start my six hundred mile journey afterwards and cross the Alaskan Range, at night.

Though riding on Sunday, is usually something I try to avoid, I have always really enjoyed touring on motorcycles for their therapeutic value. On a bike, the world becomes peaceful. I travel the living art gallery of the Lord and listen to the wind and the gentle thumping of my engine. It is my great escape, the chance to clear my mind and to be with the Savior.

Riding is one of my most effective tools for decompressing and meditation. It brings a serenity that few other activities can bring me. Literally everything I look at, testifies of Christ.

When I didn't have a bike, it was my tractor. I could get on my tractor, drop the disc in a field, pull the throttle open and then escape into a very peaceful realm, where it was just me and the Lord. It was in those moments, that I could be totally alone with Him. There were no phone calls to take, no problems to solve and no emergencies. There was nothing that could not wait, until I was done with the field. With the groaning of the motor and the gentle swaying of the tractor, I could be a thousand miles away.

With that expectation in mind and today being Sunday, I was really looking forward to being with the Lord, on my journey north. So I got up, packed my gear on the bike and rode away. As I traveled north on Spit Road, I was struggling with changing my mind and waiting instead for the party. After all, I had come so far and the party was only a couple miles away and at 4 p.m. But when I made that left turn, at the top of Spit Road, instead of turning right and heading up the Kachemak, toward Millers Landing, I left the party behind and mentally began my Sabbath with the Savior.

As I climbed the hill that led out of town, I stopped, got off the bike and took one last look. As I quietly stood there, I began remembering all the feelings of yesterday. The word, Alaska, is an Americanized word for the Russian word, *Alyeska*. It means, *the Great Land*. As I stood alongside my bike, overlooking the town and inlet below, I could feel the meaning of that Russian word, *Alyeska.* I raised my camera and captured the moment.

After a few minutes of reflection, I turned, threw my leg over my bike and rode away. Only a half mile later, I found Lizard alongside the road, starting the day, as well. I stopped and we embraced and said our goodbyes. After the party, he was flying home and shipping his bike back. Smilin' Bob was still asleep. He would be taking the Cassiar Highway home. Though the Posse had disbanded, the friendships, would last a lifetime. In our homes, the other would always be welcome and in our hearts we would always be ...*The Posse*.

Riding up the Kenai along Cook Inlet, early Sunday morning, was very peaceful. It was quiet and still. The little shops and towns, along the way, were not yet awake, so as I rode, I found myself unencumbered by traffic, shoppers or tourists.

My morning was filled with beautiful scenery. The only things that were moving, were the clouds overhead. Just before Cooper Landing, I decided to pull over, take my time and enjoy my day. To lie down alongside the road and just stare at the sky above and take in the beauty of the mountains, was like being in Heaven. As I lay there gazing at the sky and watching the clouds, I began to ponder what all had taken place and what was *about* to take place. For many, the adventure was over. For me, a brand new adventure was beginning. As I got up off the ground and again threw my leg over the bike and hit the starter, I began—The Ride Home!!

Every passing mile went well, but shortly after Anchorage, it began to sprinkle *...again.* I stopped and suited up in my rain gear. I rode through Wasilla and started making the climb up into the Alaskan Range. A few hours later, I entered Denali Park. The word, Denali, is Eskimo for *the high one* or *the great one.* Denali Park is the home of Mt. McKinley. At 23,000 feet, it is the highest mountain in North America and the third highest in the world. I have ridden through Colorado as well, and like Alaska, Colorado is incredibly beautiful. Amazingly, Colorado has fifty-four majestic mountains that are over 14,000 feet. Even so, Alaska has eleven, which are thousands of feet higher.

To my dismay, when I entered Denali Park, it was heavily overcast with dark, angry, black clouds sitting on the lower mountains. I felt as if they were only a few hundred feet above my head. As I worked my way through the park, I began hoping they would not open up on me. I didn't want to find myself in the middle of a huge, ugly storm that stretched as far as I could see.

As I rode, I started looking for openings between the mountains, hoping there might be a way out and that I might beat the dark, impending storm. Mile after mile, through the Denali, I kept looking and praying. Every so often, I would see a break in the mountains, where a logical pass would be. However, in every possible pass, there were dark clouds with heavy rain. As the road would drift toward each pass, I would pray, "Oh Heavenly Father, please not that one! It's pouring in that pass! But if that's where I have to go, please provide a way through for me."

That was literally my prayer each time and I spoke those words, with all the humility of a child, asking a loving parent for a huge favor. To my great relief, the road kept slowly twisting and turning and kept passing by each one of those passes.

After what seemed like a hundred miles of looking, hoping and praying for a dry way out, up ahead I began to see sunlight. It seemed about fifteen miles away. It too, was covered with heavy black storm clouds, but it was the only pass that had a small portion of sunlight peering through.

I started hoping and praying that the road out was through that pass. Closer and closer, turn after turn, it came and when I made that last turn into Cantwell, I was now looking straight at the opening. Still several miles away, I was sure it was the way out. I gassed up in Cantwell and quickly kept riding, hoping to exit the mountains before the heavy black clouds let loose on me.

The road turned and twisted back and forth, but finally, I started heading down hill. Closer and closer I came to the opening that led to the light of day. Finally, there I was, out of the Denali and completely through the dry pass and heading into the lower mountains. I had totally escaped the storms. That opening in the blackened sky was so spiritual to me, that I not only thanked my Heavenly Father for it, I got off my bike and took a picture of it. When I made it through the opening, I stopped and took another picture of the sun bursting through the black clouds.

Adding to my great experience was an owl perched on top of a tree. He was just sitting there, looking at me, as if to say, "All is well. The Lord is with you! All is well." Though it was not a dove, with an olive leaf in its mouth, to me, it was what the dove was to Noah. It meant that much to me. So I took a picture of my little friend on top of the tree, then waved goodbye and rode on.

My life's experiences with the Savior can be likened to that single experience in the Denali. Whenever I am surrounded by dark, looming storms and I have no one to go to and nowhere to turn, all I have to do is pray …and up ahead …will be a light.

As I left the dark and threatening clouds behind and now rode under clear skies, I thought of what Luke recorded when the Savior was baptized. He said a voice from heaven said, "This is my beloved Son: hear Him." To me, it meant I am to always look to the Savior. When the Savior dictated to John the Revelator and said, "To him that overcometh will I grant to sit with me in My throne, even as I also overcame, and am set down with My Father in His throne," to me, it meant that if I follow the Savior, I can live with Him and my Heavenly Father forever. I smiled as I rolled the throttle on and thought …it is indeed …a good day to ride!

My formula for seeking help from the Savior has always been that simple. First I pray, then I believe, then I listen and then I keep moving forward. Lastly, I watch for the miracle to happen. It is that simple and it always works.

During the last one hundred sixty miles to North Pole, the skies were much prettier and less threatening. I arrived at Steve and Alisa's home, sometime after midnight. Afterwards, I looked out their big picture window and saw a beautiful double rainbow in the eastern sky. I pointed it out and then took a picture of it. To me, as soon as I saw it—it was a salute! It was the kind of salute that comes from a Dear Friend, wearing a smile, after doing you a big favor and who is actually saying, *"You're welcome!"*

That was one of the best Sundays, I have ever spent in my entire life. It is one I will always remember. I may have been on a motorcycle and not in Church where I belonged, but even so, I had just passed through a very personal experience with the Lord. It was one that catapulted my faith forward. It was another reminder, that I can *always* turn to Christ.

In North Pole, I finally got some very much needed rest and deep sleep. I then spent the day embarrassing Alisa, by the way I looked. She drove me around Fairbanks, showing me the sights, as if I were the governor himself. She is a very remarkable person. She has had Multiple Sclerosis for several years and has to work very hard to keep the symptoms at bay. Even so, she's always happy and excited about life. She has always been incredibly positive, regardless of the situation. As we traveled together, she was never embarrassed of me and took me place after place. In my own trials and troubles, I have tried to remember her remarkable and indomitable spirit and have tried to be more like her.

As we rode around, I thought about the great State of Alaska and the time I had been here before. Alaska has over one hundred thousand glaciers, three million lakes and is only fifty-five miles from Russia. Alaska stirs something within me. I am not sure how to explain it, but it is like the *Call of the Wild.* It is incredibly rural, uninhabited and enormously beautiful.

In every other state I have ridden, cities and towns are usually, not too far apart. In between them, the landscape is dotted with rural communities, little farms or little dirt roads running off in some direction. Alaska is not that way. It is twice the size of Texas and saying it is remote, is a huge understatement.

From Fairbanks to Wasilla, is about three hundred miles with basically just outposts with maybe a general store and a gas pump. There is very little else in between. I didn't see any roads that take off into the outback, no little farms along the way, no anything …just Alaska! From Fairbanks to the Canadian border is about three hundred miles of the same thing. On the trip up, I passed the town of Tok, with fifteen hundred people and Delta Junction with one thousand people. Everything else in between is Alaska, just as it was one thousand years ago!

Just before leaving Steve and Alisa's, I refigured my one thousand mile day, from Watson Lake to Fairbanks. With no surprise to me, I realized I had made a mistake. My math is something I always have to double check. When I did, I found that my one thousand mile day was in reality, only a nine hundred and twenty-two mile day. So I packed my bike and prepared to take off! This time, I was determined to make a one thousand mile day. After all, what motorcycle rider, anywhere, could have better bragging rights, than to say he had a one thousand mile day on the ALCAN?! The thought was exhilarating!

After two days in Fairbanks, I headed through North Pole, onto the Richardson Highway, barely missing a moose and pressed on to Tok. I passed Tom and Jerry Lane and then headed for the Canadian border. At the border, I greeted the American border agent. As he looked me over and asked me a few questions, I turned around to take one last look at Alaska. I said goodbye to the state, which became a state, when I was in the second grade. Because Alaska stretches into the eastern hemisphere, it is also America's most east and most west state. I have loved Alaska since my first visit in 1971. "I'll be back." I said. "I'll be back!"

After my last, long look, I gave one more wave to the border agent, let the clutch out, gave my trusty steed some gas and entered the Yukon Territory. I was now totally focused on having a one thousand mile day. I had tried several other times in the States to have a one thousand mile day, but it's hard on a Sportster. It's even harder if you don't take freeways—and I don't. It is also very difficult because riding at night, staring into a black hole, trying to stay awake is boring and dangerous. So this time, I was very determined to make it for sure. Though I couldn't travel any longer between stops, because my tank was small, I could spend less time at every stop and I could forgo eating meals.

Trying for a one thousand mile day in the *Land of the Midnight Sun* was much easier to stay awake, than it was in the States. The reason it's easier, is because it never gets dark up there in the summer. In Phoenix the days get longer or shorter by a minute a day, thirty minutes a month. In Anchorage and most of the ALCAN, it's *four minutes* a day, *two hours* a month.

But, the ALCAN also has three big downsides. One is the speed limit, which is 100 kilometers an hour (60ish.) Another is the road conditions. Besides the frost heave damage from Alaska to Destruction Bay, there are a lot of construction areas, some with pilot cars, leading single lane traffic, through the repair work.

The third downside to the ALCAN, is the animals. On just the ALCAN alone, on the road or on the shoulder, I saw nineteen moose, one elk, about a dozen mountain goats, a dozen or more caribou, about fifty actual wild buffalo, two or three mountain sheep, seven bears, two foxes and one cougar. Consequently, between the hours of 11:30 p.m. and 2 a.m., when the sun dips under the horizon and becomes dusk, I slowed down and rode between forty and forty-five miles an hour. I traveled in third and fourth gear, dropped my RPM and strained to spot the animals, along the shoulder, before they ran in front of me. I'll never understand why a frightened animal will run in front of a vehicle, crossing the sound that scares them, instead of running away from the sound. But animals often do, just as several of these did.

Ninety-five percent of my meals, throughout the entire journey, consisted of trail mix, jerky and water. I ate, while I was filling up my tank with gas. I didn't speed because usually, I try not to, especially in another country and especially when I'm trying for a record. My plan was to stay in the saddle, stay awake and keep riding.

At the Shell station in Haines, I ran into about a dozen riders from Whitehorse, on shiny BMW's and Goldwings. Each one had a really clean and very nice bike. Surprisingly, I found I had a hard time getting a conversation going with them. If you are a rider, usually you can easily strike up a conversation with other riders. But trying to get a conversation going with these riders was tough. They would answer my questions, but not say much more. They would then turn back to their friends. Each question I asked, resulted in a similar, short and direct answer. I felt certain that my filthy bike and my badly deteriorated looks were the problem.

As I stood there, thinking about their responses, I got my first clue, of just how much my appearance was getting in the way of being fairly judged by others. I could tell, these nicely dressed riders on their nice, clean Goldwings and BMW's, didn't think much of this grubby looking guy on his mud-packed Harley.

The Yukon is extremely beautiful and gave me the same *Call of the Wild* feel that Alaska did. As remote and uninhabited as Alaska is, the Yukon is even more so. It's about twenty-five percent larger than the state of California and has one paved road, one city, two towns and about twelve settlements. Yup!! In fact, it has six times more caribou than people, twenty thousand more moose than people and one bear for every two people *...wowzers!*

I rode mile after mile, enjoying every inch of beauty along the way. My head could not stop turning from side to side, as I tried to take it all in. Suddenly, to my right was a glimpse of one of the most breathtaking scenes, I had ever seen before. I slowed, turned around and went back to what seemed to be, a window into another world. I turned off the motor, got off the bike and feasted on the beauty before me and the silence around me.

It was a narrow view between two hills that hid a small lake on the other side. I had been riding all night and the new day was dawning. The air was crisp, the sun was low and the shadows were long. The downward hillside in front of me, rapidly fell off into a canyon, which started at the edge of the road and made its way toward the lake. In front of me and on each side of the lake were two large hills that were covered with beautiful green, heavy undergrowth. There were hundreds of dark green pine trees that protruded upward toward the sky. The new sun had not yet fallen upon the hillsides. The water in the lake was a baby-blue color and was so calm that it was almost a perfect mirror. The water on the lake had only a slight shimmer and the trees on the far bank, were outlined in the water and reached out into the lake.

On the far side of the lake was a tall, rock and tree covered mountain, which caught the low sun and lit up like a beacon in the dawning of the new day. The long mountain bore the striking resemblance of Mt. Timpanogos, the *Sleeping Maiden*, in Utah. Part of the legend, was that a beautiful Indian maiden had climbed up the mountain to wait for her Nez Perce warrior to come and claim her hand. While she waited, she slept and her long hair can be seen flowing off her head and down the mountain side.

I had climbed Mt. Timpanogos, as a boy scout. Now, here was the beautiful maiden's twin, on the far side of the lake, bathing in the early morning, Canadian sun.

The sky above me was clear. The reflection of the sky, somehow, made its way through the singular cloud that lay over the lake in front of me. It was as if someone had unfolded a huge cotton blanket and covered the entire lake with it. The color of the blanket was baby-blue, with only a few specks of white. It seemed to be a hundred feet thick and maybe two hundred feet off the water. The cloud was almost a perfect outline of the lake itself. The blanket seemed to be trying to protect the lake from the rising sun, which would soon be upon its beautiful blue face.

The silence and serenity around me, held me like a magnet, as I stared at the beauty in front of me. I was in awe of the art work of the Lord. I found myself thinking of Him and the many things He had put in place that seemed to be just for me. I thought of the trials that had been before me and the obstacles that said this journey was impossible. I thought of the disappointments and the no's that I had received. Yet, through faith in Him, obstacle after obstacle had been removed. Standing there alongside the road, I thought of the many times throughout my life, where having faith in Christ had been paramount, just as it had been here.

I continued to ponder those feelings as I threw my leg over the bike and rode away. When I pulled into Liard River, British Columbia, my odometer said I did it. I had ridden one thousand miles in twenty-four hours, and I did it on the ALCAN!

As I entered the little settlement, I slowed my speed and pulled into the dirt parking lot of the lodge in the center of town. I just sat there, too sore to get off. My mind went to those who are quick to have faith in Christ when all is well, but during times of uncertainty, conflict or pain, are quick to abandon their faith and turn on Him. I thought of the times in my own life, when I had been tempted to do that myself. Times when Satan would start ranting in my ear, that I couldn't trust Christ and that He would let me down, only to find out later on, that He had been with me all along. I have learned in those moments, when Satan is ranting in our ears, that Christ will never defend Himself. Instead, He will be silent and let you choose what to believe, just as He did when He stood before Herod and Pilate. Why? Because in those moments, you either know Him …or you don't!

I finally managed to get off my bike. I held onto it while I stretched and tried to stand straight. I then went into the lodge with a huge smile on my face and ordered an omelet. It was my first one of the entire journey. It was huge and perhaps the biggest omelet, I had ever had. I was happy as I started digging in. The people probably thought I was smiling because the omelet was so delicious, but I was smiling because I just completed my first one thousand mile day. As for the omelet? It was one of the worst I had ever had! To this day I have wondered if it was just my taste buds that were out of whack, instead of the omelet being poor. After all, I had been riding for twenty-four hours and my body was pumping a lot of adrenaline into my system to keep me awake. But while sitting there, eating my omelet, I noticed lots of funny looks from the people in the lodge. It was more evidence to me that I was looking pretty bad. After finishing my omelet, I probably didn't help my image any, when I went outside, laid down on the grass and fell asleep.

About forty-five minutes later, I woke up and decided to try for another personal record. I knew I was not coming back, at least on a motorcycle. So, I decided to ride the *entire* ALCAN, all fifteen hundred miles of it! I slowly peeled myself off the grass and made it to my feet. I then smiled at the patrons in the lodge, who were looking out the window at me. I then swaggered to my motorcycle with all the *cool* that I could muster, trying not to wobble as I strutted. As I stood there, alongside my bike, I looked down the road I had just traveled. I then turned and looked up the road ahead of me.

After a few moments of trying to clear my head, I rubbed my eyes and then tried to wrap my mind around the idea of this new challenge—of riding another five-hundred miles.

I looked back at the lodge and the patrons in the window and gave them another smile and a wave. I then slowly looked into the beautiful sky above and gave a wink toward Heaven. I took a deep breath, inhaling as much fresh air as possible. Then, I slid my shades over my eyes and took another deep breath. A mischievous smile crossed my face, as I signed, turned the key and hit the starter. *"Why not?!"* I said. *"It's a good day to ride!!"*

68) Live inspired ...love life ...love the Lord ...and choose to be a *Victor*.

LoneRider…

A loner at heart began a long journey, once upon a time.
He came from a distant place and now is a good friend of mine.
He wasn't very popular in school or ever at the head of his class.
He never played basketball or baseball or caught a single pass.
He had a few friends as he grew but mostly kept to himself.
And he never had ambitions of having fame, fortune or wealth.

In motorcycles he found a new world, filled with exciting adventure.
One where he could be alone and free and be with Mother Nature.
As he rode, the heartbeat of the motor was all he ever heard.
When he stopped on some lone road, it was the chirping of some bird.
What he smelled as he rode, were the flowers, fields or the vivid scent
of farms, rivers or mountains or whatever was at, where he went.

His leathers were not new, shiny or without mar or unsightly tatter.
They were old, faded and rain damaged and often covered with splatter.
Many would look at him and would see just a grungy, old biker.
But he wasn't a biker at all, he was just a friendly, old rider.
He enjoyed being alone and riding his motorcycle down the open road.
The stories of his travels to distant places were often printed and told.

When he rode alone, he slept on the ground, next to his faithful bike.
And he usually managed to take a shower, about every fourth night.
He would lay under the stars and stare into the heavens above.
And feel an incredible feeling inside that was always filled with love.
He rode so he could be alone to travel the land or gaze at the sea.
He rode to think and ponder, through the Lord's living art gallery.

Yes, he rode so he could be alone but not totally alone you see,
for on his rides he took a Friend to talk with on his journey.
It always turned into a ride with the Lord, his best and dearest Friend.
It always became a rich encounter, as he would feel his soul mend.
I say he began a long journey ...because of who he was before.
Actually, it was those rides with the Lord ...that changed him evermore.

Ofcr. Samuel Jeppsen, #3751

Chapter Twenty-Six

The Sign read "NWT Border"

About twenty miles before I got to Fort Nelson, I passed a fairly small and very simple road sign that pointed straight north. The "T" intersection didn't even have a gas station, a general store or even a welcome sign. The narrow, little, northbound road was unceremoniously marked, N.W.T. Border, with an arrow pointing north. Is this the road to the North West Territory? I wondered? My map confirmed that it was. It said that from Fort Nelson to the N.W.T. border, was about one hundred miles. It was another forty miles to Fort Liard, which was on gravel.

What an adventure to add to my adventure!! How many could say they've ridden their bike to the Northwest Territory? The land averages seventy frost free days a year and stretches from the 60th parallel to the North Pole. "Who knows?" I smilingly said! "Maybe I'll run into Allakariallak, better known as Nanook of the North, and his family!"

My problem was that, from Fort Nelson, it would take a full tank of fuel and also full gas cans, to make the round trip. Even then, there was no guarantee I could make it back to Fort Nelson, if for some reason, the single gas station in Fort Liard was not open. It was extremely tempting for me, to take that little road to the N.W.T. on a motorcycle. However, the Liard Highway is extremely remote and mostly dirt. The population of Fort Liard is six hundred or less. I knew if I broke down, I would be lucky to see one car a day, on that road. Not willing to take that risk, I took a picture of the sign, hit the starter and moved along.

With renewed conviction, I continued on my journey to Dawson Creek. I rode mile after mile, stopping only for two more short naps. I made it to Dawson Creek in thirty-seven and a half hours, after leaving Steve and Alisa's in North Pole *and* I made it without speeding. According to my odometer, I had traveled one thousand, four hundred and ninety-seven miles. How many motorcycle riders can say that they have traveled the entire ALCAN—nonstop, on a Sportster? If I never do another Iron-Butt Ride in my life, I have bragging rights, few can match!

When I got too tired to stay awake, I would put my feet on my rear pegs and do leg presses—halfway up and hold. I did that until my thighs burned so badly, I was once again wide awake. Needless to say, I did a lot of leg presses. Yes, it was dangerous, but so is every other sport, except maybe golf or ping-pong.

At Dawson Creek, I got a room, took a shower and went to bed. I slept for ten hours straight, before waking. After packing up, I decided I wasn't ready to end my journey, so I turned west on 97 and headed for Chetwynd. After a bite to eat there, I followed 97 to Prince George. That night, I got another room in Quesnel.

The young lady, that rented me the room, was so very nice and kind to me. I knew I looked like a rat and probably smelled like one too. But somehow, she was able to see past her first impression of me. She saw me and treated me as just an old guy who loved bikes. An old rider who probably had a home and family someplace and who was just out living an adventure.

At Quesnel, I got another ten hours of much needed sleep and awoke to, yet another rain storm. So, I suited up in my rain gear and followed the road to 100 Mile House, then to Kamloops, spending the night around Peachland. The next day I headed south to Osoyoos and then home …to the good ole U.S.A.

At the U.S. Border crossing, I noticed lots of suspicious looks from the tourists in the cars who, like me, were waiting to cross the border. I was starting to become uncomfortable with the ugly leers, I was getting. I did look pretty bad. I was still wearing the same shirt and pants that I had left Key West in, three weeks ago and I had worn them every day. I hadn't shaved. My hair was greasy and matted. I was grimy from the day after day dirt and my bike was a muddy mess. Other than that, I didn't look too bad. But inside, I was becoming uncomfortable with the thought that others were thinking that I was a misfit or an outlaw biker.

The U.S. Border Agent gave me a bit of a rough time, as well. I could see his perception of me, was not the same as the young girl in Quesnel. His impression was more like those, in the cars alongside me. They were not seeing the real me, but only what I appeared to be. He was curt, never smiled and offered no small talk. He was convinced, I was a bad guy. He gave me a very stern once over, asking a lot of questions as to where I had been and what I had been doing. I told him I was part of the Hoka Hey riders that had gone from Florida to Alaska. Now, I was returning home to Arizona. He didn't smile and he wasn't impressed. As he continued his assessment of me, I was positive I was going to be ordered to the *short line* for a search.

It was only when he lifted my drooping rear bag and saw the "FOP" (Fraternal Order of Police) emblem that his attitude toward me, began to change. He then noticed my folded rider's jacket and the patches on it and said, "Are you associated with any motorcycle clubs?" (The politically correct way to say, Gangs.) I told him that I'm a Blue Knight, that I am part of the largest law enforcement motorcycle club in the world and that I am a retired cop from Mesa, Arizona. Shortly after that, he lightened up on me, smiled, waved and told me to have a good day.

I learned an interesting thing from him and from others I had recently come in contact with. People were judging me to be someone I was not. My appearance was branding me and had become my enemy and curse! I was facing constant uphill battles. Earlier on my journey, I had been getting smiles and questions. Now, I was getting suspicious stares and looks of resentment. Had I been riding a Goldwing or BMW, I probably could have gotten away with it. But riding a Harley was only adding to the negative stigma. The good in me, was blocked by what they saw.

I had seen this reaction several times in my police career. Where people would judge others or *profile*, based on what they saw. Though laws are continually enacted to stop profiling, the fact of the matter is, it is a protection mechanism, which is deeply engrained in all of us and *cannot* be legislated *out* of us. It is how we protect ourselves. The brain is the first weapon of defense and perception is its first tool. Yes, it's true to say you cannot judge a book by its cover. However, it is just as true to say that you can.

Imagine getting a knock at the door at 2 a.m. Through the peephole, you see two men in black leathers, chains, tattoos, long scraggly hair, knives, guns, sunglasses and beards. They *could be* preachers—missionaries, coming to tell you about the Lord! But in all probability, they are exactly who they look like. And that's what was happening with me. I was being categorized. My looks had indeed, become my enemy.

As a police officer, I had taught for two years in public schools. I told the youth that changing their outward appearance is the first step to changing who they are and their first step in cutting the ties to their past. Now, I was experiencing what I taught.

Had I not been on a month long motorcycle adventure and just passing through the communities and the lives of those around me, I would have changed my appearance, after that experience with the U.S. Border Agent. I had created my own enemy. Fair or unfair, the image we project, either works for us—or against us.

However, I did have two positive experiences that came as a result of my greatly deteriorated appearance. They took place in the small town of Omak, Washington. I had pulled in to a local convenience mart for fuel and a food break. I parked next to two beautiful, expensive Harleys. They were owned by two riders, out enjoying the day. Their bikes were top of the line bikes, covered in chrome and spotless. My bike, on the other hand, was a total mess. There was not a clean spot on it, except for my seat and grips. Everything else was either covered in mud or splattered with bugs. At first, their look to me was one of, "Gee pal!!! Ever thought of giving your bike a bath? You're riding a Harley, ya know!!" But when they found out I was a Hoka Hey rider, returning from Alaska, you would have thought I was a big name celebrity. Their looks of, *"Get a clue"* quickly changed to a respectful, *"Pardon me."* I have to admit …that was fun!

But the most important experience took place after they rode away. I was sitting on the edge of a small wall, just resting and thinking, when a couple in their mid-thirties came and sat down next to me. This guy and his wife were strugglers in life. They lived on the street and made it one day at a time. Their clothes were a little worse than mine and he was a little dirtier than I was. In fact, he was even more odoriferous than me. They used street language and though I did not personally know either of them, I had seen both of them a thousand times in my police career. They were transients who lived in alleys, under bridges or wherever they could find.

They began talking to me, as if I was socially one of them, as if I too, had no home, no job, no family that cared and no place to go. I didn't answer him in the colorful language he used, but I was not offended by it, either. To me, having heard it so often and for so many years, it was just another of the almost seven thousand languages spoken in the world today. I smiled and listened, more than I talked. I was most impressed with his ease in talking to me.

Over the years as a cop, I had talked to hundreds of homeless people, but I had always felt a wall between us or a holding back. They had a little sign that read, *I can't let you too close to me. You may hurt me! I know I'm a nobody. I know I've made tons of mistakes and I don't matter, but I still have feelings.*

I have never been the kind of guy who looks down my nose at anyone, regardless of their status. It's just not my style. To me, everyone is a child of God. Everyone has a story and everyone has a reason. And usually, finding the reason, their *want to,* is the key to opening the lock, changing the compass and turning that person around. To be able to find the compass inside them, you have to genuinely care. The sincerity of your feelings is *key* to reaching deep inside another human being and making that difference.

This man talked about his inner feelings and about their life and their extended family. In that five minute conversation, I realized that nobody can become so far removed from society, so covered with mistakes and spotted with blemishes that they still do not have hopes and dreams of a better life, someday.

The conversation with this couple, reminded me of the only other time, I had come this close to the deepest feelings of someone, who had so little in life to hope for. As an officer, I had received a call of a family fight, inside a local Jack in the Box. It was concerning a homeless couple by the names of Jackie and Robert. Robert began yelling at Jackie and calling her names. He then threw his drink at her and left the restaurant. When I got there, I found Jackie sitting out front, crying. It was not so much in what she said, but how she said it, that made me realize how close I was to her most tender, heartfelt feelings.

Jackie was sobbing deeply, not just outwardly, but the kind that comes from deep within the soul. Through her tears she said, "All I want is a husband who will love me. I want a man who will come home to me after work—a man I can take care of! I want a home with a front lawn! ...Why can't I have those things?"

These two people, on the wall next to me, had opened up to me the same as Jackie had, those many years ago. As I watched them walk away and disappear behind the building, I thought of all the blessings, I have so richly enjoyed in my life. I thought about my Savior and how He can make anyone's life better and can bring to pass the many unfulfilled hopes and dreams, we all have deep inside us. I thought about how much He can do, if we will just *ask* and then …just *let* Him. Dreams don't have to be shattered like a piece of china that crashes to the floor. They can actually come to pass. Deep joy and happiness can be ours, if we will follow Him.

As I sat there on the wall watching the townspeople coming and going around me, I realized that today was Sunday. I then realized that every Sunday on this trip, the Lord had blessed me with a special spiritual experience. Experiences that were just for me and that helped shape me and add to my character.

On Sunday, June 20th, Father's Day, when I took off from Key West, the Lord endowed me with His love as I began my ride and began to fulfill my dream. On Sunday, June 27th, He showed me how much He loves people of other races and faiths, as I sat and listened to Chief Oliver Red Cloud speak of the Great Spirit. On Sunday, July 4th, the anniversary of the country I love, I was kept safe from heavy, black, dangerous storms in the Denali Range and led safely toward the light. Now, on Sunday, July 11th, I reentered the good ole U.S.A. and had the opportunity to sit on a wall and visit with two people, as He showed me how much He loves them. He loves all of us, regardless of who we are. Whether we are the Chief of a great nation or a homeless couple in Omak, He knows each of us personally and loves us individually.

I smiled as I rose to my feet. I threw my leg over my bike and headed east on 155 to Coulee Dam. Still filled with the feeling of freedom and adventure and not ready to end my journey, I decided to ride east to Idaho to visit Esta and Teddy, Julie's sister and brother-in-law. I then rode to Wyoming to visit Margo and Ted, my sister and brother-in-law. While there, I learned that Smilin Bob had gone down on his bike, while riding the Cassiar Highway home. He would be okay, but he was laid up in a Canadian hospital. After my visit with Margo and Ted, I went to visit with an old police buddy of mine, Chuck Stadler and his wife Teddy. Chuck was known more by his badge number than by his name. His deep gravelly voice was known by all as, *4848.*

Chuck is a very dear friend of mine. He's one of those cops that have a huge, soft heart, but very capable of being a tough guy if needed. In my career, I was in four, noncontact shootings. I don't know how many noncontact shootings Chuck was in, but I do know he was in three contact shootings and two of the people didn't make it. Even so, Chuck is the kind of guy who has a genuine love for his Lord and his fellowman. You might say that Chuck saved my life, by following the Spirit, thirty-five years ago. He did it, by being brave enough to call me to repentance. It takes a lot of courage for a friend to do that for another friend. After all, you risk a friendship! But, as a wiser man than I, once said, "When you see a friend doing wrong and you are afraid to tell him …you are only thinking of yourself!"

Chuck had the courage, the love for a friend, and the willingness to cross that threshold and risk our friendship to help me. I remember that day as if it were yesterday. I was in the PD weight room at District Two. When Chuck came in, he lovingly, yet firmly, called me to repentance. When he did, I remember thinking, "Who are you to call me to repentance?" But I was not so far past feeling that I could not feel the power of the Holy Ghost in his words. That call to repentance was from the Lord. Being brave enough to follow that prompting inside him and call me back, is something I will always respect and love Chuck for.

After our visit, I left Wyoming and rode to Utah to visit my brother Harvey and his wife Sherry. To share this special time in my life, with these people that I love so dearly, was like enjoying a fine dessert, after a fabulous dinner.

Before I left Utah, my wife called and wanted me to call her when I was getting close to home. She told me that Jim, my son-in-law, wanted to come over and take my picture as I rode in. I called her about two hundred miles out. When I turned onto my street, to my great surprise, I found my dear wife, my children and grandchildren, all twenty-seven of them, standing in the street. They were holding a long banner across the road.

The banner read, *Welcome Home, We Are Proud of You.* They were all shouting and waving at me and they held the banner for me to ride through. What a perfect end to a perfect journey! I got off my bike and began embracing them all. My grand-children stared at me. The older ones stared in amazement and the younger ones stared in disbelief.

Their clean cut granddad had always taken pride in his appearance. He had always worn nice, clean clothing. On Sundays, he always dressed up in a suit and tie. Now, that same granddad was wearing a scruffy beard and he was in the same clothes he left in, over a month ago. He needed a haircut and had road grime all over his face. He stunk and his once beautiful bike was a dirty, mud covered mess!

I had ridden over eight hundred and fifty miles that day. Since I had left Key West, I had ridden about thirteen thousand five hundred miles. I had spent twenty-six days on my motorcycle, twenty-four of which, I rode alone. I had been away from my family for a month. I had traveled over four swamps, through thirty-three Indian Reservations, six National Parks, eight *HOT* Deserts and twenty-six National Forests. I had ridden across sixty-two mountain ranges. I had traveled through eighteen states (four of them twice,) three Canadian Provinces (all of them twice,) crossed two countries and crossed the state of Alaska twice! The fulfilling of this boyhood dream had come with a price tag,, from the first nickel to the last, of over seven thousand dollars.

I had lived on trail mix, beef jerky, water and *Trust*. I slept on the ground. I paid as much as $25.00 a gallon for gasoline. I had worn the same shirt and pants everyday for a month, was sunburned, wind burned, grimy, dirty and smelly. But now, it was over and I was at home with my family. I was standing in the driveway with my wife, my children and grandkids, all gathered around me. They were hugging me and telling me how much they loved me and how proud they were of me. The feelings inside me were almost impossible to explain. It was as if I had just walked off the stage, holding my very own Academy Award, while the audience stood, cheered and applauded and yelled out my name. Overwhelming exhilaration and gratitude were my companions as I lovingly hugged and kissed each member of my family.

My mud-packed and bug-splattered Harley went on display for six weeks at Superstition Harley-Davidson. Alongside it was a poster with my pictures and my words that said, *Live the Dream!*

69) Notice the changes taking place inside you, in your journey toward Christ and keep growing and going. Keep moving toward the Light.

Chapter Twenty-Seven

Never afraid again

"Behold, my soul delighteth in the things of the Lord; and my heart pondereth continually upon the things which I have seen and heard."

This whole journey was a once in a lifetime experience and opportunity. I had been blessed from the very beginning, at every turn, in every town, along every road and every time I slept alongside the road. My mind was filled with love for my family as I stood among them and shared my love for them. We hugged and kissed and laughed together for the next couple hours. As we did, I shared my pictures and my experiences with them. The feelings of joy and happiness inside me, were indescribable. As filled with love as I was for them, my mind was also on my Lord and Savior, Jesus Christ and my Heavenly Father. It was another dangerous journey, which had become a great collection of spiritual experiences and teaching moments, which would last a lifetime.

The organizers of the Hoka Hey told us that the ride would be life changing and it was. I think about the things I experienced, often. Like a favorite movie, they play over and over again. But the experiences I am referring to, are the spiritual experiences with my Lord and Savior. These are the memories that I relive. I am so thankful to God the Father for loving us so much that He gave the world His Only Begotten Son and I am so thankful to His Son, Jesus Christ, for giving His life that we might live and have eternal life with Him and our Father in Heaven. Christ is our Lord. He is our Shepherd. He is our God and He is the Creator of Heaven and Earth. But He is also our friend—and so He was with me on this journey to Alaska. Each day, in some new experience, He was there, reaching out, teaching me, taking my hand, expressing His love for me and drawing me closer to Him.

One of the other things, my daughter, Katina said, as she spoke that day in Stake Conference, was, "It's not enough to belong to Christ's Church, you've got to belong *to* Christ." Those few words spoken by her, have never left my thoughts. I realized that those few words require a mighty change inside us. They require a deep commitment that no person can make for another. It is a very sober decision, which finally comes after much thought. It is a decision that *only* comes when one decides, on whose side he stands—good or evil, the Lord's or the Adversary's.

After Peter had denied Christ three times, he made the commitment to belong *to* Christ. When he did, he became a new man and became more powerful than he had ever been before. When the Apostle Paul made that commitment, he went from one of the worst enemies and persecutors of Christ, to perhaps one of the greatest apostles that ever lived. The Scriptures contain several stories of people who made that commitment and then became incredibly valiant servants of Christ. In fact, there is an almost endless and ongoing list of them. You don't have to be *in* the Scriptures, to change and be like those *of* the Scriptures. One of the things I realized, is having a past full of dents, scratches and ugly baggage, makes very little difference in the Savior's ability and desire to forgive you, love you, prosper you and help make your greatest dreams, even your impossible ones, come true.

I have many favorite verses that were spoken by the Savior, but perhaps my most favorite is, "I am the light which shineth in the darkness and the darkness comprehendeth it not." It's one of those verses that I think about often. It is as the tapping of a Morse Code Machine, as the message comes over the wire and clearly says …the Savior is the answer to every problem.

The greatest journey you will ever take in your life, will be your journey with Christ. "Come unto me." He said. When you do, He will build a bridge through one unusual coincidence after another. He will hold your hand, while you cross it and He will bring you to the unseen knowledge that He is there.

It was not this motorcycle ride or any motorcycle ride that taught me these things. It was the compilation of life experiences. I could have learned these things through *any* avenue, as long as I listened to the whisperings of the Spirit. It was wanting to know, listening to the promptings and then following those feelings, that led to this knowledge.

After those basic steps, it was experimenting on the words of Christ and recognizing the changes and the patterns that were taking place in my life. It required taking the time and effort to learn the language of the Spirit and to keep moving toward the Savior. The avenue I happen to like, *motorcycling*, made little difference in the Lord's ability to reach out to me and to teach me and to bring me closer to Him.

In your journey with Christ, He will bring you to a place, where life is without fear, hope is replaced with confidence and faith is replaced with trust and knowledge. Suddenly, there you are in a different place than you have ever been before. Around you is the feeling of angels and inside you, is a deep feeling of peace. On your journey with Him, you will travel that long road that each of the Ancients traveled with Him—that long road of life and spiritual experiences labeled, *From Faith to Trust.*

When you no longer hope or believe, when faith is no longer necessary, when you know for a surety that He lives, life holds an excitement that is difficult to put into words.

When that time comes, when knowledge replaces your faith and trust is your companion, there is no circumstance to face, no threat to be afraid of and no disaster that can frighten or crush you. You are as the man in the story, whom to the amazement of his friends, can sleep in the midst of a storm.

I am a guy who has so many shortcomings, yet, I have won the three most valuable prizes of all. The very personal knowledge that my Savior actually lives and that I can trust Him in all things! Secondly, because of His Atoning sacrifice, I know that who we *were*, does not have to be who we *are*!

It was Peter that said, "For the eyes of the Lord are over the righteous, and His ears are open unto their prayers." And it was John the Revelator, who when Christ appeared to him in all His glory said, "I fell at his feet as dead." And it was Christ who lovingly reached out and laid His right hand upon him and said, "Fear not." The knowledge of "Fear not" is prize number three. When Christ said, "Fear not" it means that He is more than our Savior, He is our Friend. It means that we can go forward in total faith and trust, as He is there and He will be with us.

Recently, my oldest grandson, Austin, who is eighteen, was helping me with some computer troubles I was having. We talked as we sat side by side and worked to solve my problems.

He has made a rather dangerous career choice and said, "I've been praying, Grandpa! I don't pray the way you guys do, but I've been praying to Jesus every night. I've even been reading the Scriptures!" I smiled and said, "That's wonderful, Austin!" He continued, "I don't want to die, Grandpa, but I'm not afraid to die anymore! I used to be afraid to die, but since I've been praying to Jesus, I'm not afraid anymore! I know I'll be with Grandpa Lay and the rest of them up there and soon, I'll be with everyone here too! So I'm not afraid to die anymore!"

I said, "That's right, Austin. Life is like being at college and living on campus. We're only here for a while! If you build your life around Christ …you'll never have to be afraid again."

70) *Believe* in Christ …*believe* Christ …*trust* Christ …*belong* to Christ!!

"Moreover I will endeavour that ye may be able after my decease to have these things always in remembrance. For we have not followed cunningly devised fables, when we made known unto you the power and coming of our Lord Jesus Christ, but were eyewitnesses of his majesty. For he received from God the Father honour and glory, when there came such a voice to him from the excellent glory, This is my beloved Son, in whom I am well pleased. And this voice which came from heaven we heard, when we were with him in the holy mount."

Peter

The Trial…

I had committed many wrongs ...and one worthy of death.
I sat at the defendant's table, anxious and reaching for breath.
At the victim's table to my right was a man who was large and strong.
He'd been the victim of a violent crime and had done nothing wrong.
During the trial he sat there silent, somber, straight and tall.
He listened to the evidence, saying nothing at all.
In front of us was the Judge, powerful and regal.
My soul seemed transparent and hiding the truth, futile!
Finally the trial was over, my pitiful excuses failed.
Every detail came forth and absolute truth prevailed.
The Jury found me guilty. They called for my life.
I looked around the courtroom and saw my dear wife.
My wife and family were weeping, the rest seemed understanding.
But in their hearts, they knew it was fair what the jury was demanding.

As I sat there, alone and looking about,
I was scared and I wanted to scream out!
Ohhh, if only I could look good in the Judge's sight!
Why hadn't I always done what I knew in my heart was right?
If only my wrongs could be forgiven and excused.
But what I had done ...could not be undone or defused.
It was then that the man at the victim's table raised his hand,
"I plead for mercy for this condemned man."
Suddenly the courtroom was still as shock filled the air.
The Judge looked and said, "You want mercy?
I'm a Judge! I have to be fair!"
Then after a moment the Judge spoke again,
"No one could ask for mercy but you!
Except for you, it would be unfair for anyone to do!

For this condemned man, are you sure mercy is the right call?
For mercy and fairness are not the same thing at all!"
"I'm sure." he said as he nodded his head.
Then the Judge granted the plea of mercy, instead!
So from the hangman, I was spared.
But..., who was this man that sat in that chair?
He seemed so familiar.
But I knew not from where!
As I looked him over and tried to remember,
it was then I realized that his feet were bare.
His hands, he had kept folded throughout the trial,
but now they were out and one was raised in the air.
"In his feet and in his hands," I said with a pause,
"he has terrible scars" and I wondered at their cause.

Still..., who was this man that had saved my life?
And what was I to him that he would take on <u>my</u> strife?
As I strained for a better look at who had pleaded for me,
suddenly, my mind was made clear and I could see!
I knew Him in an instant! My heart began to pound!
The teachings of my mother came back true and profound!
His outpouring of love made my emotions hard to control,
as I felt His extreme love for me now flooding my soul!
Unable to remain silent, "It's Him!" I weepingly said!
"He's the One that died for me and in Gethsemane, bled!"
"So forgiving and loving!" I thought as I looked into His face.
"Here is the Savior of not only me, but the entire human race!"
As His eyes met mine, there was no doubt He was the One.
He was the Savior, Jesus Christ, the Father's Only Begotten Son!

Ofcr. Samuel Jeppsen #3751, defendant.

"Believe in God; believe that he is, and that he created all things, both in heaven and in earth; believe that he has all wisdom, and all power, both in heaven and in earth; believe that man doth not comprehend all the things which the Lord can comprehend."

“My home was an eight by eight wooden shack, of sorts. What if they never told me about the bear?”

“We know! We saw it! That caribou probably saved your life.”

"Mister Inspiration" along the Old Seward Highway in Alaska, 1972.

Sur de la frontera.

One of the many villages where we made camp by.

"What right did he have to smile," I thought.

Even the roads that connected the villages, held an adventure.

"It was a good place to share some of those singles in my pocket."

Steve Arduser with Humphrey Bogart ...well almost.

“I often stopped and tried to communicate with them, as my love for Central America and her people was continuing to grow.”

“The road to British Honduras was absolutely incredible! Absolutely incredibly bad that is!”

Up the PCH with friend and paramedic, Stan Petersen.

Our second night in La Paz, they fed us five pounds of home cooked shrimp. We were in the front yard. They were digging the pool ...by hand.

The Baja Gang. (LtoR) Juan, Lexie, Cory, Siria and Fearless Leader—Fernando.
"REGULATORS ...MOUNT-UP," he would yell with a smile.

Estamos aqui. Los seis aventureros. (Here we are. The six adventurers.)

"Welcome to Cabo San Lucas," the sign read.

"Si," I said, "Siete mil."

We were a quarter mile off the road, we had grass two feet thick and the sun was setting over the Pacific Ocean. The finest hotel wouldn't have been better.

Knowing the Baptists to be good people, Olin and I picked a corner of their Church parking lot, rolled out our bedrolls and bedded down for the night.

"I will always remember the lesson of the motel room."

It was the little, out-of-the way places that brought the memories.

Loaded up and ready to head out for my great Alaskan adventure and surrounded by my precious, precious family.

Live the Dream and be smart.
Always invite the Lord along.

"The slender, bearded Navy Seal with a bad limp,

…was an Eagle Scout."
(second patch under my right hand)

The Posse…
(From LtoR: Stray dog, Smilen Bob and Lizard.)

…at the gate.

Literally …it was The End of the Road.
The bottom of Spit Road, Homer, Alaska. (about 11:00pm)

"I was pumping fuel and the young lady in the next island smiled and said, 'You're one of them, aren't you?!' "

I had been gone for 5 weeks, had been riding for 26 days, 24 as a lone rider.

But when I got home, my whole family was in the street, waiting for me.

Week one,

week two,

the night I got home,

the morning after.

Chief Oliver Red Cloud.

After 8,500 miles, there it was.

The Light in the Denali.

Always there.

Finishers of the 2010, the Florida to Alaska, Hoka Hey

Ackerman, Donald
Adee, Eugene
Alexander, RIP
Anderson, Greg
Annicelli, Rodger
Backhaus, Jordan
Barclay, William
Barnak, Michael
Barnes, Peter
Bass, R. Dale
Beasley, Zack
Beckett, Jim R.
Bennett, Jeff
Berland, Larry
Bernal, Efrain
Blount, John
Boone, Timothy
Borum, Robin
Breit, Damon
Brinkley, James
Brown, Clark
Buis, Roger
Bulger, Thomas
Burmaster, Kolin
Cadena, Angel
Callen, Christopher
Carlo, Robert
Carr, Christopher
Charlton, Jeffrey
Chester, E.B.
Clark, Gail
Clermont, Paul M.
Clevenger, Cliff
Clower, John
Cody, M.B.
Conner, Michael
Cook, Todd
Corella, Jacob
Crawford, John
Cross, Cherie
Curley, Nate
Darby, Greg
Davis, Josh
Denbrock, Raymond
DePari, Charles
Dickins, Don
Dillé, Steve
Dillé, Brian
Donohue, Michael
Doyle, William
Drake, Richard
Ellis, John
Evans, Clifford
Ezell, Marion
Fisher, Gerald
Flickinger, Russell
Frauenkron, Gary
Gearhiser, Charles
Gillard, Scott
Glaves, Robert
Goff, Mark
Goldweber, Barry
Goss, John
Gregory, Stephen
Grieve, Grant
Griffin, Robert
Halsey, Tymothy
Hartman, Scott
Hartman, Carl
Haynes, Doug
Herold, Jim
Hewlett, Kenneth
Hilliard Jr., Henry
Hirchert, Earl
Hodge, Mark
Hoehn, Sheila
Holt, Gregory
Hopkins, Mark
Hotchkiss, Robert
Hrytazy, Arthur
Hudson, Robert
Inman, Ron
Ivins, Marty
Jensen, Arnie
Jeppsen, Samuel
Johnson, Chris
Kacki, Piotr
Karner, Helmut
Kelly, Frank
King, Richard
Klan, Joseph
Klima, Ron
Klima, Chuck
Kohn, Jeff
Lacke, Mark
Laird, Gregory
Lambert, Anthony
Landrum, Carl
Laughlin, Dennis
Laws, Charles R.
Leclair, Joseph
Ledig, Walter
Lees, Lenette
LePelley, Lynn
Lewis, Edward
Lowman, Carl
Lutes, David
Madison, Christopher
Mailloux, Eden
Mallett, Jeffrey
Malone, James
Markasky, Richard
Martinelli, Michael
Mason, Bryana
Matzek, Mitchell
Maxcy, Charles
McConnell, Kelly
McGuire, Michael
McKelvey, Kristin
McMurrin, Doug
Mead, Greg
Mech, Gregory
Meindertsma, Dale
Mendell, Michael
Meredith, Josh
Metcalfe, Travis
Meyer, William
Meyer, Terry
Middleton, Don
Miller, Michael
Miller, John A.
Mills, Dale E.
Mirgliotta, Dale
Mosby, Jeff
Myers, Marshall
Naaktgeboren, Martin
Nelson, Kerry
Nesson, Bob
Newell, Sherie
Noffsinger, Terry
Normandin, Yves
Novak, Michael
O'Barr, Ricky
Oberquell, Donald
O'Brien, Marcus
O'Brien, William
O'Donnell, Mary
Olinger, Arnold
Parry, William
Paschke, Rod
Perkins, Kelly
Peterson, Robert
Petterson, William
Phelps, Raymond
Phipps, James
Pimentel, Edgardo
Pineiro, Alex
Pixler, William
Poole, Jeffrey
Pylant, Tom
Ramos, Louis
Reese, George
Reidy, Jeremiah
Reynolds, William
Sampsel, Curtis
Sawyer, Jeremy
Schall, Ronald
Scheirer, Gary
Scofield, Thomas
Scott, Alan
Scott, Paula
Scott, Andrew
Sehnert, Jim
Shackelford, Dan
Shook, Paul
Short, Allen
Smith, Jack L. Jr.
Smith, John
Smith, Terry
Smith, CW
Smith, Sandford
Spielvogel, Heinz
Stapleford, Robert
Steele, Rory
Stephens, Mark
Stinnett, Richard
Story, Marc
Strayer, David
Surry, George
Swaby, Clyde
Sweeney, Alex
Thacker, Darryl
Tomsic, Harry
Trejo, Jesus
Trewin, Geoff
Trumper, Gary
Vaughan, Timothy
Vaughn, L. Russel
Vieira, Carlos
Vincent, Milton
Walck, Lewis
Walters, John
Weyers, Terry
Whirlwind Horse, Arlin
Whirlwind Horse, Elijah
Wickre, Eric
Widmayer, James
Wight, Dannie
Wilson, Edward
Wilson, Mark
Wolfe, Allen
Zakrzewski, Paul
Zommer-Webster,Theresa
Zubaugh, Robert

Three generations. My son Clay and his oldest son, Reed.
And my favorite tie, The Three Wisemen, following the star. Estamos aqui!

With my beautiful wife Julie and Law Enforcement Chaplain Joe Avila.
International Conference of Police Chaplains, 2011, Scottsdale, AZ.

On a life long journey with my dream girl, Julie.

And because of the Lord, we can be together forever.

"But whosoever drinketh of the water that I shall give him shall never thirst; but the water that I shall give him shall be in him a well of water springing up into everlasting life," He said.

If you want to view the pictures of the rides, visit us at:

www.ArizonaCharityRiders.com
or
www.BelieveTheDreamWithin.com

Available through Amazon.com
Samueljeppsen@cox.net

Special dedication to:
My son, Clayton Samuel Jeppsen. Return Missionary, Writer, Motivator, Exemplar.
My oldest grandchild, Austin Michael Boubelik. Soldier, US Army, 25th. Infantry.

Your dearest and very best Friend

"And I will also be your light in the wilderness; and I will prepare the way before you…and ye shall know that it is by me that ye are led."

Jesus Christ

Police Retirement Day

From our home to yours …con amor.

Made in the USA
Lexington, KY
13 June 2013